Australia Human Resource Management

Current trends in management practice

Volume 2

Australian Human Resources Management

Current trends in management practice

Volume 2

Edited by
Graham O'Neill
Robin Kramar

Business & Professional Publishing Pty Limited

Unit 7/5 Vuko Place
Warriewood NSW 2102
Australia

Email: info@woodslane.com.au

First published 1999

Australian human resources management : current trends in
management practice.

ISBN 0 582 87691 51 (v. 1).
ISBN 1 875680 61 61 (v. 2).

1. Personnel management – Australia. I. O'Neill, Graham L.
(Graham Leslie), 1946– . II. Kramar, Robin.

658.300994

Publisher: Robert Coco
Edited by Carla Taines
Designed by Designpoint
Set in 11/12 pt Bembo by Lauren Statham
Printed in Australia by McPherson's Printing Group

Distributed in Australia and New Zealand by Woodslane Pty
Limited. Business & Professional Publishing publications are
available through booksellers and other resellers. For further
information contact Woodslane Australia on +61 2 9970 5111 or
Woodslane Ltd, New Zealand on +64 6 347 6543, or email
info@woodslane.com.au

Preface

All organisations seek some competitive advantage to maintain and enhance their long-term viability and growth. The key to competitive advantage is time—the speed with which the organisation can respond to its clients, its competitors, and the economic and business environment in which it operates. The capacity and ability to make maximum use of the workforce is a primary determinant of how effective an organisation will be in achieving the necessary speed of response. The competitive advantage of the organisation is enhanced by the effectiveness of those processes that relate to securing and utilising a skilled workforce and earning and maintaining its commitment.

Volume 1 of *Australian Human Resources Management: Current trends in management practice* was published in 1995. It 'sought to provide human resource practitioners with an authoritative reference source for their work in planning, development and utilisation of employees' by capturing current and emerging trends in Australian human resource management. Volume 2 has a wider agenda—it seeks to provide students and practitioners with ideas and case study examples of effective people management.

Managing people is a major concern for all managers. A survey of chief executive officers (CEOs) in Australia revealed that they spend more than 40 per cent of their time on 'people issues'—mostly on issues concerning leadership and communication. Their main concern is how to best attract, retain and develop people, particularly the top management team. 'They realize that if they are going to grow their businesses and build their revenue base they will need to attract the people who can handle these sorts of issues' (Bagwell 1997, p. 16).

During the 1990s line managers took a more active role in managing people. The Price Waterhouse-Cranfield survey of more than 330 large Australian organisations revealed that in the first half of the 1990s line managers were taking a greater responsibility for decisions in many areas of human resource management, particularly training and development, recruitment and selection, occupational health and safety, and workforce expansion/contraction (Kramar & Lake 1997, p. 6). Line managers and human resource managers are in partnership and share responsibility for many people management decisions. However, as the *Report of the Industry Task Force on Leadership and Management Skills* (the Karpin Report) and the survey of 119 senior executives by Arthur D. Little showed, most managers lack the people skills necessary to manage in modern organisations. They lack the skills to manage cultural issues and change, and to provide leadership (Macleay 1997, p. 45).

Legislation in areas such as industrial relations, affirmative action and discrimination, and occupational health and safety, influences the competitiveness of organisations by setting out frameworks for human resource management policies. Since the publication of the first volume, major developments have occurred in the industrial relations area, with particular encouragement of enterprise level industrial relations. Legislation establishes minimum standards, but the standards need to be integrated into the business requirements of the organisation for it to be effective in enhancing an organisation's performance. An emerging trend has been the greater awareness of the need to manage the diverse interests of employees and the diverse subcultures existing in organisations rather than merely to comply with affirmative action legislation. Diversity management is one way competitive advantage can be encouraged.

Reward systems can be used to improve organisational effectiveness. The methods and criteria for rewarding employees, especially the criteria for determining pay, are undergoing significant changes. With pay increasingly influenced by enterprise results, rather than industry awards, interest has grown in the relationship between pay and individual performance. Pay for performance systems have become more popular (Kramar & Lake 1997, p. 13). Superannuation arrangements have been continuously changing for the last decade and further changes will occur to this aspect of post-employment financial security.

A central concern for human resource managers is managing organisational change and preparing individuals through the personal transitions associated with these changes. Transitions require an understanding of how contextual issues, including human resource management issues, influence the change process. A particularly important difficulty is overcoming the interdepartmental 'turf battles' which contribute to low levels of trust (Macleay 1997, p. 45).

Globalisation has been a major motivator for change in Australian organisations. In many organisations, globalisation has also necessitated the development of broader competencies and skill sets to manage an international workforce. As organisations move people around the world, greater understanding is required of the needs of employees who are expatriated and repatriated. Members of the international workforce provide a source of competitive advantage for organisations operating in the global marketplace. This competitive advantage can be facilitated by assisting the transfer of the international workforce's increased skill and learning to other employees.

This book brings together some of Australia's foremost academics and practitioners. They outline emerging trends and issues in areas of their expertise. The editors would like to wholeheartedly thank the authors for their enthusiastic response to the opportunity to contribute to the second volume and for their patience during its preparation. Carla Taines provided outstanding editorial assistance with her usual patience and good humour. The editors sincerely thank her for her commitment to the project.

GRAHAM O'NEILL
ROBIN KRAMAR
1998

References

Bagwell, S. 1997, 'What keeps chief executives awake at night', *Australian Financial Review*, 24 July, pp. 1, 16.

Kramar, R. & Lake, N. 1997, *The Price Waterhouse-Cranfield Project on International strategic human resource management*, Macquarie University, Sydney.

Macleay, J. 1997, 'Our managers fail the test of leadership', *Australian Financial Review*, 10 December, p. 45.

Contents

Preface   v

Contributors/Editors   xi

Chapter 1
The future role of human resource management
Graham Andrewartha   1

    Case Study A
    From personnel manager to HR consultant—The Auschain
    experience
    Daryl Wightman and Jenni Werner   17

Chapter 2
Executive recruitment and selection
Ross Johnston   27

Chapter 3
Planning and managing employee performance
Helen Scotts   43

    Case Study B
    Performance management at Optus Communications
    George Abramowicz   61

Chapter 4
Development, training and learning
Andrew Smith   69

    Case Study C
    Training and development in change management: An energy
    industry example
    Denva Scott   89

Chapter 5
Industrial relations and human resource systems
Max Ogden with Robin Kramar   97

Case Study D
Transforming employee relations from adversarial to
problem-solving: ICI Botany
Tony Mealor   115

Chapter 6
Understanding the process of organisational change
Patrick Dawson   125

Case Study E
Managing change: Culture building at Texicom
Robin Kramar   143

Chapter 7
Issues in the design and structure of executive remuneration
Graham L. O'Neill   155

Case Study F
Changing reward and recognition processes in SGS Australia
Cynthia Mundy   171

Chapter 8
Superannuation—A changing landscape
Michaela Anderson   181

Chapter 9
Managing diversity
Robin Kramar   193

Case Study G
Profiting from diversity: The Westpac experience
Jacqueline Gillespie   207

Chapter 10
Managing an international workforce
Alan Fish   217

Case Study H
Human resource issues involved in establishing a joint venture
in Indonesia
Jasmine Sliger   237

Chapter 11
Developing an ethical culture
Ron Miller   245

Chapter 12
Sources of information
Margaret Patrickson   261

Contributors

Editors

Graham O'Neill

Graham O'Neill is Director, Business Development for the Hay Group. He has 20 years consulting experience in areas related to organisation structure, work design, performance management and reward planning. Apart from his consulting career, Graham has also held corporate management roles as Chief Manager, Remuneration & Benefits for the ANZ Banking Group, Group Manager Personnel & Employee Relations for the Australian operations of Daimler-Benz, and as an Organisation Development Consultant with General Motors. He commenced his working career undertaking teaching and research in Psychology at various Australian tertiary institutions.

Graham has a first class BA (Hons) degree in Psychology and a post-graduate Diploma in Applied Psychology. He was elected a Fellow of the Australian Human Resource Institute in 1988 and is a member of the American Compensation Association.

He has published two other books, *Corporate Remuneration in the 90s: Strategies for Decision Makers* and, with Dr Robin Kramar of Macquarie University, volume I of *Australian Human Resources Management: Trends in Management Practice*. He is the author of some 30 papers that have appeared in Australian and overseas journals, magazines and books. Graham is a past editor of the AHRI journal *Human Resource Management* (now *Asia Pacific Journal of Human Resources*) and remains on the editorial board of that journal; he is also on the editorial board of *Reward Management Bulletin* published by John Libby & Company.

Robin Kramar

Robin Kramar (PhD) is a Senior Lecturer in Management at Macquarie Graduate School of Management, Macquarie University.

She has more than twenty years experience lecturing in Australian universities. Robin has lectured, researched and published internationally and in Australia in a range of areas such as human resource management, strategic human resource management, industrial relations, management strategy and labour market economics. Robin has served as a consultant for a number of organisations in the public and the private sector. Her work includes the development of human resource strategies, performance management, assessment of management development programs, managing professionals, equal employment opportunities, diversity management, work and family policies and managing organisational change.

Robin has received funding for a number of projects, including a study of youth unemployment and labour market programs, the development of work and family policies, the management of professionals and managers and labour flexibility. Her most recent project involves an international study of developments in strategic human resource management policies and practices. This study is part of the Cranfield survey, an international study of human resource practices in more than 25 countries.

In addition to lecturing, she is the Director of the Centre of Australasian Human Resource Management, Book Review Editor of the *Asia Pacific Journal of Human Resources,* on the Editorial Board of two journals and is the Director of the Master of Management at MGSM.

Contributors

George Abramowicz

George Abramowicz is the Managing Director of Development Training and Motivation, a company specialising in optimising the human resource potential, and unlocking creativity in organisations.

Initially trained as a Mechanical Engineer, George shifted his focus from Engineering to Management and Human Resources in 1978 when he joined Esso Australia. He served in a wide variety of roles including Corporate Training and Development Consultant and was responsible for all management development programs. In 1992, he joined Optus Communication as their Corporate Training and Organisation Development Manager.

George has worked with the highly creative Accelerated Learning Process and is the only Master Trainer for Accelerated Learning System 2000 in Australia. He is also an accredited trainer with the Edward de Bono Institute and a member of A.I.T.D. (Australian Institute of Training and Development), A.S.T.D. (Australian Society of Training and Development) and World Future Society.

Michaela Anderson

Michaela Anderson is the Director, Policy and Research at the Association of Superannuation Funds of Australia (A.S.F.A.), the peak industry body for superannuation funds. Michaela leads a team which consults with government on policy and implementation issues, provides expert technical advice to Government, and assists A.S.F.A. to remain a key contributor to public debate on retirement income policy issues. Michaela has worked in the superannuation industry for 14 years.

Prior to her A.S.F.A. appointment in mid-1994, Michaela was the Manager of Policy Advice to the trustees for the superannuation funds for NSW public sector employees. Michaela is also a director of the trustee board of a superannuation fund.

Graham Andrewartha

Graham Andrewartha is an organisational psychologist and partner of McPhee Andrewartha, a human resources consultancy firm based in Adelaide, and consulting in Australia and Asia. He is a past President of the Australian Human Resources Institute and has over twenty years experience in the training and development of managers. He is the co-author of the text *Developing Management Skills in Australia*.

Patrick Dawson

Patrick Dawson's main research interest centres on various aspects of organisational change, where he has published numerous articles in scholarly books and refereed journals. His latest book is entitled *Technology and Quality: Change in the Workplace,* London: International Thomson Business Press, 1996.

Patrick gained his PhD from the University of Southampton and then held academic appointments at the University of Surrey and the University of Edinburgh. Between 1988–1997 he was employed at the University of Adelaide and during 1992 he held the position of Honorary Principal Fellow at the University of Wollongong. He is currently Professor and holder of the Salvesen Chair of Management in the Department of Management Studies at the University of Aberdeen.

Alan Fish

Alan Fish is a senior lecturer at Charles Sturt University and Director of Postgraduate Programs in HRM. His studies were undertaken in Sydney culminating in a PhD from Sydney University.

Alan has an extensive local and international publication record, and he has recently been appointed Editor of *Career Development International*. His work has been presented at conferences in England, Germany, the United States, Hong Kong and Australia and he has been Visiting Professor in HRM at Paderborn in Germany.

Alan's research interests are in expatriate management and the selection, development and retention of key international staff.

Jacqueline Gillespie

Jacqueline is the Head of HR Policy at Westpac Banking Corporation. Over the last three years, she has been responsible for the HR policy and diversity strategy for the Bank. During this time, Westpac has been the recipient of the 1997 and 1998 Silver Award for the Corporate Work and Family Awards and in 1998 received a 5 rating for Westpac's Affirmative Action Report.

Prior to Westpac, Jacqueline worked in a range of HR and management development roles at TNT and Grace Bros.

Jacqueline has worked in the area of policy and diversity for many years and was the President of NSW EEO Practitioners Association from 1993 to 1995.

Ross Johnston

Ross Johnston is the principal of Ross Johnston and Associates, a Melbourne-based consultancy specialising in career management, outplacement, executive assessment, top level HR advice and employee relations.

Ross worked with Shell for nearly 24 years including roles as Industrial Relations Coordinator Australia, Personnel Director Shell UK Oil, and more recently as Group General Manager Personnel for the ANZ Bank.

Tony Mealor

Tony Mealor holds a first-class Bachelor of Social Science honours degree from UNSW in research methodology, industrial relations and psychology.

From 1982-1992, Tony worked at the ICI Botany (Sydney) petrochemical complex and drafted and negotiated the site's first enterprise agreement, which included annualised salaries, self-managed work teams and flexible shift systems. Tony's research interest is in organisational capability and the diffusion of such innovations.

In 1994, with Paul Gollan, he undertook a study of changing work practices in the metal trades industries which produced fourteen case studies in 'best practice'. In 1995 he took on the role of Project Manager for the Change Management Qualification in the Australian Graduate School of Management, Australia's first post-graduate qualification in change management.

Ron Miller

His company, Ron Miller & Associates, provides confidential advisory services and counsel to senior executives and board members on strategic issues including organisational development, ethics, culture change, leadership and compensation.

Ron was previously CEO and Director of Hastings Deering and formerly an executive with Caterpillar Tractor Co.

Cynthia Mundy

Cynthia Mundy is a consultant with the Victorian Employers' Chamber of Commerce and Industry. She has a Bachelor of Business in Human Resource Management from the Victorian University of Technology and a Graduate Diploma in Industrial Relations and Human Resource Management from the University of Melbourne. Cynthia's principal areas of practice are human resource strategy, reward management and equal opportunity. Her experience includes extensive involvement in reward and recognition strategy design, enterprise bargaining and performance management.

Cynthia's focus is developing practical reward management solutions for individual companies that enable them to measure their return and ongoing effectiveness.

Max Ogden

Max Ogden is an Industrial Officer with the Australian Council of Trade Unions. His involvement with the Union movement stretches over 40 years and includes the Amalgamated Metal Workers Union where he was the first full-time education officer for the Victorian branch and subsequently National Industrial Democracy Officer with responsibility for negotiating workplace change at industry and enterprise level.

In 1993 Max published the book, *Towards Best Practice Unionism* and between 1992-1995 he was the Unions' representative on the Federal Government's Best Practice Program which encouraged new management systems in industry.

Max has spoken at international conferences and worked overseas on assignments relating to Union interests over many years. He is presently a member of the National Food Industry Training Council.

Margaret Patrickson

Margaret Patrickson is Associate Professor in Human Resource Management at the International Graduate School of Management at The University of South Australia.

Her research interests cover workforce diversity with a special interest in older workers and she is also involved in research into women in late career. She is the author/editor of several refereed books and papers in these fields including *Managing an Ageing Workforce* (1998) and is an Associate Editor of *Asia Pacific Journal of Human Resources*.

Denva Scott

Denva Scott is Director of Denva Adele & Associates. Her work covers the analysis, diagnosis and solution of complex HR problems, management and people development, succession planning, facilitation of consultative processes and the development of reward systems.

She is particularly interested in the impact of leadership, organisation structure, HR systems and processes, individual employees and employee-management relationships, and the interplay between these five factors, on the success of business strategy.

Helen Scotts

Helen Scotts has worked in the field of organisation and management consulting for the past ten years.

Currently she is Director of Consulting Operations for the Hay Group, New South Wales. In this role, Helen leads a team of twenty consultants in the delivery of consulting services to organisations in the areas of Organisation Change, Strategy and Implementation, Leadership, Individual and Team Performance and Work Design.

Jasmine Sliger

Jasmine Sliger is the Managing Director of JSA International Communications Pty Ltd. She is a communications specialist and cross cultural corporate psychologist who has run an international corporate communication consultancy since 1987. The focus is on reviewing communications at an organisational level, interpersonally and especially in teams.

Jasmine's projects, across a variety of industries and major corporations, have included international company improvement, large training programs, building cross–cultural teams and assisting companies to set up strategic planning necessary to successfully communicate globally.

Andrew Smith

Associate Professor Andrew Smith, MA (Camb), MBA (Aston), PhD (Tas), is Head of the School of Management at Charles Sturt University and Director of the Group for Research in Employment and Training (GREAT). He has made the study of training at the enterprise level his specialist area of research. He is currently researching the impact of new management practices on enterprise training.

Before becoming an academic in1987, Andrew worked for ten years in a variety of training and development positions in manufacturing industry.

Jenni Werner

Jenni Werner, Master of Education (Human Resource Studies) and a Bachelor of Arts (Applied Psychology), is a human resource consultant specialising in organisational development and effectiveness and executive resource management.

Prior to consulting, she held senior corporate appointments with Westpac Banking Corporation, Rio Tinto Ltd and Coles Myer Limited. In these roles she was responsible for the development of strategy, policy and procedures relating to a broad range of Human Resource activities across business units and corporate departments. She has extensive commercial experience in organisational change and development, competency development, recruitment, executive development, performance management and succession planning in the retail, mining, financial services and consulting industries.

Daryl Wightman

Daryl Wightman is Managing Director of Performance Dynamics, a Sydney-based organisational development consultancy. He has 20 years experience as a management consultant, previously with Price Waterhouse and Andersen Consulting in London. He regularly facilitates business planning and change management initiatives and runs courses on internal consultancy throughout Australia.

Daryl's academic achievements include an MA in Physics and Psychology from Cambridge University. He is also a Chartered Psychologist in the British Psychological Society.

The future role of human resource management

Graham Andrewartha

This chapter proposes that human resource management (HRM) is a management specialty that has not yet achieved professional status. Further, because of its monopoly over the people management area, it has diverted other managers from taking responsibility for 'people' issues and unintentionally contributed to the continuing decline in people skills in Australian organisations. As an established business function it is likely to dissipate through outsourcing, and be absorbed back into mainstream management through ineffectiveness unless it discovers its true professionalism.

HRM has always been reshaping itself, continuously changing and innovating, yet not really changing at all. It requires foundation—not innovation—to be effective. That is, HRM needs to identify its basic principles and make its fundamental mission concrete. Failure to do this will see devolution become dilution, and strategic HRM become adopted by managers with no people skills background.

In a study by Ulrich, Brockbank and Yeung (1989), 10 000 managers across 91 firms were asked to comment on the most important business contributions to be made by the HRM function. The results highlight three areas of contribution:

- managing change (43% of HRM time);
- delivery of HRM practices (40%); and,
- knowledge of the business (17%).

1

These results indicate a considerable change in the requisite HRM competencies for the future compared with the previous period of transition from personnel to human resources. Over the transition period, the rate of change in organisations has accelerated, and the nature of organisations themselves has shifted and changed (Limerick 1992). On this basis, a prediction for the year 2010 is likely to have some subtle differences. For example, knowledge of the business will probably still constitute 17 per cent of the HRM contribution whereas delivery of HRM practices may drop to a mere 2 per cent, with an overwhelming emphasis on managing organisational learning (81 per cent).

Knowledge of business requires the HRM manager to understand the objectives, structure and operating environment of the organisation. This includes a detailed understanding of the products or services, and the organisation's marketing strategies and customer requirements. While future HRM involves knowlege and understanding of all traditional HRM activities, these are increasingly being outsourced. However, these services still need to be understood and be effectively and competently managed from within the organisation. This should remain the HRM manager's responsibility.

Managing change needs to be transformed into managing organisational learning. It covers much the same area, but with a different focus on the process and attitude of learning in small groups, and the connection between the learning relationship and the larger organisational systems. This change in the HRM role would mean even more substantial changes in the skills and mindset of future HRM managers.

HRM: A struggling management practice

Australian HRM had its roots in administration and industrial welfare in the 1940s (Smart & Pontifex 1993, 1995). The body of knowledge has tended to be defined in response to organisational and social requirements; in many ways it is a reaction to what the organisation does not practice very well. Consequently, HRM has always had a specific functional focus (e.g. recruitment, remuneration, occupational health and safety). However, none of these functions necessarily requires a HRM specialist. Many of them, once initiated within the personnel department, have been developed, refined—and often given a touch of class—by outside consultants and functional specialists. Current views of the future suggest that this functional provision of HRM services will continue; the changing expectations of organisations and the community about the role of HRM make it likely that they will increasingly be provided externally.

Walker (1982) identified four criteria necessary for professional status in Australian society:

1   mastery of a discipline and specialised body of knowledge and skills;
2   completion of a prescribed pre-service preparation program at tertiary level;

3 acceptance of legal sanctions controlling the behaviour of practitioners; and
4 acceptance of a system of self-policing by practitioners.

On the basis of these criteria, HRM was deemed not to be a profession in 1985 (Smart 1985), nor in 1992 (Smart & Pontifex 1993). To achieve that professionalism HRM needs to demonstrate credibility, not superiority. In recent years HRM has had significant critics, and even its advocates and enthusiasts tend to describe it in terms of potential rather than practice. The following comments illustrate some current perceptions of HRM:

- 'Disbanding human resources departments and appointing three chief executive officers instead of one were some of the ideas canvassed by a group of specialists at a recent brainstorming session' (*Weekend Australian* 14–15 September 1996, p. 69).
- Staw (1986) highlights the lack of a coherent strategy as one cause of the failure of organisational psychology over the years to deliver measurable improvements in work satisfaction and productivity.
- John Storey's (1995a) book, *Human Resource Management: A Critical Text*, highlights the pieces of HRM which are not formed into a whole cloth.
- Kochan et al. (1986) estimated that no more than 23 per cent of employees are affected by human resource management policies.

In a similar vein, David Guest (1990) considers HRM is merely a part of the American Dream. He says HRM is a novelty because of its claim that full use of human resources will enable a firm to gain competitive advantage. He concludes 'It follows from this that HRM is too important to be left to personnel managers but is instead a key strategic issue demanding the attention of all managers' (p. 378). He also observes that HRM should be integrated with business strategy, and that the various elements of HRM policy should be integrated into the values and behaviours of line managers and owned by them. 'In short it is the intention of behavioural science and business strategy to provide a distinctive HRM path to competitive advantage' (p. 379). He queries the implication that there is strategic choice about how best to use human resources. Guest argues that HRM takes as its starting point the view that organisations should be designed on the basis of assumptions inherent in McGregor's (1960) Theory Y. These assert that a) workers have talents that are rarely fully utilised at work, and they show a desire to experience growth through work; b) if management trusts workers and gives them responsible and challenging assignments, workers will respond with high motivation, high commitment and high performance. To the extent that a) is true, b) requires a degree in organisational psychology to render it practicable. McGregor was correct but the issue is irrelevant. The dilemma facing HRM is that in practice it has been unable to distinguish the difference between the assumptions of McGregor's Theory Y and organisational social work. HRM takes a profound mindset but fails to translate a position about people at work into a practical process that finds acceptance in our workplaces.

There has been unprecedented change in Australian working life in the 1990s. This has prompted calls for a new approach that places greater value on people in organisations (e.g. O'Neill & Kramar 1995). Others have pointed to the increasing need to involve line managers in the delivery and development of HRM policies (Downie & Coates 1995; Storey 1995c). Empowerment of line managers is one feature distinguishing HRM from traditional personnel management. But people have not always been seen as a key success factor compared with other traditional resources in Australia (Dowling & Boxall 1994). More generally, Kramar (1992) suggests there has been a slow uptake of the HRM philosophy in the Australian environment.

The HRM function has moved away from a reactive administrative, pro-cedural role, to one that involves strategic planning, organisational design, enterprise-based employee relations, and the initiation of change (Dowling & Schuler 1990; Lawler 1995). In this context, the HRM professional needs to be a generalist who understands as many areas in the organisation as possible. In this way HRM has shifted ground, to involve itself in strategic enterprise-level relationships while engaging more effectively in individual relationships.

However, Storey and Sisson (1993) have suggested that developing a strategic approach to managing human resources is not easy. Kessler (1995) argues, for example, that reward systems are not being used strategically; Rothwell (1995) reported little evidence of the effective use of planning tech-niques; Legge (1995) suggests that labour practices and employment relation-ships have not improved significantly; Lawler (1986) believes that much of the innovation in HRM is piecemeal and lacking in strategic integration; greater financial and analytical expertise is required in HRM (Boudreau 1990); and several writers argue the importance of formal education in the development of management skills (Dowling & Boxall 1994; Karpin 1995).

Restructuring HRM

Legge (1995) has defined the shape of the transition from personnel to HRM. First, she sees a shift of focus from HR processes and procedures onto the development of managers and their team in HR and people skills. Second, HRM will operate proactively with a focus on developing core business, not merely supporting it; and finally, HRM will generate an emphasis on defining and shaping organisational culture. Storey (1995a) has a 25 point scale of differences between personnel and HRM that focuses on four areas of belief and assumptions, strategic aspects, line management roles, and key levers. Storey also notices the beginnings of the interpersonal skills approach into HRM, blurring the boundary between the disciplines of organisational behaviour and HRM. In an international context, but with suitable implica-tions for domestic HRM, this has also been noted by Dowling and DeCieri (1995).

This transition of HRM has accentuated a longstanding paradox in HR— that key people specialists in our organisations do not possess core competencies in strategic planning nor in personal and interpersonal skills. This paradox challenges the nature of HRM itself. Without a radical restructure HRM will continue to be reactive, a contributor rather than a cause. HRM has yet to really define itself as qualified with people stuff. It has never defined how it can manage people in a way which captures real commitment to competitive advantage. This should be its core business.

People issues are not just symbolically or sympathetically the heart of organisations: they are the essence of organisations. Every issue in every organisation depends on social relationships. This requires us to face the complexities of people and relationships at work (Andrewartha 1994). Buber (1990, p. 28) said, 'The origin of all conflict between me and my fellow-man is that I do not say what I mean, and that I do not do what I say'. This is as true at work as it is in social situations, yet management skills (including HRM skills) still focus on technical developments and ability (see Karpin 1995).

The basis of this need to manage human psychology in the workplace is the issue of responsibility. Most of us have difficulty being responsible organisational members. One of the substantial roles of a future HRM practice is to assist in the growth of responsibility and autonomy of our corporate citizens consistent with the description of mature learning relationships described by Argyris (1992) and Senge (1990). This conjunction of people, paradox and responsibility is neatly summarised by Argyris:

> A theory that purports to explain human paradoxes is also a theory about self responsibility. For example, the theory should explain the predisposition to blame others for the defensive routines, to insist that one is helpless to change them, and to be unaware of one's own causal contributions. (p. 43)

Such a theory would be a blueprint for leadership learning that the HRM function could embrace. It is vital to focus on the individual and the organisation; this requires that management of both systems should overlap. Recent HRM literature discusses just such an integration of micro (individual/psychological) and macro (organisational/socioeconomic) processes in organisations. This *meso* or middle approach requires that people and organisations be treated as interdependent, not in isolation (DeCieri et al. 1997; Rousseau & House 1994). This framing of HRM places it firmly back as a management discipline in which the characteristics of the management skills are behavioural, paradoxical and interrelated (see Carlopio, Andrewartha & Armstrong 1997). The human resource function is the best area for investing in people, connecting with the organisation's goals and ensuring that organisations fulfill their obligations of being part of the larger community and society.

Four areas of HRM focus stand out with this sharp-angled view of the current context. They are meaning, practitioners, behaviour and target—the *what, who, how* and *which* of HRM.

1 *Meaning*—the 'what' of HRM. Currently, meaning is blurred; HRM has a need to be specialised, and yet also to devolve. Line managers need to

accept responsibility for HR and own it as a normal part of their management skills; this shift will need to be supported and managed by HR specialists. Discussions highlight role confusion between hard and soft HRM, tangling in Theory X and Y, and swinging between people, systems, and procedures. It is unclear whether it is a management discipline or a separate specialty, and currently it is extolling the virtues of strategic planning and strategic positioning. As a management specialty, HRM needs to derive its meaning from the value of individual differences, and the complexities and challenges of people working in small groups, to create an environment of competitive advantage for the organisation and socialisation for employees.

2 *Practitioners*—the 'who' of HRM. This group will include normal line managers, comprehensively trained and with the capacity and authority to provide proactive and fully integrated HRM practices in their daily work. Other practitioners will be HRM specialists at senior levels, external consultants and other outsourced providers who administer and provide a range of practical administrative HRM services. This scenario will require a new form of networking for HRM to be managed effectively. While the supplier/stakeholder/customer relationship will become blurred, the responsibility will need to be very clear. HRM will need to manage the process by precisely connecting all parties in an ongoing way in order to gain maximum effectiveness.

3 *Behaviour*—the 'how' of HRM. The methodologies will require sophisticated managerial competencies, including a strategic focus using the *meso* approach to build learning relationships. This approach will draw upon expertise from psychology, organisational behaviour, strategic management and education. Key competencies include personal competencies (personal mastery, integrity, responsibility, self-awareness, personal and interpersonal skills); business competencies (technical and HR knowledge, financial expertise, strategic skills); and organisational learning competencies (leadership skills, consulting expertise, systems thinking, innovative problem-solving). (See Ulrich (1997) for further discussion.)

4 *Target*—the 'which' of HRM. With the changing nature of HRM this will include some of the same groups identified in 'Practitioners' above;

Line managers The devolution of HRM principles and practices to line managers in the organisation will be conducted as a complex learning process. Such devolution provides creative ownership of HRM by line managers, not irresponsible delegation. Although the line managers' workload increases, so does their acceptance and understanding of the practical vitality of HRM as part of their normal daily work. Following devolution, the continuous process of consulting with line managers by senior HR specialists is essential.

Outsourced providers The next ten years will see the outsourcing of as many HRM functions as possible. The corollary of this is to maintain competent management of those outsourced functions rather than outsourcing the responsibility as well as the function.

Senior executives HRM will focus the executive on the learning culture and the strategic HRM input, discussed by such writers as Ulrich (1997), and Dowling and Schuler (1990). The aim is to develop the organisation's values and culture to more effectively link the organisation with customers and the community.

Management groups HRM will be responsible for ensuring that managers continuously support a learning context for their work groups and teams.

External stakeholders HRM activities will focuse on the external customers and involve them in the HR function, linking customer service and HRM activities commprehensively.

In summary, the HRM future will include:

- full devolution of HRM activities to line managers;
- development of line managers in HRM;
- HRM professionals acting as consultants to line managers;
- provision of strategic HRM expertise to the executive;
- outsourcing of administrative tasks;
- customer focused HRM;
- creation of a genuine learning culture.

Given this scenario, a definition of HRM for the future is: the capacity to link all stakeholders (employees, customers and the community) by creating and maintaining an effective learning culture that will enable people to achieve the strategic and operational goals of the organisation.

A learning culture

Twenty years of working with organisations in Australia confirms for me that more competitive advantage is diminished, more productivity is lost, and more time is wasted by incompetent handling of normal human interactions in the workplace than by any other cause. Conversely, a real competitive edge, increased productivity and effective time management can be gained if we practice better people management skills with a learning focus. 'Organisations are designed and managed in order to make management less difficult, but human beings act in ways that make management more difficult' (Argyris 1992, p. 40). The transition to the new HRM means a combined strategy that blends management and employee needs. We all have built-in cultural structures from our families, education, class and ethnic background: the goal is to unify these diverse individual structures with the management structure to achieve an organisational learning culture. This is a socialisation process that can only commence at the individual level. Currently, we approach 'people problems' as if they can be fixed. We target a concrete destination rather than an uncertain journey. As a result, performance management is full of 'poor performers' and ineffective appraisals. Like the medical condition of referred pain, where the disease is situated at a different site from where the pain is experienced, so in our work systems we attack symptoms but ignore the source.

People in their work interactions need a focus that combines personal, interpersonal and organisational perspectives. The lack of integration has continued because we separate one thing from the other when things are complex and uncomfortable. We compartmentalise people and systems; problems and performance. HRM with a learning focus is in a good position to provide this reintegration.

There are two reasons why the 1995 Karpin Report identifies people management, particularly personal and interpersonal skills, as the major deficit for Australian managers. First, we overlook that employees in our organisations actually have a complex range and depth of experience, emotions, motivations, and drives; by missing this we also miss the opportunity to benefit from this complexity of experience. Second, we are too timid to challenge this oversight. We support people with words but we rarely challenge a downsizing process which is ill-considered; we help staff with problems but are reluctant to disagree with the boss who intimidates them; we manage the consequences of poor recruitment practices but fail to change them.

There are four ways in which managers (including HR managers) demonstrate this tyranny of timidity:

Aggressive timidity When a dynamic leader pushes the organisation (or section) in a particular direction with charisma and energy, he/she may well be demonstrating aggressive timidity. These leaders hide their own fear behind their power, and deny others their natural reluctance and resistance: 'The intention to move the whole organisation at one time towards one culture, by one means, is destined to evoke compliance not commitment, it becomes high persuasion not high performance' (Block 1993, p. 200).

Benevolent timidity Often, well-meaning CEOs, HR practitioners and trainers want to help people realise their potential; in doing so, they introduce rules and procedures to help regulate attitudes and prejudice. They aim to modify reactions and energy to help the lowest common denominator in a way that makes change safe and attempts to guarantee empowerment. These are the people who help others, but don't ask for help themselves.

Denial timidity Many who would rather just get on and do the work demonstrate denial timidity. They don't want to take on difficult decisions for which they may make waves and be held responsible. They don't want to make an unpopular decision. They don't want to handle a difficult staff confrontation or face the anger and distress of people in difficult circumstances. The problem is denied and therefore doesn't exist.

Messianic timidity The 'quick-fix' messengers and leaders show messianic timidity. They advocate management by walking around; the one-minute managers and incentive movitators are the used car salesmen of organisational change. If it looks good, if it stirs the blood and gets people moving, then it must be the way to go—as long as it doesn't require continuous thoughtful effort.

If these forms of tyranny do not change, the timid might inherit the earth. High-performance organisations are places where a climate of individual acceptance and creativity is developed for all employees. The condescension of the benevolent can be traded for honesty; aggressive leaders can learn to accept the differing energies of people who contribute in other ways; those who deny will accept personal responsibility; and messiahs will get their hands dirty. Timidity will be overcome by acceptance, openness and integrity. Paradoxically the tyranny of timidity will be eradicated by the display of vulnerability.

One of the major contributions and responsibilities of the new HRM is to overcome this timidity. To achieve this HRM needs to have the vision and tools to develop a genuine people-based organisational culture. The *Macquarie Dictionary* (1981) defines culture as 'the sum total of learned ways of living, built up by a group of human beings, which is transmitted from one generation to another'. Thus culture is a part of learning in groups. It is demonstrated as behaviour, and as a mindset of cultural values. We do not realise how much culture influences our behaviour until we meet other ways of doing things. Inside the same culture we still tend not to recognise diversity as a (sub)cultural difference, regarding it usually as an irritation or discomfort to be discounted, labelled or 'fixed'. Utilising differences in a focused learning environment is the new HRM. Approached in this way, diversity produces real gains for the organisation as it values 'the varied perspectives and approaches to work that members of different identity groups bring' (Thomas & Ely 1996, p. 80).

Establishing and maintaining the learning culture is not simple: it means a change in behavioural strategies with a concomitant matched change in governing values (see Argyris 1992). The sort of changes required include the following:

Focused understanding of organisational errors Current HRM tends to treat mistakes or errors as problems that need to be fixed: we find out who is to blame and then we apply a strategy to fix things. Once fixed, we expect that everything will be satisfactory. If it is not, we blame the person who caused it all in the first place. This first order change approach is simplistic and is commonly used because of its simplicity. It is action/reaction management that actually contributes to the recurrence and worsening of the original problem (see Watzlawick et al. 1974).

Another frame of reference views errors as genuine learning and development opportunities. 'An error is any mismatch between plan or intention and what actually happened when either is implemented' (Argyris 1992, p. 1). This learning approach needs a prerequisite change in individual mind maps. Simply asserting that it is so is not sufficient. Argyris (1992), Harvey (1988) and others have demonstrated that managers are very reluctant to reveal organisational problems or their own difficulties or objections. When problems are embarrassing or threatening, adopting a learning approach becomes more difficult. Managing this personal aspect is crucial to ensure the learning approach is more than another organisational gimmick.

Respect for differing perspectives of employees Acceptance that different employees actually do perceive the same things differently comes before respect. Diversity is so often experienced as discomfort not discovery. Mostly the differences are not distinguished as such and are judged resistance, laziness or some other negative attribute. Such is the case in every misunderstanding at work, every conflict, and virtually every communication. Cultural difference misperceived is the source of much wasted time and effort, and the cause of the majority of work problems. It is the reason people wrongly assign blame and are dismissive, rather than experience options and are inclusive. Much of the early social psychology research convincingly established the power of the group, its impact on individuals to conform, and issues of control in interpersonal relationships (see Newcomb 1952). In the workplace control produces employees who are dependently loyal, and non-sustaining in their attitudes, or employees who are difficult, critical and hard to get on with.

This kind of conformity and control results in anti-learning, and shared protective routines (Argyris 1992; Harvey 1988). Yet organisational cultural reality might more effectively be constructed along learning lines.

Willingness of employees to be open and vulnerable Psychologists have pointed out the paradox that in order to gain trust, people must first take a risk and trust others. They need to be open, and therefore vulnerable. That this might be considered improper or naive in a work context is astounding; people are still people when at work. Under Taylorism they left their brains at the door. Under empowerment they are expected to leave their personality behind. Trust is a major ingredient of effective relationships and therefore effective learning. With people, problem-solving is rarely objective—it is usually subjective. Examining ourselves, our fears, our hidden assumptions and our values is an essential part of learning and adding value to our organisation. Openness diminishes defensiveness and expands new possibilities. Unfortunately, it is uncomfortable. Yet so is much of business life with its hidden rules and pressures, and we could be uncomfortable with better outcomes!

Acceptance of the recurring nature of interpersonal relationships Problem-solving with people is a continuous learning project. It is not quality control. Difficulties, misunderstandings, conflicts and negative reactions recur again and again. You do not 'fix' things, you build on the last exchange. The ideas of many recent HRM articles have posited excellent outcomes and 'best practice' results. The hope hides the handicap and manoeuvres against lasting gains. Considering work relationships through a learning lens means that normal recurring human difficulties, coexisting with daily schedules and project demands, are not experienced as so frustrating and unresolvable.

Commitment to mess with the real 'people stuff' Work relationships continue to be messy: we are contradictory and complex and mostly remain unaware of our own contradictions. (This is why properly conducted performance feedback is so valuable.) In our work environments we commonly encounter statements like 'Be quiet. The trouble with you is you never listen to others.' We are normally unaware of our own self-contradictions, and often deny what has occurred, despite being confronted with evidence. This self-una-wareness, coupled with a tendency to try to keep people happy and not cause upsets, is the everyday context in which our HRM practices occur. To pretend it isn't like this is naïve. To recognise it and simply react is a waste. To understand and utilise it is learning. Rationality is necessary at work but not to the exclusion of feelings. Both are fully present in every work situation and both should be faced and dealt with if we are to have really potent HRM programs.

As Argyris (1992) says,

> Learning is defined as occurring under two conditions. First, learning occurs when an organisation achieves what is intended; that is, there is a match between its design for action and the actuality or outcome. Second, learning occurs when a mismatch between intentions and outcomes is identified and it is corrected; that is, a mismatch is turned into a match (p. 8).

Limerick et al. (1994) have suggested that this is an action learning process. They argue that this approach straddles continuous and discontinuous change and relies on chaos theory to be successful.

Tools for a learning cuture

Language and learning relationships

Language is the daily currency of our work relationships, yet its power and subtlety are usually taken for granted. However, verbal and non-verbal language is the most significant tool we have to build our learning culture. The work of Alexander Luria (see Vocate 1987) established that the development of words is directly linked to non-verbal actions, gestures and expressions. The language we use is cemented by the relationships between the child and its inner workings in connection with external people. Luria argues the child plays an active part in structuring his own world of language and his own understanding of it. 'Every function in our development appears twice. First between people, then inside the child. All higher functions originate as actual relations between human individuals' (Vocate 1987, p. 11). Repetitive relations between people determine our learnings. Relations are the foundation of our language and our learning The learning culture therefore is dependent upon the organisation's diverse learning relationships. Language reflects conceptual differences; a person's language and conceptions may limit or enhance what facts he or she can envisage.

Luria's early work on the brain suggested the likelihood that perception was shaped by our internal language and 'learnt' from others during early development. Other work further suggests that all our perceptions (and learnings) are uniquely formed and developed inside our own brains—that is, we create our own unique reality (Maturana & Varella 1988). Our words and language create new metaphors or paradigms, and each separate person uses words and language differently to create their own metaphors and paradigms (Andrewartha et al. 1997). Thus language (verbal and non-verbal) is a tool for such learning.

Chaos and productivity

Luria further observed that, 'Differentiation precedes generalisation in development' (Vocate 1987, p. 4). This is why we discriminate and differentiate things before we can form generalisations about things. If we do not discriminate and differentiate sufficiently, intelligently and effectively, then our later generalisations (learnings) are tainted in a corresponding manner. This process is at the root of chaos theory, which is another tool of the learning culture.

Handy (1994) and others have identified the presence of paradox in progress. The excitement and complexity of paradox and its usefulness in effective motivation and transformation of people have been explored in some detail (Watzlawick 1974; Rossi 1980; Argyris 1992).

Paradox is about contradiction, ambiguity and vagueness. Fuzzy logic is a theory of fuzzy sets that calibrate vagueness. Fuzzy logic rests on the idea that all things admit of degrees—temperature, distance, beauty, friendliness, greenness, pleasure: all come on a sliding scale. Sliding scales often make it impossible to distinguish members of a class from non-members. Traditional logic and set theory have forced us to define the world in black and white terms. Fuzzy logic reflects how people think; it partly models our sense of words, our decision-making, our recognition of sights and sounds. It unveils a corner of intuition (McNeil & Freiberger 1993). All that exists is part of a continuum: work is a continuum as is time; politeness, anger, joy, and other feelings and behaviours come in continua. Competence, leadership, best practice and HRM are also part of a variable range and are not fixed entities. Peter Block (1993) has thoughtfully addressed these issues and delicately unravels the threads of predictability, control and disorder. His book is an excellent blueprint for planned chaotic learning in an organisation which reinforces the respectful use of disorder as another tool for the new HRM.

Conclusion

The HR professionals of the future will have redefined themselves out of a functional job. Their technical expertise will mean they know the business of their organisation; they will manage a complex array of others who provide functional HR services; and their primary role will be to effect organisational learning at the individual and systems level.

With HRM focused on creating a learning environment, the present differing views of HRM (as strategic or procedural; linked to the business or linked to people; proactive or reactive) are all integrated. Strategic HRM which employs interpersonal skills, understanding and competence, combines these features. A learning culture develops in a real way. Our organisations will be more real and alive. HRM will be more real and active. HR practitioners will be champions who are connected.

HRM, operating as the steward of the leaning culture, will develop organisations that operate with experimentation, expectancy and respect. The new HRM will help us achieve the difficult middle road of autonomy: rights with responsibility, obligation with commitment, caring with contribution. The result will be a productive interdependence between the person and their organisation, family, colleagues, and society.

References

Andrewartha, G., McPhee, S. & Budden, A. 1997, *Influence Dimensions*, McPhee Andrewartha, Adelaide.

Andrewartha, G. 1994, 'The personal changes required', paper presented at AHRMI/Quality Council Conference, *Making Employee Involvement Work*, Sydney, Melbourne, Brisbane, July.

Argyris, C. 1992, *On Organisational Learning*, Blackwell Publishers, Cambridge, Mass.

Block, P. 1993, *Stewardship*, Bennett-Koehler Publishers, San Francisco, CA.

Boudreau, J.B. 1990, 'Utility analysis for decisions in HRM', in M. Dunnette (ed.), *Handbook of Industrial-Organisational Psychology*, Consulting Psychology Press, Palo Alto, CA.

Boxall, P.F. & Dowling, P.J. 1990, 'Human resource management and the industrial relations tradition', *Labour & Industry*, vol. 3, nos 2 & 3, pp. 195–214.

Buber, M. 1990, *The Way of Man, According to the Teaching of Hasidism*, Carol Publishers, New York.

Carlopio, J., Andrewartha, G. & Armstrong, H. 1997, *Developing Management Skills in Australia*, Addison Wesley Longman, Sydney.

De Cieri, H., McGaughey, S.L. & Dowling, P.J. 1997, 'A conceptual framework of organisational factors and processes: An application to international human resources management', in Earley, P.C., and Erez, M. (eds), *New Perspectives on International and Organizational Psychology*, Jossey-Bass, San Francisco.

Dowling, P. & De Cieri, H. 1995, 'Cross cultural issues in organisational behaviour in trends', in Cooper, C.L. & Russo, D.M. (eds), *Organisational Behaviour*, vol. 2, John Wiley & Sons, New York.

Dowling, P.J. & Boxall, P.F. 1994, 'Shifting the emphasis from natural resources to human resources: The challenge of the new competitive context in Australia and New Zealand', *Zeitschrift fur Personalforschung*, vol. 8, no. 3, pp. 302–16.

Dowling, P.J. & Schuler, R. 1990, 'Human resource management', in Blanpain, R. (ed.), *Comparative Labour Law and Industrial Relations in Industrialised Market Economies*, 4th edn, vol. 2 (pp. 125–49), Kluwer Law and Taxation Publishers, Boston.

Downie, B. & Coates, M.L. (eds) 1995, *Managing Human Resources in the 1990s and Beyond: Is the Workplace Being Transformed?*, Queen's University Press, Ontario.

Guest, D.E. 1990, 'Human resource management and the American dream', *Journal of Management Studies*, vol. 27, 4 July, pp. 378–97.

Handy, C. 1994, *The Empty Raincoat*, Hutchinson, London.

Harvey, J. 1988, *The Abilene Paradox*, Lexington Publishers, San Diego, CA.

Karpin, D. 1995, *Enterprising Nation, Report of the Industry Task Force on Leadership and Management Skills*, Australian Government Publishing Service, Canberra.

Kessler, I. 1995, 'Reward systems', in Storey, J. (ed.), *Human Resource Management: A Critical Text*, Routledge, London, pp. 254–79.

Kochan, T., Katz, H. & McKersie, R. 1986, *The Transformation of American Industrial Relations*, Basic Books, New York.

Kramar, R. 1992, 'Strategic HRM: Are the promises fulfilled?', *Asia Pacific Journal of Human Resources*, vol. 30, no. 1, pp. 1–15.

Lawler, E. 1986, *High Involvement Management*, Jossey-Bass, San Francisco, CA.

—— 1995, 'Strategic human resource management: An idea whose time has come', in Downie, B. & Coates, M.L. (eds), *Managing Human Resources in the 1990s and Beyond: Is the Workplace Being Transformed?*, Queen's University Press, Ontario, pp. 46–70.

Legge, K. 1995, 'HRM: Rhetoric, reality and hidden agendas', in Storey, J. (ed.), *Human Resource Management: A Critical Text*, Routledge, London, pp. 33–62.

Limerick, D. 1992, 'The shape of the new organisation: Implications for human resource management', *Asia Pacific Journal of Human Resources*, vol. 30, no. 1, pp. 38–52.

—— 1994, 'High performance and the socially sustainable organisation', paper presented at the AHRI National Convention, *Exploring the High Performance Organisation*, Hobart, October.

Limerick, D., Pasfield, R. & Cunnington, B. 1994, 'Towards an action learning organisation', *The Learning Organisation*, vol. 1, no. 2, pp. 29–40.

McGregor, D. 1960, *The Human Side of Enterprise*, McGraw-Hill, New York.

McNeil, D. & Freiberger, P. 1993, *Fuzzy Logic*, Bookman Press, Melbourne.

Macquarie Dictionary 1981, Macquarie Library Pty Ltd, St Leonards, NSW.

Maturana, H.R. & Varella F.J. 1988, *The Tree of Knowledge*, New Science Library, Shambhala, Boston and London.

Newcomb, T. 1952, *Readings in Social Psychology*, Henry Holt, New York.

O'Neill, G. & Kramar, R. 1995, *Australian Human Resources Management: Current Trends in Management Practice*, Pitman; Melbourne.

Rosseau, D.M. & House, R.J. 1994, 'Meso organisational behaviour: Avoiding three fundamental biases', in Cooper, C.L. and Rousseau, D.M. (eds), *Trends in Organisational Behaviour*, Wiley, Chicester, UK.

Rossi, E.L. (ed.) 1980, *The Collected Papers of Milton H. Erickson*, Irvington Publishers Inc., New York.

Rothwell, S. 1995, 'Human resource planning', in Storey, J. (ed.), *Human Resource Management: A Critical Text*, Routledge, London, pp. 167–202.

Schuler, R.S. & Dowling, P.J. 1990, 'Human resource management and organisational strategy: Implications for industrial relations', in Blanpain, R. (ed.), *Comparative Labour Law and Industrial Relations in Industrialised Market Economies*, 4th edn, Kluwer, Deventer, Netherlands.

Senge, P. 1990, *The Fifth Discipline*, Doubleday, New York.

Smart, J.P. 1985, 'Personnel management and the pursuit of professionalism', *Human Resource Management Australia*, vol. 23, no. 2, pp. 29–31.

Smart, J. & Pontifex, M. 1995, 'Human resource management: The profession and its society', in O'Neill, G. and Kramar, R. (eds), *Australian Human Resources Management: Current Trends in Management Practice*, Vol. I, Woodslane, Melbourne.

Smart J.P. & Pontifex, M.R. 1993, 'Human resources management and the Australian Human Resources Institute: The profession and its professional body', *Asia Pacific Journal of Human Resources*, vol. 31, no. 1, pp. 1–19.

Staw, B. 1986, 'Organisational psychology and the pursuit of the happy/productive worker', *California Management Review*, vol. XXVIII, no. 4, pp. 40–53.

Storey J. (ed.) 1995a, *Human Resource Management: A Critical Text*, Routledge, London.

—— 1995b, 'From personnel management to HRM: The implications for teaching', *Asia Pacific Journal of Human Resources*, vol. 33, no. 3, Spring/Summer, pp. 4–14.

—— 1995c, 'Human resource management: still marching on, or marching out?', in Storey, J. (ed.), *Human Resource Management: A Critical Text*, Routledge, London pp. 3–32.

Storey, J. & Sisson, K. 1993, *Managing Human Resources and Industrial Relations*, Open University Press, Buckingham.

Thomas, D. & Ely, R. 1996, 'Making differences matter', *Harvard Business Review*, Sept.–Oct., pp. 79-90.

Ulrich, D. 1997, *Human Resource Champions*, Harvard Business School Press, Cambridge, Mass.

Ulrich, D., Brockbank, W. and DeYeung, A. 1989, 'HRM competencies in the 1990s: An empirical assessment of what the future holds', *Personnel Administrator*, vol. 34, no. 11, pp. 91–3.

Vocate, D.R. 1987, *The Theory of A.R. Luria—Functions of Spoken Language in the Development of Higher Mental Processes*, Lawrence Erlbaum Associates Publishers, London.

Walker, J.W. 1982, 'The Ralph Report, Implications for the Australian Institute of Training and Development', *Training and Development in Australia*, vol. 19, no. 4, p. 10.

Watzlawick, P., Weakland, J. & Fisch, R. 1974, *Change: Principles of Problem Formation and Problem Resolution*, W.W. Norton & Company, New York and London.

The Weekend Australian, 1996, 14–15 Sept., p. 69.

Case Study A

From personnel manager to HR consultant—The Auschain experience

Daryl Wightman and Jenni Werner

Is your human resources function providing value for money? Although most of us would agree the HR function plays an important role, few chief executives today are willing to tolerate functions that consume resources without demonstrating a real contribution to the business. This demanding attitude is a result of increasing national and global competition, cost pressures, and a new emphasis on 'added value'. Process re-engineering asks the fundamental question: 'does this activity add value?'. In other words, does this activity give customers something they are prepared to pay for? Unfortunately, many HR functions are extremely good at performing tasks of questionable real value to the business.

In response to these demands to add measurable value, many organisations are now attempting to transform their human resources functions to an 'internal consulting' mode of operating. This, they hope, will bring them closer to the business units, and enable them to be more responsive to the specific needs of the business. Although this change in operating style sounds fairly straightforward, it needs careful planning and execution, and can present a number of pitfalls for the unwary.

The following case study shows how a large Australian organisation attempted to 're-badge' its

HR professionals as internal consultants and highlights some of the potential problems and how they might be overcome.

The Auschain story

Auschain is a large retailer with some 100 retail outlets around Australia. The personnel function was organised on traditional lines, with a central corporate department and a small personnel group in each regional office. An in-store personnel manager in each outlet was responsible for day-to-day personnel activities.

Margins in the Australian retail industry had come under considerable pressure in the early 1990s and Auschain was facing fierce competition in a diminishing market. In an attempt to reduce costs and increase profitability, the company embarked on a significant restructuring. To increase account-ability for profit and service delivery, store managers were now to take responsibility for staffing as well as for store operations. The job of in-store personnel manager was abolished, and the size of the personnel function was to be reduced from 150 to 20. These remaining personnel professionals were to operate as HR consultants.

The planning process

No single factor was driving the changes in Auschain's personnel function, although market pressures had a large role to play. The pressure on margins in an already depressed market was having an adverse effect on Auschain's business. Some stores were not performing well, a number of products were under-performing and the customer focus was not quite right. This poor performance was the result of the accumulation of a number of issues affecting business performance rather than of a single issue or event.

The changes in Auschain were part of an overall process of organisational development. Changes in top management positions and the increased emphasis on profitability opened up opportunities to challenge the *status quo* and inject new ideas. The main targets for change were the retail outlets. Each outlet had a management team comprising product managers responsible for different types of goods, and headed by a store manager. Staffing levels were being reviewed, particularly in under-performing stores, and store managers were being asked to manage their stores as individual business units.

It was against this backdrop of organisational change that the restructuring of the personnel function began. The impetus for the changes came from within the personnel function itself. The process was initiated by an enthusiastic and energetic manager with a strong desire to see things done differently. The issue at the heart of the changes was that management roles and responsibilities within each store tended to split the responsibility for product and people: the product managers and store manager were responsible for the product and for achieving financial and sales targets, while the in-store personnel manager was responsible for managing the people issues. How could store managers be held accountable for service and profitability if they were only responsible for half the store's resources? And if responsibility for people was given to store managers, where did that leave the in-store personnel managers? The answer was to abolish the role of in-store personnel manager and set up a team of HR consultants responsible for servicing all stores within a geographic area.

The key to this change lay in the content of the personnel manager's job. The job included a large element of administration that did not make full use of the personnel manager's capability. As shown in Table A1 (see p. 20), most administrative tasks could easily be handled by a general administration function. Overall responsibility for staffing issues within each store was to rest with individual product and store managers. The administration and recordkeeping activities were given to a new in-store administration manager who also handled aspects of store administration and paperwork. This arrangement allowed the new HR consultants to concentrate on specialist HR activities.

The idea seemed quite attractive, particularly when it became apparent that cost savings would accompany the change. The initiating manager and the head of HR, who was at the same time lobbying the rest of the management team, discussed the proposal. A formal case was put to the top management team to restructure the HR function. As shown in Figure A1 (see p. 21), the new group of HR consultants reported to a district manager responsible for store operations within a geographic area. The main steps in the proposed implementation plan were:

- communicate the nature of the proposed changes to all employees; the aim of this step was to explain the aims and reasons for the changes, allay possible anxieties and gain personnel managers' commitment to the process;
- select 20 HR consultants from the existing pool of 150 in-store personnel managers using a competency profile for the new consulting role;
- redeploy as many as possible of the remaining 130 personnel managers in other roles, and deal with any necessary redundancies.

The heart of the selection process for HR consultants was a profile of competencies—the attitudes, knowledge, skills and behaviour expected in the new role. The content of these competencies was similar to what is set out in 'the new demands' column in Table A2 (see p. 23), except that consulting skills were not explicitly mentioned. This omission was also to have a critical impact on the initial success of the project.

The detailed project plan was submitted to the top management team for approval. At first the team regarded the competency profile as 'too academic'. However, the HR group argued that without the competency profile there would be no systematic template for selecting the new consultants; they saw

Table A1   The change in roles

	THE OLD REGIME	NEW ROLES		
	Personnel manager	HR consultant	Administration manager	Line managers
Payroll administration	• Administers the Award • Timekeeping (recording hours worked)	Advice & guidance (e.g. how best to pay people, interpretation of the Award)	Administration (runs the payroll)	
Rostering & scheduling	Determines number of staff needed each day and allocates individuals	Advice & guidance (e.g. on number of hours part-time staff can work)	Administration	Define business need (i.e. staff levels required)
Leave management	Administers: • sick leave • leave accrual • long-service leave	Advice & guidance (e.g. whether to pay someone who is out of sick leave)	Administration (recordkeeping)	
Occupational health & safety	• Monitors claims • Organises safety committees • Records incidents	Interprets regulations	Administration (recordkeeping)	
Training & development	Delivers on-site training	Runs 'train-the-trainer' courses for line managers	Records training attendance	Deliver training using guides and materials developed by HR function
Recruitment	• Advertises position • Interviews & shortlists	• Helps develop specification • Interviews applicants with line manager		• Interview applicants with HR consultant • Make final decision
Industrial relations (IR)	• Manages site IR issues • Deals with the union	• Advises corporate head office on local impact of IR issues • Advises line managers on how to handle IR issues	Collects union subscriptions	Greater responsibility for meeting IR obligations and taking action

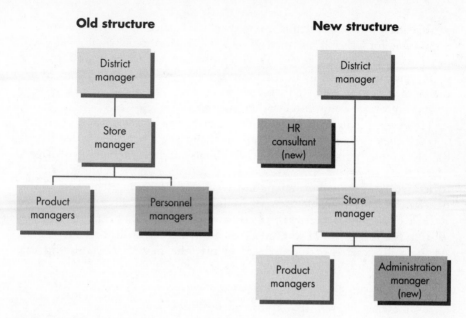

Figure A1 How the structure changed

this profile as a practical and necessary implementation tool. The top team concurred and the project received formal approval.

Implementation and outcomes

The first step was to inform managers and staff of the proposed changes. A 'road show' was developed including videos and small group briefings. These briefings were cascaded down the organisation from regional managers to store managers and finally to employees in each outlet. This exercise was supported by detailed briefing notes (including questions and answers) to ensure information was conveyed accurately and consistently. The briefings covered all aspects of the restructuring, including the new responsibilities of product and store managers, and the in-store administration managers and the HR consultants. The changes in the HR function were therefore conveyed as part of the overall change in store structure to deliver better service.

The next step was to use the HR consultant competency profile to assess existing personnel managers. This assessment was made by the regional manager and regional personnel manager based on each in-store personnel manager's past performance and degree of fit with the target competency profile. Most personnel managers were redeployed in other roles including the new administration manager role in each outlet. However, the large reduction in the size of the personnel function led inevitably to a number of redundancies. These were dealt with prior to the introduction of the new structure and were handled through an outplacement program.

The new HR consultants were then established as a mobile resource responsible for assisting line managers in a number of retail outlets. The style of the job changed fundamentally: although they had access to desk-space at their regional office, many now (almost literally) lived out of their car. At first the new structure seemed to be working. HR consultants had a positive attitude and were committed to their new roles.

However, gradually it became clear that all was not well. Many consultants felt they were not doing as well as they should be. Some were having difficulty pinpointing the needs of their clients and influencing line managers. Many were finding it hard to operate within their more nebulous and less structured working environment and were not clear what their role should be. Why did these problems arise? Mainly because the differences between the role of personnel manager and HR consultant had not been fully appreciated. In fact the new role was fundamentally different, as shown in Table A2. As we will explore in more detail below, the new HR consulting role demanded:

- a new set of skills and style of working;
- a somewhat different set of personal attributes.

New skills and style of working

Whereas the old personnel manager role was well defined and had a large administrative content, the new consulting role was less task focused (and hence less clearly defined); in addition it required a more proactive style of operating. Although the new consultants had HR expertise, many did not have a sufficient understanding of the wider HR framework, and in particular they did not understand how HR contributes to a business result. They had moved from a position of being personnel administrators to a new role of giving advice and guidance to the business. Whereas their original HR expertise was heavily focused on day-to-day operational issues, they now needed an understanding of how HR could make a positive contribution to help the organisation achieve its business objectives. Furthermore, they had moved from maintaining stability in a narrow and clearly defined unit to improving the way a much broader part of the organisation operated. This meant working in a less stable and more fluid environment, which required an understanding of organisational dynamics and how to overcome inertia to influence line managers and make things happen.

To help HR consultants deal with these new demands, an external consultant was engaged to run a series of consulting skills courses. This training gave the new consultants a better understanding of their role as consultants and how they should be managing and establishing relationships with line managers as 'clients'. It gave them a deeper understanding of how to initiate and manage change, and equipped them with practical consulting tools and skills. This new set of 'consulting skills' had been missing from the original competency profile.

Table A2 The new competency demands

Traditional personnel role	HR consultant—the new demands
Business competencies	
Often focused on narrow personnel issues rather than the broader aims of the business. Focused more on day-to-day operational matters than longer term business objectives.	'Business people who deal in HR matters': • Understands the client's area of business • Sees the HR implications of business issues • Focuses on achieving business objectives • Thinks like a chief executive!
'Consulting' skills	
More administrative and to do with implementing HR policies rather than assisting line managers to achieve their business objectives. Seen as a functional specialist rather than a business partner.	• Plans and manages consultancy assignments • Establishes professional consulting relationships • Prepares formal proposals setting out terms of reference for assignments • Actively manages the client's involvement and expectations—no surprises! • Overcomes inertia and obstacles to change • Applies consulting tools and techniques for information gathering, analysis and reporting • Spots opportunities and 'markets' their services
HR expertise	
Often limited to interpreting the current requirements of the law and ensuring this is effectively put into practice. Includes setting up and operating appropriate administrative procedures.	Understands the wider HR framework (e.g. can advise on the likely impact of legislative change, and the accompanying business opportunities or threats).
Interpersonal skills	
Some have highly developed interpersonal skills. However, they often derive their authority and influence more from their positional status and the authority vested in them to police legal requirements, or decisions and policies laid down by more senior managers.	Rely more on their personal assertiveness, social confidence and perceived professionalism. Often have less formal 'authority' or positional power: • Builds internal relationships • Gains respect of senior management • Can 'read' the attitudes and motives of others • Can 'sell' new ideas and approaches • Prepared to challenge people if appropriate • Can handle difficult people • Can cope with being rebuffed or attacked
Personal characteristics	
• Well organised and methodical • Not always comfortable with a loose role definition • Often reactive rather than proactive • May be wary of the power and status of others • Often very nice people!	• Goal and results oriented • Comfortable with ambiguity • Thick-skinned; comfortable under pressure • Proactive; takes the initiative • Eloquent, convincing communicator • Insightful about people ('emotional intelligence') • Confident • Analytical

Personal attributes

While most HR consultants benefited from the consulting skills training, a few still struggled. Their new role was placing them under new pressures. They now had to confront line managers and ask difficult questions, and many were finding these new challenges hard to cope with. Although they worked well in an administrative role, some did not have the required assertiveness, drive and resilience to perform well as a consultant. However, these limitations had not been apparent in their old roles. In this respect, the retrospective performance assessment had not always given a complete picture of each personnel manager's potential to work as a consultant. Past performance as a personnel manager is not necessarily a good indication of future potential as a consultant.

Perceptions of line managers

There was still another and more subtle obstacle in the way. Line managers regarded HR consultants as personnel managers who had simply been re-badged and given responsibility for a larger pool of staff. The consultants often did not have the 'status' to operate independently and were seen as playing second-fiddle to the district managers. When they visited a store, the district manager would talk about stock, and the HR consultant would talk about people. Instead of operating as business partners, the consultants were seen as subservient, and people issues were still regarded as secondary. This perception limited their credibility and their ability to discuss business issues on equal terms with line managers; as a result, they could not achieve their full potential as agents of change and performance improvement. Inadvertently, the old structure had simply been duplicated one level higher in the organisation.

Lessons from the case study

Auschain was one of the first large organisations in Australia to attempt to move their personnel function to an HR consulting role. The new structure reduced costs and encouraged line managers and the new HR consulting function to concentrate on improving business performance. However, the changes did not take place as smoothly as expected or deliver all the potential benefits of an internal consulting function. The main lessons from Auschain's experience are:

1 The role of HR consultant is fundamentally different from the traditional role of personnel professionals. Rather than performing a set of predefined tasks, consultants must focus on building relationships, giving advice, challenging management thinking and achieving business objectives. Because of these differences, past performance is not necessarily a good indicator of future capability as a consultant. Steps should be taken to provide a reliable

measure of the gap between existing and required capability, and to take suitable action to close the gap. Additional measures of future potential (e.g. psychometric measures of aptitude and occupational personality) may be required to supplement information on past performance.

2   In addition to a good understanding of HR issues, the HR consulting role requires a broader understanding of business and organisational dynamics, and a new set of skills and techniques. Even the best personnel managers may need formal training and development in consulting skills.

3   The structure of the new HR consulting function should help consultants build their credibility and perceived 'independence'. Setting up individual reporting lines to specific line managers as we saw in Auschain tends to undermine a consultant's ability to act. Although an experienced consultant may be able to cope with this situation, those new to the role are likely to find this type of working relationship very hard to deal with. If possible, we believe a separate consulting unit or stream should be established, and that this should report through to a manager on the top team (at least formally). In addition to giving the consultant greater flexibility and autonomy, this line of accountability should help build the consultant's credibility. Rather than being tied to the narrower interests of a particular unit or section, this structure will reinforce their objectivity and should encourage line managers to regard them as valued business partners.

4   Line managers may need to be educated in how the new consulting function operates and how best to make use of the new resource. In fact we believe that one of the first 'marketing' tasks of the new function should involve meeting line managers, redefining old relationships and positioning HR consultants as business partners rather than narrow personnel specialists.

There is good news emerging from Auschain's experience: although a number of HR consultants struggled, many eventually developed the professionalism and skills to operate effectively in their new roles. Their success suggests that many within our existing pools of personnel professionals have the potential to make this transition to consultancy. The challenge is to ensure the transition is properly planned, executed and supported. Only then will personnel professionals take their seats as fully fledged business partners.

2 Executive recruitment and selection

Ross Johnston

The executive recruitment and selection process is a key element of the human resources management (HRM) cycle. Many Australian companies are now finding the need to review their recruitment processes as they change and upgrade the skills mix of their senior employees. It is important that management have the skills to take advantage of a rapidly changing business environment, a key element of which is workforce flexibility. It is also essential in today's legal environment where mistakes are expensive, both in terms of time and money. This chapter gives an overview of current practices used in Australia and overseas, and raises a number of issues that need to be considered in any executive recruitment exercise.

The HRM cycle depicted in Figure 2.1 (see p. 28) assumes that the organisation needs to continuously improve the quality and performance of its human capital to match the continually changing business environment. In order to improve its human capital, the organisation must assess and measure the skills and competencies needed to achieve its business plan against its current workforce and address any shortfalls through recruitment, training, personal development and performance management. The evidence suggests that single careers streams will be shorter and personal skills will need to be

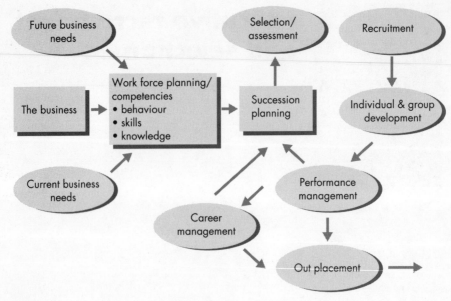

Figure 2.1 Human resources cycle

upgraded more frequently. In the words of Charles Handy, 'Time's paradoxes mean that the old blocks of time, the 40-hour week and the 50-year career are probably gone for ever as a way of life' (Handy 1994, p. 167). In this future scenario, the injection of new, higher skilled or more experienced employees will be a fact of organisational life. Therefore, the success of the recruitment process, and the filling of key vacancies, is fundamental to the ongoing health and continuity of the organisation.

A series of steps are involved in the selection and recruitment process of key staff. These need to be considered each time an organisation seeks an alternative to filling an existing or new position on a planned basis. The final recruitment might be an internal or external candidate; in either case, the following issues need careful consideration:

- *the organisation*: What is the current culture of the organisation? What is the culture required to achieve its vision and business objectives? What understanding is there of its staffing needs now—and for the future—against its planned business strategies and objectives?
- *skills and competencies:* What competencies are required for the position and for the individual, now and in the future? What are the most appropriate measures for successful performance in the role?
- *sources of recruitment:* Will the recruitment process be internal, external or a combination of both? Where are likely candidates for the position to be found? Will candidates be drawn from the same or similar industries and will it be necessary to consider international resources? Is the organisation's HR function capable of managing and executing the process, or is an external

search firm required? Has the organisation considered the high cost of recruitment using external resources, and has it planned for this?

- *selection processes:* Who will be involved in the selection process, and at what stages? Should there be a structured interview process? Will psychological assessment be useful to the process? Does the organisation's culture require a personality profile to ensure the appropriate 'fit'? Is there a role for assessment centres? How will references be checked?
- *the recruitment decision:* Are the prime candidates compatible with the organisation and its culture? What future career path opportunities may be available, or is this a specialist area? How relevant is the candidate's previous experience? Where is the remuneration package positioned? Are there any cautions to be considered and thought through? Is an employment contract necessary from either—or both—the organisation and candidate's perspective?
- *commencement:* What will be the induction process to the organisation, the specific work area and how can this best accelerate the assimilation process? How does the individual become aligned with the corporate goals and strategies? Does the employer build in insurance—mentoring, counselling and networking assistance? What personal development is planned for the recruit? What and when will be the review processes?

The organisation

'Culture' is an unpopular term in a number of large Australian companies. This is probably due to a surfeit of enthusiasm from some of the early organisation development proponents of the 1970s and 1980s. Nevertheless, all major organisations have characteristic ways of operating, individual 'rituals' or behaviours that distinguish them from others, even in the same industry and in similar business environments. Edgar Schein (1985, p. 15), a major contributor to our current understanding of organisational behaviour, described culture as:

> the deeper level of basic assumptions and beliefs that are shared by members of an organisation, that operate unconsciously and define the organisation's view of itself and its environment ... these assumptions and beliefs are learned responses to a Group's problems of survival in its external environment and its problems of internal integration.

Brief examples of strong and very different characteristics of organisational cultures experienced by the author, are Shell International Petroleum Company, ANZ Banking Group and BHP.

Shell has remained a successful top-ten *Fortune 500* company by maintaining a strong international management cadre of home grown and trained executives. They share such common characteristics as high academic qualifications, strong analytical, general management and networking skills. Arie de Geus (1997), Shell International Petroleum's planning guru of the 1980s, wrote that living companies—companies that have enjoyed long-term business success—regard the optimisation of capital as no more than a necessary complement to optimisation of people. He drew the analogy that 'birds that flock together learn faster, and so do organisations that encourage their employees to flock' (Geus 1997, p. 57). All senior managers in Shell are part of an international network that encourages them to manage in a similar operational approach across more than 50 countries. They are recruited, 'parented' or sponsored by a business function or country (or both), and it is here that their development and future careers are planned. Only in recent years, as the power of the strong internal culture and its barriers have faded, have external recruits of mature age been successfully integrated into this culture at senior levels.

Several years ago, the ANZ Banking Group conducted a cultural evaluation of its senior executive team using the Organisational Character Index (OCI). The OCI is based on the popular Myers Briggs Personality Indicator and is designed to assist organisations understand their own capacity for change and the responses they are likely to exhibit. In a sense, it identifies the organisational 'personality' as seen through the eyes its employees. The employee responses are sorted into the four primary characteristics of the Myers Briggs Personality Indicator, namely:

1 *extroversion/introversion*—where does the organisation focus its energies?
2 *sensing/intuition*—what does the organisation pay attention to?
3 *thinking/feeling*—how does the organisation make decisions?
4 *judging/perceiving*—reliance on information-gathering versus decision-making?

The survey recorded an overall ESTJ profile (extroverted/sensing/ thinking/judging) for this executive group. In practice, this means that top management of ANZ Banking Group was, at that time, perceived by its employees as being:

- *extroverted*—focused outward and responding to external stimuli;
- *sensing*—concerned with realities, facts and attention to detail;
- *thinking*—heavy reliance on impersonal procedures and objective principles; and
- *judging*—a clear preference for things to be spelled out, planned, fixed and settled.

In contrast to Shell, the ANZ Bank has had significant success in recruiting mature age staff over a number of years; but has also had major disappointments when the importance of candidates' ability to manage within the culture had been undervalued. For example, several senior executives coming from organisations with strong but very different cultures to ANZ were not perceived to 'deliver' because of difficulties in coming to grips with elements of the culture. In particular the *thinking* and *judging* characteristics referred to above did not sit comfortably with recruits possessing the opposite *perceiving* or *intuitive* skills.

BHP is an organisation with a pronounced organisation culture. The company has been accused of staying in a 1960s time-warp with an implied promotion advantage to Anglo-Australian men over women and people from non-English speaking backgrounds (Bagwell, 1997). For many years successful managerial experience in the traditional steel business appeared a prerequisite for elevation to executive ranks. However, BHP brought in a much broader base of experience and management skills as the company's minerals, gas and petroleum business expanded rapidly through the 1980s and 1990s. The perception of the closed nature of the culture remains strong despite these changes.

According to the business press, BHP is aware of the strong cultural difficulties in operating in male-dominated industries and recognises the significance of the issue in its multinational operating environment. Presumably, with this background, the company will increase its focus on designing and monitoring HR processes to change this current state.

It is not suggested that organisations need to go through a major cultural analysis as part of the recruitment process, nor is deliberate 'cloning' an appropriate strategy for long-term growth and survival. However, recruitment and separation of staff are expensive exercises. In choosing staff, companies need to be more systematic and rigorous than simply attempting to assess the interpersonal 'chemistry' in an unstructured interview process. The harder issue to resolve during the recruitment process relates to how the organisational culture and particularly senior appointments within that culture reinforce the business environment and long-term objectives.

Most major Australian companies face market pressures of increasing competition, reducing margins and a need to contain costs. A major challenge is to control staffing costs while remaining competitive in the labour market. The response to this challenge is often to focus on short-term behaviour. Today's competent line manager or supervisor may be capable of achieving short-term objectives, but may not have the skills required for longer term success. Some of the skills required for the future may be developed over time, yet in many cases the manager of today does not have a long-term future. Organisations need to recruit tomorrow's senior managers while managing the issue of developing these 'newcomers' over today's existing—and probably, long-serving—managers.

The much discussed Karpin Report (Industry Task Force on Leadership and Management Skills 1995) raised the question of a new paradigm of management. Part of the report dealt with a definition of the senior manager profile for the year 2010. Table 2.1 (see p. 32) illustrates the changing business and management skills required, and highlights the urgency in defining the future organisation. Having a clear idea of future requirements needs to be part of all recruitment exercises directed at key management and executive positions.

In addition to the culture 'fit' and management skills required, the third element an organisation must consider is what its workforce requirements are, now and in the future. Planning too far into the future can be useless because

Table 2.1 The emerging senior manager profile

1970	Today	2010
The autocrat	**The communicator**	**The leader/enabler**
• Male	• Male	• Male or female
• Anglo-Celt, British or Australian citizenship	• Anglo-Celt, Australian citizenship	• Wide range of ethnicities, citizenships
• Started as message boy, rose through ranks; all management training on-the-job	• Graduate, possibly postgraduate qualification; career in corporate centre; product of internal management development program	• Graduate, probably MBA as well; wide ranging career, many placements; product of major development program including placements
• Very local focus, possible one Australian state; has travelled once, to England	• Expanding focus, travels regularly to Asia, USA, and Europe	• Global focus, travels regularly, has lived in two or more countries
• Established competitors, cartels	• Recently deregulated marketplace, rapidly changing competitors	• Manages in both regulated and deregulated economies
• Paternal view of workplace	• Sees workforce as stakeholder in business, working hard on communication and information sharing	• Manages workforces in several countries; shares information and delegates heavily
• Stable environment; relatively low stress, home to see kids most nights, long-term position	• Turbulent environment; high stress, long hours, fears burnout	• Environment typified by rapid change; limited term appointment, high pressure, results driven

Source: Industry Task Force on Leadership and Management Skills 1995, p. xi.

both internal and external events can make strategies irrelevant, but it is necessary to plan a supply and potential progression of senior management at least up to ten years ahead if long-term continuity is to be achieved. An interesting example of this is De Geus' Shell-sponsored study in 1983. This involved 30 companies identified as having strong corporate identities, being successful in their respective industries, and ranging in age from 100 to 700 years (De Geus 1997). The third question an organisation must consider is what its workforce needs are, now and in the future. Planning too far in advance is useless because external as well as internal events can make strategies irrelevant, but it is necessary to plan senior management progression/succession up to ten years ahead if long-term continuity is to be achieved.

To define the gap between their current supply of high potential management and assessment of future job requirements, Shell has, for many years, used the Staff Structure Planning model. This model matches the supply of jobs available now, and in the future (e.g. 3, 5 and 10 years out), against the supply of people available to do those jobs, using the current estimate of potential (CEP) for each employee in the population under review. The CEP was established by a ranking process based on Shell's leadership competency clusters. The clusters were the famous Helicopter competency grouping (which combined the skills of Power of Analysis, Imagination and Sense of Reality; in order to provide an enlightened overview), business skills and leadership skills. Like all models this one is susceptible to incorrect assumptions on individuals, confusion between generalists and specialists, discounting of entrepreneurial skills, and rapid organisational change. Nevertheless, the system has provided Shell with a continuing 'pipeline' of talent progressing through to top management positions, without the gaps or unpleasant surprises experienced by many organisations. It is in this context that forward-thinking organisations need to understand current recruitment requirements, likely future needs and possible career paths for a talented individual, when they commence the recruitment process.

Skills and competencies

As with 'culture', the word 'competencies' does not sit well with many Australian companies. The term 'competencies' has led to much confusion because of contrasting usages. In recent years many major Australian companies have introduced competencies into their selection and recruitment, training, development or performance management processes; nevertheless, there is no common definition of the term (see for example O'Neill & Doig 1997). One definition of competencies refers to requirements for entry level or adequate performance in a position; another sees competencies as the characteristics that differentiate superior performance.

Boyatzis (1982) proposed that a competency model should include two dimensions; one dimension is the *type* of competency, the other is the *level* of competency that may exist in the individual. His study found that superior managerial performance was also affected by factors other than the competencies of the individual. The demands of the job and organisational environment (or culture) also influence job performance. He concluded that maximum performance requires an appropriate fit between three things—

individual competencies, specific job requirements, and the organisational culture and environment in which these come together.

In some companies senior managers are recruited against a detailed job description. The job description can be a good starting point for setting out the role expectations for an individual, but only if it recognises the context and complexity of the role, its interaction with other roles, and the key performance indicators. Recognition of the context and impact of a role will not occur if the job description is simply an aggregation of tasks (Gerstein & Reisman 1983).

Hay McBer studied organisations across fifteen countries to determine the characteristics of outstanding CEOs (Dalzeil 1996). While there is no simple recipe for executive success, the study concluded that two dimensions were required to master global leadership:

- *international adaptability*—the ability to align business strategies, policies and behaviours with cultural requirements in given parts of the world. Such adaptability becomes evident in the assumptions CEOs make about building business relationships, choosing a basis for action, and the way in which authority and leadership is exercised.
- *universal competencies*—this dimension focuses on critical issues and alliances. The competencies are measureable through the way executives sharpen their business focus, build commitment within their organisation for the business direction, and drive for success.

Another example of the definition of personal dimensions or competencies is the Career Architect system, developed in the US by Lominger and licensed in Australia by the DBM consulting organisation. This system lists 67 separate competencies—or portfolio skills—and 18 'career stallers and stoppers'. It has been used by a number of companies in Australia and elsewhere as the basis for management discussions and definition of competencies required for a role, or for future senior manager development.

Whether one uses a competency cluster approach such as Hay McBer, or a more exhaustive competency definitional approach like the Career Architect, is a matter for individual management teams to work through. The key element is to have a shared management understanding of the competencies seen as critical for senior management success and a process for measurement of these competencies. The process need not be as sophisticated as the Shell CEP approach, but without a process of evaluation, Boyatzis' comments on the need for a comprehensive and integrated understanding of the role context remain a cautionary warning. It is much easier to develop a recruitment profile and to compare a candidate against other candidates when the job and organisational context is provided.

It also provides a firm basis for more sophisticated selection and recruitment processes, including structured interviewing and assessment centres.

Sources of recruitment

The decision on how to source recruitment is an important step towards a successful outcome. However, the decision should not be determined solely on cost. High level international searches for world-class executives or professional specialists may take more than six months to complete. For positions at senior levels, the opportunity cost of a six-month delay may be a small cost to pay against the need to find the individual with the skills required. Timeframes vary considerably: in 1993 when Westpac was teetering on the brink of a financial collapse, the chairman used an international search firm to scour the world for a successor to CEO Frank Conroy. The search—concluding with the announcement of Bob Joss' appointment as chief executive—lasted 30 days (Carew 1997). Yet, in a much more secure environment in 1997, the ANZ bank waited more than five months to announce a successor to CEO Don Mercer. Clearly, short-term cost was not a consideration in either case, but each company needed to balance thoroughness of the search against a sense of urgency.

There is a sequence of questions to be worked through in determining how to go about a particular recruitment exercise. The most obvious question is where are likely candidates to be found? Will they be with local industry competitors in the same geographic area? Are similar skills used in other industries, and can they be transported readily with the added benefits of outside breadth of expertise? For example, major Australian banks have found that corporate finance executives, experienced in the management of balance sheets and raising finance, quickly adapt to senior banking roles involving portfolio investment or credit and risk management. Also, is geography or international experience a key factor, in which case the net needs to be cast much wider? Senior managers with specific technical backgrounds in particular fields often fall in this category, as BHP and Rio Tinto have found.

The next question is how should the recruitment process be managed? Is the organisation's human resources function capable of managing the process by advertising in major newspapers, trade journals, association memberships and the like? Or should the recruitment exercise be delegated to a specialist with interstate or international linkages?

Recruitment specialists vary in their practices. At the top end of the market are specialist executive search firms, often subsidiaries or allied with major international firms, and with specialisation in particular disciplines or fields. They have the necessary network to mount an international search.

The initial issue for any search firm is to determine—or clarify—the client's particular requirements. Detailed person and job specifications are necessary, which is why issues of organisation, culture and competencies are so important. Search firms are expensive, particularly for international searches. To avoid wasting money (and time), the client needs to state clearly the required result and negotiate the fee payable.

Executive search firms may be also used when potentially suitable external names have been identified. Often, these potential candidates are with opposition companies or customers. It is far better for an independent party to make the initial approach without revealing the source. This protects the organisation from possible retaliatory reaction from the other company, and the individual from the embarrassment of an ill-timed or clumsy approach. A search firm can also provide an independent assessment of the potential recruit's suitability, which can be valuable if management or the board is under pressure to make an urgent appointment.

Potential internal candidates are another source of recruitment. In large corporations formal succession plans are usually reviewed before commencing an external search. It is possible that internal candidates not currently included in the succession planning lists may be interested in the position. Some companies are reluctant to advertise internally for senior positions for which they are recruiting externally. Fear of creating precedents (such as always advertising internally) and the inconvenience of establishing extensive internal interview—and appeal—processes are the usual reasons for this reluctance. However, internal advertising does maintain good employee relations, and the process provides useful internal benchmarks against which external candidates can be matched.

Most successful recruitment exercises result from using multiple sources. For example, the power of a well-respected brand name will galvanise the formal and informal networks and ensure broad search coverage. Time, and timing, is also important to the success of the exercise. Even if the ideal candidate is found in the first week, it can take months to work through outstanding contractual obligations of both the new and the current employer, and sort out issues such as visas, interstate or international transfers.

Selection processes

The selection process is critical for two reasons: first, it brings the preferred candidate into the organisation; second, it is the starting point for ensuring the success of the recruit in their new role. The supervisor, line management and the human resources function, together with any internal customers of the role, need to be involved in the selection process. Their involvement lays an essential foundation for creating acceptance of the role and the new incumbent, and removes the potential for any initial internal politics. It also makes it much easier for the new appointee to develop an internal network, often an essential prerequisite for an outsider to succeed in large organisations.

By way of illustration, the ideal selection process for a divisional manager in a large company could take the following sequence:

1 Preparation of a role/person specification that includes:
   • reporting relationship
   • technical details of the role, including the dimensions of the activities and the need for any specific technical or professional mastery

- details of essential prior experience, including previous roles or activities expected, as well as any international experience
- a description of the management and integrative activities required of the role, including the need for business acumen beyond the specific role but necessary for membership of a broader management group such as executive committees
- possible future roles and career expectations, including the timescale required to demonstrate suitable performance
- requirements for special attributes such as leadership and change management skills
- details of the proposed salary package range and its positioning within the organisation's remuneration structure

Gerstein and Reisman (1983) see this degree of detail as fundamental, not only as a selection tool but for induction purposes and for establishment of objectives for subsequent appraisal.

2 A corporate profile summarising the company's business objectives, together with its cultural characteristics and values, to provide a suitable background brief for an executive search firm.

3 Profiles of the supervisor to whom the role reports, together with those of other key members of the management team with whom the role may interact.

4 The search firm produces a short-list of candidates capable of meeting the specification. Each will have been vetted for background career and references, and have been discussed with the assignment manager. This may include any psychological assessments required, the results of which will be discussed with the candidate by the search consultant, prior to being passed on to the company with the candidate's approval.

5 Initial interviews of no more than six short-listed candidates to be carried out by the future supervisor, head of HR, and two other senior managers. Typically, this panel meets before the interviews to discuss background papers, assessment data and possible strengths and weaknesses of each candidate. Interviewing may follow a formally structured process or be semi-structured. The company might use assessment centre processes (combining individual and group interviews, presentation skills, solution of a case study, and a group interaction session) for middle level and junior management positions. Woodruffe (1993) points out that there is a great difference between self-reported behaviour and a person's actual behaviour in a specific job. Assessment processes can give a direct preview of behaviour.

6 A short-list of two candidates is identified and the preferred candidate meets individually with key peers and potential subordinates to validate technical skills and industry knowledge. This is also the time to identify and discuss any areas of reservation from either side. The second candidate is kept in reserve until this process is completed and evaluated.

There should be sufficient information available at the completion of these steps to make an informed decision. Some companies do not bother about steps 2 and 3, defining corporate culture and the types of personalities involved. They argue that this is as important for the candidate to assess during the selection process as for the company. However, face-to-face assessment based on personal interview has a low reliability. Further, if one accepts Boyatzis' premise that maximum performance requires an optimal fit of individual competencies, job requirements and organisational environment, including these steps maximises the likelihood of a successful recruitment.

The use of psychological assessments is continuously debated, but there is sufficient evidence available to answer many of the concerns. Table 2.2 shows the statistical reliability of a range of common assessment procedures. There is a dramatic improvement in selection reliability as the traditional interview gives way to ability testing and ultimately to assessment centres.

An assessment centre process is an integrated system of behavioural techniques (job simulations, exercises, tests and interviews) designed to assess the critical skills knowledge and competencies required for success in a target role. A number of organisations including Shell International, the UK Civil Service and Sprint Telecommunications have used asessment centres for over ten years and have achieved reliability ratings on recruitment and promotion consistent with those shown in Table 2.2. The centres are designed to assess candidates against a clearly defined set of dimensions, usually developed to meet the specific needs of the company. Table 2.3 lists typical activities conducted in an assessment centre along with the particular competencies that each tests.

The purpose of psychological and personality tests is not to 'clone' existing management characteristics. Doing so would only perpetuate an existing culture and company performance, which, in a rapidly changing business environment, would be a serious disadvantage. The purpose of such tests is to collect and assess as broad a range of data about an individual as possible in order to make an informed choice, taking into account the demands of the role, the competencies of the individual, and the culture of the organisation. The objective is to minimise the possibility of a poor selection decision, which would incur expense to the individual (perhaps recruited out of a role and an organisation where he or she is successful) and to the organisation (which has spent considerable time, and perhaps relocation and separation costs).

Table 2.2 Statistical reliability of assessment methods

Assessment method	Reliability
Assessment centres	0.65
Behavioural interview	0.48–0.61
Ability tests	0.53
Modern personality tests	0.39
Traditional interviews	0.05–0.19

Source: British Psychological Society quoted in *Australian Financial Review* 24 June 1996, p. 1.

Table 2.3 Assessment centre design

Dimension	Interview	Tests	In-basket exercise	Interaction with subordinate	Interaction with peer
Individual leadership					■
Planning & organising			■		
Adaptability	■				
Results orientation	■				
Delegation			■		
Decision-making			■		
Coaching				■	
Applied learning		■			

Source: DDI Asia Pacific International Limited

The recruitment decision

The organisation has now identified a prime candidate for the vacant position. Does the manager simply offer the person the role, or are there further considerations? The question of organisation culture and fit has been discussed earlier, but consideration of broader human resource issues is required. Although a career appointment may have been envisaged, is that important for this identified candidate? If it is, and the candidate is coming from a career role in another company, then a reasonable rule of thumb is to ensure at least two roles the candidate could reasonably be expected to fill. This is fair to the individual and, more importantly, enhances the organisation's future staffing flexibility. If the recruitment co-ordinator is unable to envisage another role for the individual, then the organisation is really recruiting a specialist to stay in a role or department for a finite period of time. Is this a worthwhile investment for the individual or the company?

These considerations make it important to carefully consider the relevance of the candidate's previous experience. Technical experience and overseas background may be key elements of the specification. Consideration also needs to be given to examples of broader managerial scope, and delivery of results, outside the candidate's known areas of expertise. If a candidate's 15 years of relevant experience has been achieved with three companies, the person is less likely to be concerned about a career role than someone who has had a career in only one organisation.

Career path is an issue for the recruits from overseas. The financial services sector in Australia frequently has to deal with this problem. Companies such as the ANZ Bank, National Australia Bank and Colonial face the challenge of convincing high calibre international staff to relocate to a centre which represents no more than 5 per cent of the global market. Irrespective of travel, the financial 'backwater' concern becomes real to the candidate who wishes to return to mainstream financial centres in the longer term. In these circumstances, it is sometimes better to recognise that a three-to-five year assignment (suitable to the candidate's family) might be the most appropriate, and structure the employment contract and remuneration package accordingly.

The salary package needs to take account of four elements:

1 the ability to attract the candidate, often including a premium over current remuneration;
2 assessment of the worth of the candidate's current package (including superannuation benefits, health coverage, taxation, and other benefits) compared with Australian conditions in terms of gross and net of tax benefit;
3 can the company justify any added advantage in remuneration compared to other staff? For example, a rough rule of thumb on international staffing in Shell was to double the cost of an Australian manager for a UK manager of similar experience, treble the cost for Dutch and French managers, and nearly double that again for Swiss managers;
4 employment contracts may provide for greater flexibility—the package can be more innovative without offending internal equity if the recruit is on a three-year contract, than if made permanent.

Taking these factors into account, the package should reflect the individual's market worth and potential value to the company. Details need to be clarified in the contract, including any bonus or incentive schemes and most importantly, a separation clause. Even the best recruitment exercise can go wrong, or circumstances can change. However, if a recruit relocates to another continent, it is not reasonable for them to be subject to changed circumstances without some protection. Otherwise they are likely (and entitled) to seek legal redress, which is certainly not in the interests of the company.

The final task is to watch carefully for anomalies or warning signs. Are there minor discrepancies in the job history that need further clarification? Do some moves appear illogical in terms of career or experience development? Are referees the people who would be expected? Is there evidence of stress behaviour? What has actually been delivered in a previous role, and can this be verified? All recruitment exercises need to have been completed yesterday in the minds of management, and time pressures are unavoidable, but there is no substitute for thoroughness in the recruitment process.

Commencement

The selection and recruitment process is the first part of the human resources management cycle. The process is not complete when the recruit formally joins the organisation. The individual needs to align with the organisation's corporate goals and strategies, and to put the new position into context with other roles and (potentially conflicting) objectives. This stage requires a systematic induction that introduces the individual to the organisation, the department and to the job, and all in a way that speeds up the individual's integration into the company and allows for the development of appropriate networks. These steps involve mentoring, counselling and regular review processes that take account of personal development and job specific training needs. These steps recognise that no two organisations are the same, and that trial and error can be an expensive way to learn how a company operates, and how decisions are made. If the recruit comes from the west coast of the US or a South East Asian business background, their business acumen may be similar, but their experience of organisational operating environments is most likely to be significantly different.

The human resources cycle described in Figure 2.1 (ref. p. 28) is an appropriate place to finish. The concept of regular review and monitoring of performance is nothing new. It maintains a continuous improvement and review process, and keeps the individual alert to the changing organisation. The need for regular review is even more vital in a rapidly changing business and human resource management environment, particularly as organisations of the 1990s require more cosmopolitan skill sets and experience than did the organisations of the 1970s and 1980s. These demands place more responsibility upon organisations to manage their people resources—the key factor in achieving competitive advantage—more professionally than in the past. As the career move of a particular recruit into a specific role may be for only three to five years, the organisation needs to make every effort to minimise the length of the learning curve of the recruit so as to maximise the company's return on investment.

References

Bagwell, S. 1997, 'Only one woman in BHP top 117 managers', *Australian Financial Review*, 20 May, p. 7.

Boyatzis, R. 1982, *The Competent Manager: A Model for Effective Performance,* John Wiley & Sons, New York.

Carew E. 1997, *Westpac: The Bank That Broke The Bank*, Doubleday, Sydney.

De Geus, A. 1997, 'The living company', *Harvard Business Review*, March–April, pp. 51–9.

Dalzeil, M. 1996, *Predicting Leadership Success and Accelerating the Development of Leaders,* Hay/McBer, Boston.

41

Gerstein, M. & Reisman, H. 1983, 'Strategic selection: Matching executives to business conditions', *Sloan Management Review*, vol. 24, no. 2, Winter, pp. 118–40.

O'Neill, G. & Doig, D. 1997, 'Definition and use of competencies by Australian organisations: A survey of HR practitioners', *American Compensation Association Journal*, vol. 6, no. 3, pp. 1–28.

Handy, C. 1994, *The Empty Raincoat*, Arrow Business Books, Sydney.

Report of the Industry Task Force on Leadership and Management Skills 1995, *Enterprising Nation: Reviewing Australia's Managers to Meet the Challenges of the Asia-Pacific Century*, AGPS, Canberra.

Schein, E. 1985, *Organisational Culture and Leadership,* Jossey Bass Inc. Publishers, San Francisco, CA.

Woodruffe, C. 1993, *Assessment Centres: Identifying and Developing Competence*, 2nd edn, Institute of Personnel and Development, London.

3 Planning and managing employee performance

Helen Scotts

Organisational literature is rich in accounts, descriptions, research and theory related to performance management. Knowledge and experience on what works, what does not and why are offered by academics, theorists, consultants, human resource practitioners and managers alike. The views and thoughts on performance management presented in this chapter are based on the perspective of an external consultant. Over the past ten years, my colleagues and I have spent many hours talking to managers and employees in organisations about performance management, often responding to the same question of 'Why can't we get it right?' The perspective of a consultant is clearly different to that of a line manager grappling with the task of managing employee performance on the job. It is different to the perspective of an internal human resource management professional working to provide infrastructure and support mechanisms to aid line managers with the task of managing performance. These individuals face the performance management challenge daily and are in the position to offer insights based on valuable, practical experience. There is no substitute for the value of that insight.

As an external consultant I come from a different perspective, one most often sought by client organisations in our interactions with them around performance management. First, consultants offer an external perspective. We are able to observe, review and comment on organisational needs for and experience with performance management as outsiders. We can advise on design, processes and support structures for performance management without the influence of internal 'politics' and experiences. This position is particularly important in circumstances where negative experiences have become associated with performance management processes. In these circumstances the enthusiasm and willingness required to try an alternative approach can be adversely affected by previous unsatisfactory experience. As outsiders, consultants are in the position to encourage line managers and internal practitioners to leave the baggage of past experience behind and see the implementation of a new performance management approach in a more positive light.

Second, consultants bring a cross-organisational view. In our work, we have the opportunity to talk with and listen to managers, practitioners and employees who relate their experience on what works and what does not. Their input provides a constant challenge to us to develop and offer new ways of managing performance, and to learn from the experiences of a range of other organisations grappling with similar issues.

This chapter explores performance management in Australia and seeks to provide ideas about how to make the process work. The starting point for the chapter is a brief history of performance management in Australia over the past 20 years as a means of tracking the changes in views on performance and performance management. It explores what organisations have learned from that experience and what they are currently looking for from performance management. The second part of the chapter identifies a set of five key principles that help to get performance management right.

A brief history of performance management in Australia

Trends and developments around performance management in Australia over the past 15–20 years have been influenced by major developments throughout the world. It is useful to reflect on these developments and the key lessons arising from them. They help explain how Australian organisations have responded to the performance management challenge and what they are now seeking as key features for more successful processes.

During the late 1960s and 1970s, performance management, particularly in the US, was represented by organisational processes focused on individual performance—the link with organisational performance objectives was not well articulated. Performance management took the form of performance appraisal where the individual and the results he or she achieved over a defined review period were appraised. Performance appraisals generally occurred once every year. Line managers (often reluctantly) took on the appraising role, and control over the process was generally held by personnel departments.

Performance appraisal plans provided a basis for making systematic judgements about how an individual employee was performing against targets and provided data to support salary increases, transfers, promotions and on occasions, terminations. They also provided a basis for identifying performance shortfalls, addressed by counselling or training and development responses. Appraisals frequently took the form of one-way 'judgement', that is the manager judged the employee. Collaboration was not a strong feature of early appraisal schemes. Consequently, appraisal programs met a great deal of resistance and criticism, particularly from line managers who found aspects of the process difficult, particularly the burden of making such judgements about individuals.

McGregor (1972) identifies the nature of, and reasons for the difficulties experienced by managers in their role as appraisers He found the managers' resistance to performance appraisals were usually attributed to the following causes:

- a normal dislike of criticising a subordinate (and perhaps having to argue about it);
- lack of skill needed to handle (appraisal) interviews;
- dislike of a new procedure with its accompanying changes in ways of operating;
- mistrust of the validity of the appraisal instrument.(McGregor 1972, p. 2)

McGregor's description of these causes for resistance are similar to the views of many organisational observers during this period. Managers disliked the experience of 'playing God' and at the same time the prevailing social values called for greater employee involvement in the process. Alternatives were sought through processes such as Management by Objectives (MBO), which sought to provide a much more rational basis for performance planning and review. This process was based on an agreed job description and it sought to facilitate employee collaboration and motivation to improve performance. MBO flourished over the late 1970s and 1980s until it, too, fell into disrepute.

A number of criticisms of MBO have been made. Levinson (1970) argues that the problems encountered by MBO programs relate largely to the fact that the process, built as it was around an agreed job description, gave little recognition to an employee's discretionary performance. That is, performance above and beyond the boundaries of the job, did not take account of 'environmental' factors impinging on an employee's capacity to achieve objectives and the process of setting objectives occurred in too limited a timeframe and did not allow for processes such as team objective setting.

Levinson (1970, p. 3) continued: 'Coupled with these problems is the difficulty supervisors experience when they undertake appraisals'. MBO did little to overcome this key problem previously ascribed to performance appraisal—managers' difficulties in being constructively critical of subordinates.

In Australia, from the 1980s it is possible to track some significant trends in organisational approaches to performance management. These trends can be seen as responses to the difficult experiences encountered through attempts at implementing performance appraisal and MBO type programs worldwide. First, the concept of performance appraisal was being slowly replaced with a concept of performance management with some key differences identified between the two approaches (see Table 3.1).

Second, Australian organisations began to take notice of widespread criticism that performance appraisal systems were insufficiently aligned with business. They began to accept the notion that the management of individual performance needed to cascade down from organisation/business objectives and that a key purpose for the process was to achieve a connection between business performance and the individual (see Figure 3.1).

While performance management was still largely results-focused during this period, a growing acceptance of performance management as a year-round cycle of planning, coaching and review was evident (see Figure 3.2). The role of line managers as appraisers and as coaches assumed greater importance, leading to a flourishing business in performance management training.

During the late 1980s and into the early 1990s Australian organisations began to express concerns about the limitations of results-driven performance management processes. While this emphasis had delivered a clear focus on achieving business results, these achievements were often gained at the expense of effective people management practices. Results-focused processes tended to be short term. They tended to reinforce and reward negative management behaviours which valued results rather than process. The dawn of the 'competencies' era in Australia shifted the focus of Australian organisations to consider behaviours as equally important to results. Organisations actively sought to implement performance management processes which focused on the 'what' (results) and the 'how' (competencies) to achieve more sustainable business outcomes. This shift prompted a growing recognition of the need to articulate and define competencies for a variety of human resource processes, including job performance.

Table 3.1 What is the difference?

Performance management	Performance appraisal
• Performance is planned motivated, and coached	• Evaluation factors are subjectively identified • Performance is judged after the fact
• Process is emphasised	• Form is emphasised
• Results and competencies are critical	• Results are critical
• Process conducted by line management	• Procedure housed in the personnel department

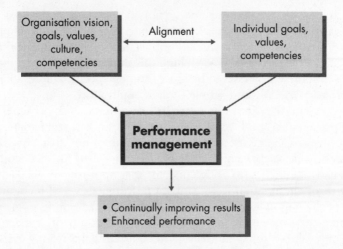

Figure 3.1   Connection between business performance and the individual

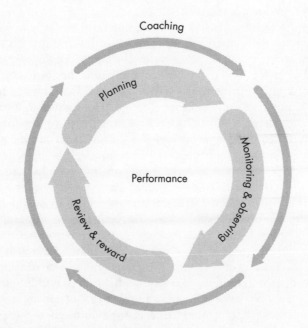

Figure 3.2   The performance management

Into the mid-1990s, many of the organisations which had adopted competencies as an integral part of performance management began to explore and implement processes which integrated job evaluation, performance management and competency-based pay. Behind this shift was a consistent interest in re-engineering these processes to be more business specific and responsive and to be more user-friendly and simple in their application.

Finally, another key trend in Australian organisations' approaches to performance management has been the recognition that a 'one size fits all' approach is inappropriate. Organisations often made assumptions that processes that were successful in one organisation would be successful in their companies, and they had a tendency to adopt one singular approach to managing performance throughout an entire organisation. In recent years, recognition has increased of the importance for every organisation to develop its own approach to performance management—one suited to its environment, strategic aspirations and culture. No single model is perfect, no model is readily transferable. Even within a single organisation, a diverse range of market pressures, processes and demands will impinge on activities in different ways. The nature of work and performance expectations will differ and consequently, performance management processes will need to be different to support the organisation in achieving its performance goals.

Companies seeking the successful alignment of performance with strategic objectives have recognised the importance of linking human resource processes with strategic drivers, by reinforcing those employee behaviours and management styles which will move individual performance in the right direction. Not all organisations have sought the same *type* of movement or direction. Some have sought change through an empowered, team-based work culture; others have sought to develop a totally customer-focused culture. Others have succeeded by developing a culture built around specialisation, risk minimisation and high degrees of product reliability achieved through control and strict attention to detail. Some organisations have sought to create and sustain a hybrid of cultures matching the requirement for a range of outcomes. Just as organisational structure should reflect an organisation's desired work culture, so too successful firms now recognise the importance of organising their key human resource processes, such as performance management, to support and reinforce that culture. Today, many Australian organisations have seen the benefit of reaching consensus on and articulating a target culture. Performance management is an essential part of building these cultures.

The last ten years have delivered a number of key lessons around performance management. Companies have learned through the experience, and today are seeking five key features as the basis for effective performance management. These features are:

1 *Alignment:* organisations are seeking performance management processes which will function as a key strategy for change—aligning employee performance with organisation objectives.
2 *Cultural fit*: organisations are seeking to articulate a target work culture and consensus on priorities for achieving it. Understanding and utilising a

concept of work culture helps organisations to connect strategy to people management processes and performance.

3 *Improved organisational climate:* organisations are seeking to create and sustain workplace climates which motivate employee performance. Organisations today recognise that managers, through the behaviours and styles they demonstrate, can create a climate which taps into the discretionary effort of all employees. Management style is, therefore, regarded as a key ingredient in making performance management work.

4 *Focus on results and competencies:* organisations are working to define and incorporate into performance management the behaviours or competencies required for superior performance by all employees. By linking results required (the 'what') to the desired competencies to achieve them (the 'how'), organisations are working to create an environment for self-development and sustained performance.

5 *Simplicity:* organisations today recognise that their own preoccupation with performance management over the past ten years has led to a tendency to overly complex documentation and rigid processes which burden line managers. Today, organisations work towards simpler processes which tap the energy and interest of employees and line managers alike by bringing performance management to life as an active part of workplace behaviour.

These features are explored in detail in the next section.

Performance management today

Alignment

In Australian organisations today, the focus on performance management is almost always in the context of a general focus on change. Performance management, together with several other human resource processes (selection, assessment and reward), is seen as a key change strategy offering the potential to achieve alignment between employee behaviour and performance and an organisation's change and growth objectives. The manner in which performance management is deployed as a change strategy is dependent on the scale of change the organisation is seeking. The scale of change in turn is dependent upon the nature of the organisation's change environment, i.e. the forces of change both internal (resistance) and external (market, competitor activity, technology changes) and the way these forces are experienced and interpreted within the organisation.

Goodstein and Burke (1991, p. 6) put the view that 'organisations tend to change primarily because of external pressure rather than an internal desire or need to change'. They describe two different levels of change, each of which corresponds to the level of pressure applied on an organisation by an external factor. They refer to 'large scale change in the organisation's strategy and culture—a transformation, re-focus, re-orientation ... and fine-tuning, fixing problems, making adjustments, modifying pressures'. Transformation, as described by Goodstein and Burke (1991) is the level of change required when an organisation faces a threat to its survival. Fundamental change to the manner in which it operates is critical to its continued existence. Fine-tuning, on the other hand, refers to implementing modest changes that improve performance, but do not fundamentally transform the organisation. They argue that understanding the level of change required by an organisation is useful in determining the purpose and design of change strategies, such as performance management.

Strebel (1994) holds a similar view that strategies to achieve change in organisation performance should be carefully considered:

> Change management is suffering from competing approaches. On the one hand, chief executives put their companies through radical restructuring, with little account taken of the time and process needed to change skills and behaviour. Then they are surprised to find that they have to repeat the exercise a few years later, because once restructuring is over, change stops. On the other hand, executives influenced by theories on organisational behaviour encourage deep cultural change in their companies from the bottom up and are surprised to find that financial performance, rather than improving, is suffering from the impact of external change drivers. (Strebel 1994, p. 29)

Like Goodstein and Burke (1991), Strebel is concerned with the preconditions of change—the nature and strength of change drivers influencing an organisation's need to respond. He gives more consideration, however, to the effect of internal resistance in an organisation and the tension or force field created between them and external pressures. He argues that change strategies will be more successful when the strength of change forces and resistance is accurately assessed and change strategies are selected and implemented accordingly. Performance management as a process provides a key opportunity to promote employee awareness of the nature of change in the external environment and the need to respond and to manage internal resistance to change by building greater understanding.

Dunphy and Stace (1991, p. 72) also identify the relationship between the scale and scope of change needed in an organisation and the strategies selected to respond to it. They recommend the use of a 'situational model' to assess the environment within which an organisation operates. The model considers the degree of 'fit' between an organisation and its environment, and emphasises the importance of considering how much change an organisation needs to restore 'fit'. They identify four different levels or scales of change which they describe as 'types':

Type 1   *Fine-tuning:* refining policies and procedures;

Type 2   *Incremental adjustment:* distinct modification to structure, people, processes;

Type 3   *Modular transformation:* major realignment of one or more divisions;

Type 4   *Corporate transformation:* corporate-wide, radical shift.

Dunphy and Stace argue that the assessed level of change required should influence the change strategies and leadership style adopted to respond to the need for change. When an organisation is considered to be generally 'in fit' with the external environment but in need of minor adjustment, the need is for incremental change, whereby strategies will be implemented participatively or by force, depending upon the support for, or resistance to change within the organisation. When organisations are assessed as being significantly 'out of fit' with the external environment, change of a transformative type is required. Change strategies for transformation will be either of a charismatic type, i.e. drawing on and marshalling support for change within the organisation; or of a dictatorial type, i.e. where little or no support for change is present in the organisation (Dunphy & Stace 1991, p. 90).

There is general agreement among organisation change theorists that the approach to change adopted by an organisation should never be accidental. Successful change relies heavily on reading the external environment (change forces) and the internal environment (resistance) to determine the scale of required change. The scale of change defines the questions of 'how much' and 'how quickly' change is required. The strategy or intervention is the 'how to' of change and must match the scale determined.

In grappling with the management of change, organisations consistently turn to performance management as a key tool for achieving the alignment of employees with the organisation's change direction (see Figure 3.2). An organisation with a good performance management system identifies and articulates the explicit results and behaviours required to achieve change through that system. It has the potential to focus and mobilise effort to move the organisation forward through change. How performance management is designed and deployed as a change strategy is dependent upon the scale of change the organisation is experiencing. In transformational change environments, the implementation of a system which crystallises new behaviours and explicit results will often play a significant part in a broad-scale, managed change effort. Planned change efforts of a transformational type are often led strongly from the top layer of management and incorporate radical shifts in strategy, structure, performance and pay systems.

In 1995, the Hay Group worked with a global organisation in the oil and gas industry on a 15-month transformation program aimed at spurring short-term profitability improvements and longer-term changes to realise significant opportunities. The need for change was urgent and turnaround needed to occur in a narrow timeframe. Over the 15-month period, the organisation set new strategies in place, restructured, developed a new work culture and a range of specific, targeted work process changes that produced measurable impact on organisational performance. Key to the change effort was a focus on people and performance. In conjunction with Hay, the organisation developed a new framework of competencies for leadership which were utilised as the basis for assessment, feedback and development planning for the management group. Competencies for all salaried employees were then developed. Human resources processes across the company were re-engineered to drive the competency-based processes for performance management, selection and succession planning. Competency-based performance management was used as a key platform for driving behavioural change and performance improvement. For this organisation the shift in mode of managing performance was significant, fast and intense.

Not all organisations experience change of such a transformational type. When change is more of a fine-tuning or continuous improvement nature, performance management processes may well be reviewed or modified to provide greater reinforcement for an emerging issue of strategic importance (e.g. to emphasise a greater focus on customer service or teamwork) or to respond to the feedback of line managers. For example, a large Australian resources organisation required assistance in the development and implementation of an integrated job evaluation and performance management system. The new process, developed over eight months, built on the foundations of traditional job evaluation but was designed to respond to the needs of line managers wishing to identify a new way of defining work and performance that took account of job content and behaviours. The design process was highly participative, drawing on the input of a wide range of employees as a strategy to secure ownership.

Cultural fit

Work culture expresses itself as the collective behaviour, values, expectations and attitudes of an organisation and its people. It reflects 'the way things are done around here'. It includes the ways in which an organisation selects and develops people, the way performance is managed, the way the organisation is structured and roles are defined, the way people are rewarded, and the way processes and technology are designed to enable and support performance (see Figure 3.3).

Organisations are not victims of work culture. Culture can be used as a conscious vehicle for change. Hay has worked with many organisations undergoing change which have articulated both a current work culture type and a target culture type as a framework for change. Hay utilises a diagnostic instrument (Culture Sort Survey) which requires senior managers to rank 56 work culture attributes from 'most like' to 'least like' for both the current and the target work culture. The model matching technique uses correlation and gap analysis to provide a picture of current versus target culture against four 'pure' work culture paradigms and a basis for assessing organisational action necessary to achieve culture change objectives. The process effectively builds consensus on a target culture that aligns with business strategy, identifies the gaps between current and target cultures, establishes priorities for closing the gaps and a context for prescriptive action steps to achieve alignment with the target culture.

The four work culture types are:

1 *functional*—focused on traditional management hierarchies, emphasising internal order, cost control, job specialisation and limited risk;

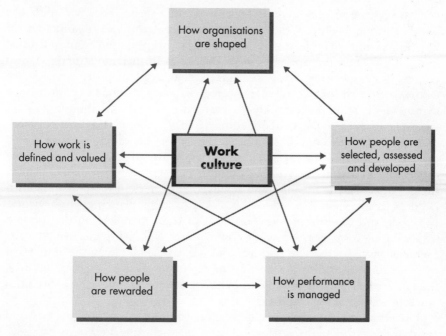

Figure 3.3   Work culture
Source: Hay Group Work Culture Presentation documents 1997

2 *process*—focused on customer satisfaction; emphasising work teams and
   continuous improvement by crossing functional boundaries;
3 *time-based*—focused on speed to market and the ability to satisfy customer
   preferences; emphasising fast asset return or market domination during
   high profitability phases, such as early in the market cycle;
4 *network*—focused on flexibility, innovation and calculated risk-taking in
   project industries such as entertainment or construction; emphasising
   temporary work groups bring required talents together to complete a
   specific venture.

In working to define the target work culture type best suited to them, many
organisations will see all or most of these four as desirable; however, most
organisations can only focus on a limited number of top change priorities.
Placing a high priority on speed and flexibility, for example, usually displaces
cultural attributes such as control and limiting risk. Accordingly, systems that
foster the displaced attributes have to give way to alternatives that support the
new priorities.

The work culture modelling process is a tool that enables organisations to
crystallise change priorities. Arguably, there are other ways to determine
target work culture. Whatever mode is used, the key value for organisations
in articulating target culture is to focus energy and resources around change
initiatives that support strategic goals. It will also assist the design of key processes for change such as selection, reward and performance management.

Performance management will take a different shape and serve a different purpose depending upon the work culture targeted by an organisation. In functional cultures, performance is valued in terms of output from individual jobs. The process for managing performance is formal and structured, and designed to track progress against agreed objectives. In process-type work cultures, performance is often managed via 'mixed-models' performance management schemes that are concerned with the demonstration of customer-focused and team-work competencies in the achievement of objectives. In time-based work cultures, striving for market dominance and a capacity to move with speed to beat competitors to market, performance management is again likely to be competency based, emphasising behaviours such as flexibility, innovation and achievement drive. In such organisational cultures, team members often play a key role in planning performance, observing and monitoring the behaviour of team members on the job and reviewing performance. Network type cultures will seek performance management processes that are informal and self-managed. Given the absence of many traditional or formal reporting arrangements in these types of cultures, the team leader plays a key role in performance management by continuous communication of goals and strategies.

Understanding their work culture helps organisations to think through and design a performance management process that best suits their strategic direction. It is quite possible that within a single organisation, a range of work cultures is desirable. A customer service division is likely to target a process-type work culture while the sales and marketing function may seek to become more time-based. The approach to performance management within an organisation will need to be similarly varied to support these target sub-cultures. One size does *not* fit all.

Creating the right climate—The role of managers

Our experience in working with hundreds of organisations in Australia and the Asia Pacific region has continuously reinforced the connection between organisational climate and performance management. Where managers are focused on creating a motivating climate for their own divisions and work teams, there is an increased likelihood of tapping the discretionary effort of employees—their willingness and enthusiasm to perform. Where climate is effectively managed, employee motivation levels are higher. Measures of organisational climate are strongly related to bottom-line performance (e.g. sales growth, profitability, productivity, efficiency and customer service). Key to effective climate management is the active management of six climate dimensions (described below) and the conscious use by managers of specific behaviours and styles which promote them. A performance management system that is designed to support these behaviours and to reinforce the importance of climate will generally achieve success.

Organisational climate can best be defined as the 'atmosphere' of the workplace— 'what it's like to work here'. It relates to employee perceptions of the workplace, particularly of those aspects of their environment that directly influence their ability to perform well. Employee perceptions about the quality of their workplace climate can be both observed and measured (via survey instruments) against six key dimensions:

1 *flexibility*—the extent to which unnecessary rules and procedures are minimised and creativity is encouraged;
2 *responsibility*—the extent to which initiative, decision-making and ownership are encouraged.
3 *standards*—performance improvement is encouraged and challenging, yet attainable goals are set;
4 *rewards*—where recognition is directly related to levels of performance;
5 *clarity*—goals, roles, procedures are clear for individuals, work groups and the organisation;
6 *team commitment*—people work co-operatively and are proud to be a part of the organisation.

Managers can greatly influence their organisation's climate by the behaviours they demonstrate generally, but particularly in relation to their performance management practices. The managerial styles that have the most significant impact on the development of a sustainable, motivating climate include *authoritative leadership,* which is characterised by setting and consistently reinforcing direction linked to vision and by setting standards and monitoring performance in relation to the broader vision, and *coaching*, which involves encouragement of employees to establish long-range development goals, and the provision of feedback on performance.

Of the six climate dimensions described, four are critical in performance management and are influenced by the effective demonstration of the abovementioned behaviours—clarity, standards, responsibility and rewards.

Managers can achieve effective climate outcomes through their performance management practices in the following areas:

- setting work group objectives that support organisation and business objectives;
- communicating work group objectives clearly, explaining the employees' role in organisational performance;
- encouraging employees to set challenging and realistic objectives, to participate in their performance management and to identify the competencies needed for success;
- monitoring and coaching employees' competencies and providing regular feedback;
- planning for training and development requirements which will assist employees' long-term development;
- recognising and rewarding employee performance based on performance.

The use of authoritative leadership and the coaching management style throughout the entire performance management cycle (planning, observing and monitoring, and review) will produce a climate where employees actively participate in assessing and managing their own performance. Employees who perceive their workplace climate as positive and motivating will be more likely to proactively seek feedback, take responsibility for developing their own competencies and strive to improve their own performance. In such environments, performance management systems that support the connection between management behaviour and climate management with simple, straightforward infrastructure which is well understood and well administered will be well received by managers and employees alike. It is critical that these systems be experienced as supportive of employee and management efforts rather than an added burden.

Focus on results and competencies

Today in Australia, competency-based performance management schemes are plentiful. Often referred to as 'mixed model' schemes, these processes combine a focus on specific measurable results with an ever-increasing focus on the competencies required for effective performance on the job. The shift towards incorporating competencies into the performance management picture reflects a growing desire to find a new way of measuring performance, beyond the numbers. The shift reflects the desire to motivate employees to adopt behaviours consistent with organisational values and strategies—to operationalise them through their work. It also denotes a recognition that employees who perform at the highest level frequently do so as an outcome of particular traits and qualities that they bring to their work in addition to required skills and knowledge, and organisations want to define and capture that 'value added' as a standard of performance for all.

Over the past ten years, there has been a proliferation of approaches to the definition of competencies and the design of competency-based performance management processes. The concept of competencies is based on the premise that in every job, some individuals perform better than others and that the better performers do their jobs differently and bring a number of different characteristics to their work. These differences are valuable, accounting for a higher standard of output, better results or greater quality. Competencies are defined as personal characteristics that can be shown to cause or predict outstanding performance in a particular job. They can be readily observed skills and knowledge or more deep-seated traits. They are observable on the job and measurable in their impact on performance. Hay utilises an iceberg model to depict the relationship of competencies to performance (see Figure 3.4).

The iceberg identifies six levels of competencies:

1 *Skill*—proficiency in an activity learned through repetition; examples include typing, selling, or balancing a budget;
2 *Knowledge*—visible information in a given area; examples are knowing how to process documents with Word Perfect, and knowing company policies and procedures for developing an annual business plan;

3 *Social role*—a pattern of individual behaviours that is reinforced by membership of a social group or organisation; this is the 'outer' self: you can be either a leader or a follower, for example, or initiate change or resist it;

4 *Self image*—an individual's conception of his or her identity, personality, and worth as a person—the 'inner' self: you can see yourself as a leader, or a motivator and developer of people, or simply a cog in the corporate machine; self-image is an issue for performance management only when it is expressed as an observable behaviour;

5 *Trait*—a relatively enduring characteristic of an individual's behaviour; some people are good listeners, others have natural sense of urgency; traits become part of performance management only when they can be expressed as observable behaviours;

6 *Motives*—thoughts in a particular area of achievement, affiliation, or power that drive, direct, and select an individual's behaviour; examples are wanting to achieve individually or wanting to influence the performance of others; motives are also a part of performance management, but only when they can be expressed as observable behaviours.

The identification of competencies required for outstanding performance in a job is not guesswork. To use competencies to their optimal effect, it is essential to research the behaviours that differentiate superior from average performance—in other words, define what it is that characterises superior performers and sets them apart. Once defined, these differentiating competencies provide a standard against which the performance of all job holders may be assessed and developed.

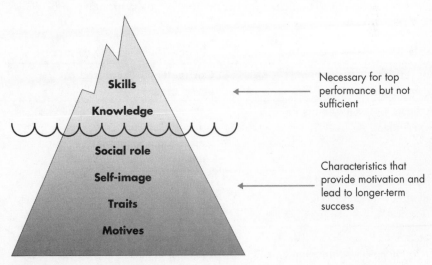

Figure 3.4   The iceberg model

Hay's competency-modelling work with organisations utilises a research process to uncover differentiating competencies. The process begins with an analysis of the business context and culture in which a particular role is placed. It will usually incorporate panel sessions involving stakeholder analysis on the performance requirements of the role under review. It will also incorporate the use of an intensive interviewing technique (the behavioural event interview) to discover in detail the behavioural patterns (thoughts, actions) of superior performers in the job. All these data are brought together to identify key performance themes and ultimately, a model of defined competencies for superior job performance.

Competency models provide a basis for a range of human resource processes including training and development, succession planning and performance management. In performance management, competencies provide a framework and guide for how results and critical performance goals will be accomplished. While critical goals define *what* the job holder is expected to accomplish within a performance management cycle, competencies define the manner in which they will be achieved, i.e. *how* the job holder will be expected to achieve the results. For example, a sales manager role may be expected to achieve some specific results in relation to a sales budget, the setting of a sales team's objectives and the identification of new accounts within the market. A mixed-model performance management system links specific competencies to the achievement of these results both as a guide to the type of behaviour the organisation expects and as a means of achieving results to the level expected. The competencies are not merely about the 'right behaviour' but about the behaviours known to lead to success. In a mixed model process, the link would involve the components set out in Table 3.2.

In implementing competency-based performance management, organisations make a commitment to implement processes for the observation of competencies

Table 3.2   The link between results and behaviours leading to success

Key results outstanding	Competencies required for performance
• Achieve and exceed units and revenue sales budget	• *Results focus*—works to achieve a standard of excellence; creates opportunities, undertakes new initiatives to achieve results
• Identify needs within the market, target new business	• *Influencing*—calculates the impact of a presentation on an audience. Works to influence and gain support of others
• Set sales team objectives • Determine skills required, train and coach team members	• *Developing others*—shows a genuine interest in developing others; arranges assignments and training to assist learning

on the job. This act of observation can be carried out by managers or team members but requires certain disciplines around active observation and data recording to have best effect.

Organisations utilising mixed model performance management are finding it of particular benefit where competencies are defined to reflect future as well as current requirements and where the need exists to drive an organisation forward via the active demonstration of defined behaviours.

Keeping it simple

Regardless of the methodology or approach to performance management chosen by organisations over the past ten years, the paper and system work tools intended to support the process have often been their undoing. Human resources departments in their pursuit of acceptance of and compliance with performance management systems by managers and employees have attempted to design, engineer and re-engineer the paperwork supporting the systems. The effect has often been to over-engineer performance management systems.

One case in point is the efforts of a senior human resources practitioner in a large transport company who devoted enormous energy and effort to winning the support of line managers for the incorporation of competencies into performance management. The human resources practitioner then designed a new mixed-model process around results and capabilities, which doubled the time requirement and created an image of complexity within the system. While the incorporation of competencies into performance management was intended to simplify the process, the paper tools made it appear more complex. Ground was lost rather than support gained.

In contrast, other organisations have embarked on campaigns to simplify the paper work supporting all key human resource processes, implementing one- to two-page documents which serve a range of human resource purposes including job evaluation, recruitment, performance management and development planning. This has proven successful, providing the documentation contains the following information:

- organisational context—industry, structure, key strategies;
- job data—accountabilities (4–6 maximum); performance measures; key results for review period; job size data (resources managed, number of direct reports);
- competencies for superior performance, level required, observable indicators;
- rating scales;
- comments;
- development recommendations.

Invariably, taking the step to simplify paperwork has required a capacity to focus clearly on the minimum information requirements about jobs needed to drive these processes effectively, and the courage to let go of the superfluous information that is more 'historical' than actually required. It also requires the confidence in the willingness and commitment of managers and employees to demonstrate the behaviours and skills to make the process a success. In organisations where this courage and confidence exist, performance management will be successful—it will seem as a part of managing well, rather than as an additional burden.

Conclusion

Performance management processes are now recognised as essential for building an organisational culture that aligns employee behaviours with organisational objectives. Effective performance management systems require the identification of a work culture that fits the organisation's strategy, a management style that elicits discretionary effort, and the identification of competencies and behaviours required for superior performance. In addition the system needs to be simple and not too time consuming. Given some of the unfortunate experiences with performance systems in the past, one of the challenges facing human resource experts is to convince managers and other organisational members of the value of these process-based performance management systems.

References

Dunphy, D. & Stace, D. 1991, *Under New Management*, McGraw-Hill, Roseville, NSW.

Goodstein, L.D. & Burke, W.W. 1991, 'Creating successful organisation change', *Organisation Dynamics*, Spring, pp. 5–17.

Levinson, H. 1970, 'Management by whose objectives?', *Harvard Business Review*, July–August. Reprinted in *Appraising Performance Appraisal*, Harvard Business Review, Boston MA, 1988.

McGregor, D. 1972, 'An uneasy look at performance management', *Harvard Business Review*, September–October. Reprinted in *Appraising Performance Appraisal*, Harvard Business Review, Boston MA, 1988.

Strebel, P. 1994, 'Choosing the right change path', *California Management Review*, Winter, pp. 29–50.

Case Study B

Performance management at Optus Communications

George Abramowicz

In November 1990, the federal government proposed reforms for the Australian telecommunications industry. The objectives were to improve telecommunications services and reduce the cost of their provision. Optus tendered successfully to acquire AUSSAT, the domestic satellite operator and holder of the general carrier licence. The company simultaneously acquired Mobilcom (now named Optus Mobile), the holder of the second mobile carrier licence. The total acquisition price for AUSSAT and Mobilcom was $800 million.

Optus Communications is owned by six major shareholders. The 51 per cent Australian share of the company is held by Mayne Nickless (25 per cent), AMP and AIDC each have 10 per cent and National Mutual 6 per cent. UK-based Cable & Wireless holds the remaining 49 per cent. This blend of partners provided the skills and experience required to successfully roll out the fully integrated, state-of-the art systems required to provide customer service and technology to the Australian market.

The initial planning group's strategy and its highly accurate forecasting made this the fastest roll-out of a sophisticated telecommunications network anywhere in the world. This resulted in the organisation growing at a rapid pace—it started with 15 employees and by 1997 had a workforce of some 7000.

The initial need was for technical expertise in the latest telecommunications technology and processes to meet the roll-out plan for an Australia-wide network. Special expertise was brought from around the globe, and expatriates from UK and USA formed a major part of that thrust. Attracting the necessary technical expertise also involved joint partnerships and alliances with external providers such as Digital and Fujitsu.

By the time the workforce began to reach planned capacity, it became increasingly evident that a significant change had to occur if the company was to remain successful into the future. This change required a stronger focus on its greatest resource, its people. The focus was always there, but what was required was a greater emphasis on the *how* rather than the *what*. Managers needed to pay more attention to *how* they were doing their job, and not be rewarded solely for achievement of their quantitative targets and objectives.

Existing performance and development process

The original performance management system was introduced with an understanding that it would need to be reviewed at a later stage. In essence, it consisted of an interaction booklet with hardcopy forms and development guides for managers to use at the review time. Clearly, this interim process had some weaknesses resulting from the fact that it was introduced at the formative stage of the company's growth. At this early stage, managers were (of necessity) very task focused, and many saw 'people management' issues as something that human resource specialists would handle. Furthermore, there was also a shared perception that no direct consequence would occur if the performance management process was not undertaken, and so, there was no way to ensure that objectives were set or employee performance reviewed.

In addition, the existing system had some inherent weaknesses. These included:

- objectives in some areas were not set in time for the review to affect performance;
- an overriding emphasis on achievement of *quantitative* objectives;
- no formal process to ensure that reviews took place;
- lack of management accountability for 'people' management;
- no opportunity for employee input into individual development plans;
- no process to ensure the quality and effectiveness of reviews;
- lack of systems and process to capture data for internal management (e.g. training and development needs, and succession planning).

Defining what was needed

Although the initial implementation of a basic performance review process was adequate for the start-up role, the corporate human resources group recognised that a more focused review process would better address important factors for this stage of the business and its development. Two teams were formed, drawn from the company's line and corporate human resource consultants (see Figure B1). The role of the corporate group was to ensure that the end result provided consistency across all Optus operations and alignment with the company's values. The line human resource team focused on issues to do with implementation and delivery to line managers and employees. The initial step was for the two teams to work together to identify the outcomes that the new system needed to deliver.

The teams came up with the following outcomes:

Values—ensure that all employees 'walk the talk' and role model the values to others.

Job skills—ensure each employee is equipped with the necessary job specific skills, at the required level of competence, to do his/her role.

Objectives—ensure that objectives are set ahead of time with appropriate measurements aligned to the company business objectives in place for each employee.

Interpersonal skills—acknowledge that each role is based on people interaction and requires a level of interpersonal skills.

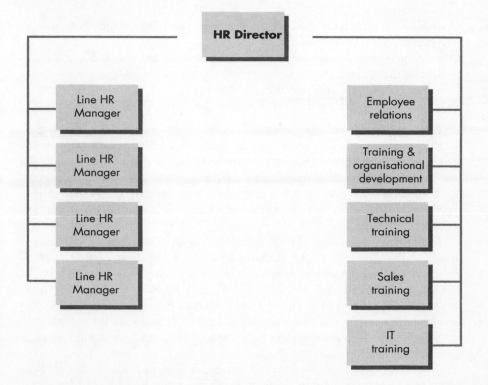

Figure B1   Optus human resources organisation chart

People management skills—managers with people reporting to them have an added responsibility to get things done through their team. Skills in areas such as counselling, coaching, delegating, developing and motivating people and teams are their accountability.

Further training & development—ensure that renewal takes place for current and future roles, as well as meeting the realistic career aspirations of employees.

Continue to reward performance—assess performance by measuring results, and reward achievement of each individual against goals set for that period.

Working from this list of end outcomes, the group then defined the characteristics required of the new performance management process. Six key issues emerged from this stage of analysis; the process needed to:

1 provide for frequent and high quality face-to-face dialogue between the manager and the employee;
2 ensure a high level of preparation by the manager and employee for the review. This was to include opportunity to reflect on achievements, development needs, areas for improvement and input from 'significant' others (e.g. customers);
3 have ability to capture data for proposed organisational development processes, trend analysis, report generation and other human resource information;
4 highlight and measure the balance of task and people management for those in charge of employees;
5 have the capacity to consider individual employee training and development needs in the current role, together with his/her own realistic career aspirations within the company;
6 further enforce the need to work within the strong Optus value system.

While still at the planning stage, it was decided to create hardcopy forms for the review, but with a computerised option available for those that preferred technology. Reservations were expressed that the use of the computerised version could reduce the quality of the personal interaction between employee and their manager. For example, managers may spend their time typing employee comments during the review, rather than actively participate and provide feedback.

The Optus values are meant to define for all employees 'how we do business' and the company prides itself on having a value-driven culture. The seven values are high ethical standards, leadership, empowerment, achievement, teamwork, personal renewal and customer satisfaction. The company uses these values in recruitment and to develop its policies and systems; they are also reinforced in company training programs. It was logical therefore to use these corporate values as a basis for assessing managers on their 'people management' performance.

The corporate human resource group, using in-house technology, designed a computerised upward team feedback system to provide managers with a people management performance rating. The process commences with the manager inviting team members to respond to a confidential, computer-driven questionnaire. Completing the questionnaire is voluntary. At a given time, the manager signals the close of the survey to the system which then consolidates any responses. To further protect individual confidentiality, the system is designed to close off and report only if a minimum of four employees have responded. The manager then accesses and reviews the employee feedback. In a meeting, the feedback is shared with the team; the manager also has the opportunity to seek further clarification if required. It is then the responsibility of the manager to create plans to act on this feedback.

This upward team feedback process allows managers to receive confidential feedback from their employees on their individual performance and behaviours. This provides them with a major developmental tool designed to increase their own managerial effectiveness and build effective work teams. The feedback forms part of each manager's overall rating at his/her own performance review.

Apart from the benefit to individual managers, the process meets several key objectives from the company's perspectives. The feedback and action planning process enables the company to:

- reinforce the importance of the Optus values by holding all mangers responsible for continual role modelling, and measuring their effectiveness in doing so;
- build trust and relationships within the team over time through disclosure by the manger;
- improve the overall capability of management by linking individual performance to the review process;
- increase the level and quality of communication with employees as each manager shares the collective output from the feedback with their team, which leads to joint discussions about individual and team perceptions and team effectiveness;
- provide an open communication environment to deal with issues constructively;
- allow the manger to share the output and enlist the assistance of their own manager.

Phasing-in the changes

The change to the new performance and development review system began with a series of briefing sessions to introduce the new process and its supporting tools. All employees had the opportunity to attend these, during the normal hours of operations. The briefings addressed the differences between the old system by emphasising the proposed enhancements, how they were to be used, and the implementation timeline.

Most employees and managers attended these sessions. Managers also received a preliminary brief to better position them to answer any employee's questions during implementation. The upward team feedback was the subject of most interest as well as the well received role that individual employees now had in providing input to their own appraisal through the new system and data collection. The previous system did not provide for data to be collected from employees.

Upward team feedback was to be piloted over an 18-month experimental stage before becoming a formal part of the performance and development review process. After that time, the results of each manager's survey data were to be shared with his/her manager and a copy included with the review on the individual's personal file. As most managers were already exploring some sort of 360 degree feedback mechanism, the new tool was welcomed as a standard approach across the corporation.

Implementation issues

Senior executives started the process with their own teams to model the way forward, and the process cascaded down the organisation to a short timetable. This allowed managers to experience the process and replicate it quickly within their respective areas. As with any change process, the most effective modelling came from a select group of influential 'early adopters'.

In general, the group managers and employees responded positively with little resistance to the process. Employees responding to the surveys and their mangers took a responsible role in sharing good news as well as making the opportunity to start further team development. One major benefit of the feedback process was evident in the actions taken to better align manager and team perceptions.

As the roll-out continued, it became evident that once the manager received feedback, the result would be enhanced if the manager's sharing of the output with the team was facilitated by an independent facilitator. Dealing through a third party with no vested interest in the feedback allowed the team to be more open and candid. Typically the manager leaves the room once the output has been shared with the team; the facilitator then works with the group to understand and absorb the output and further refine the message to the manager. The facilitation process addresses four areas:

1 What is the manager doing and should continue to do?
2 What is the manager doing, but should stop doing as it gets in the way of productivity and morale?
3 What should the manager start doing to assist the team?
4 What will the team do for the manager to assist in making these things happen?

The manager is then called back and the collective message delivered by the facilitator. Again, this maintains confidentiality of the feedback process. Any team member is able to address the manager directly, either during this session or privately should they wish.

The performance and development review process is for managers to review the performance of employees in their respective teams and to discuss their individual development objectives and career aspirations. The process has been designed to provide for the continuous development of each employee by:

- providing a specific venue for a two-way dialogue on performance and development;
- maintaining a common performance management framework through Optus, with a common understanding of the accountabilities and expectations of team members and their manager;

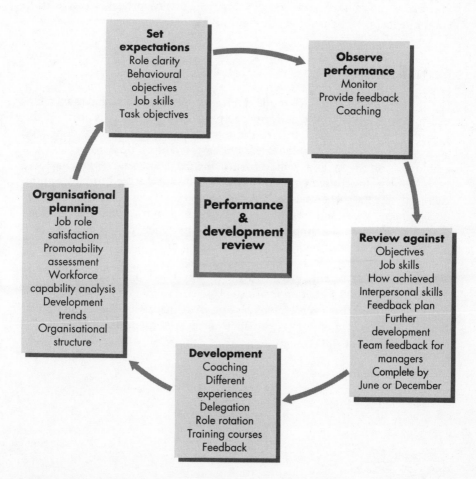

Figure B2 Performance and development review cycle

- providing a framework within which informal and formal performance and development discussions and feedback will take place;
- ensuring that individual performance objectives and targets are set and that they reflect corporate objectives.

In this way, the effective use and implementation of the performance management system contributes to performance of the company and its employees. Optus views the management of performance and employee development as a critical responsibility of all 'people managers' within the company as a key factor in its business success.

At Optus, the performance cycle extends from 1 July to 30 June, with a mid-year review completed by the end of December. This annual timeframe is not suitable for all roles or all parts of the organisation. For example, in some areas it is more appropriate to set performance objectives that have a three- or six-month achievement span. Whatever the timeframe that is agreed for the objectives, the performance and development review process has five basic components or stages as shown in Figure B2.

Conclusion

At Optus many benefits have resulted from establishing and maintaining a formal review at the end of a performance plan period. Clearly, it provides the opportunity for the manager and the employee to express their respective views on performance achievements. There is ample time to review the employee's strengths and achievements, discuss consistency of behaviours with Optus values, review the skills and knowledge required to perform the role and discuss the employee's career goals—including any training and development needs and how these might be built into a personal development plan. Where the employee is a people manager, the employee's performance in respect of people management and development is also assessed and discussed.

The outcome of this process leads to improved understanding of the employee's role in Optus and forms the basis for a more open and improved work relationship between employees and their managers. And importantly, it provides an assessment of performance and achievement that can be used as the basis of reward and recognition.

Development, training and learning

Andrew Smith

In recent years human resource development (HRD) has assumed centre stage in the effort to restructure the Australian economy to meet the demands of global competition. The reasons for this include the growing realisation that training and development can play a critical role in improving the international competitiveness of Australian industry; changes to the industrial relations system that emphasise the importance of training and development at the enterprise level; reforms to the national training system that attempt to improve the provision of training for all employees. These factors have led to the emergence of a multi-million dollar training industry in Australia and to a significant enhancement of the role of the HRD practitioner in Australian industry.

HRD and HRM

Since the late 1970s, the old paradigm of personnel management has given way to human resource management (HRM). Various factors have led to the emergence of human resource management. These include first, the globalisation of competition which led to the development of a more strategic approach to the management of human resources. Second, Japanese enterprises were held up in the early 1980s as exemplars for western enterprises, particularly in their management of human resources and finally, the growth of the 'enterprise culture' under the impact of neoclassical macroeconomic policies that provided a benign environment for the growth of a new approach to employee relations (Legge 1995).

From its earliest formulation, HRD has always occupied an important role in models of HRM. Often the discussion of HRD-related issues has been in the broader context of employee development, but HRD, as a strategy to ensure the development of employees, has been viewed as central to the implementation of human resource management. HRD has been referred to as the 'litmus test' of whether an enterprise is serious about the implementation of HRM (Keep 1989).

In their ground-breaking work on human resource management, *Managing Human Assets*, Beer and his colleagues at Harvard University gave employee development a critical role in gaining the commitment of employees and increasing their competence (Beer et al. 1984). Beer regarded employee development as an investment that will result in flexibility and adaptability. However, Beer's interpretation of employee development is far wider than the skills training of human capital theory. Training was identified as one among a number of methods that can be used by the enterprise to develop the careers of employees. Other tools for employee development include job enrichment, assessment centres for developmental feedback and temporary assignments. Beer's emphasis is on the development of the employee's career rather than simply training to meet the objectives of the enterprise. Thus, the process of employee development is as much about meeting the needs of the individuals as about achieving the objectives of the enterprise.

Walton, one of Beer's co-authors, made the goal of commitment explicit in his later typology of control and commitment models of HRM (Walton 1985). Walton described how many US enterprises were moving from an old strategy based on workforce control. This involved tightly specified job descriptions, measured work standards, hierarchical structures and adversarial labour management policies. The emerging workforce strategy was based on commitment and involved greater employee autonomy, flat structures, job security and mutuality in labour relations.

Many other models of HRM have been developed but as Dyer and Kochan (1995) have observed, these models share a number of common characteristics:

high levels of employee participation, involvement or empowerment at the workplace level, primarily through enriched jobs and/or self-managed work teams; high selection standards; extensive investments in training and development; opportunities for high levels of earnings through skills-based and / or performance-based schemes; free flow of information up as well as down the organisation, and stability of employment. All also emphasise the need for mutual trust and co-operation through the organisation. (Dyer & Kochan 1995, p. 143)

Although these models may differ in terms of emphases placed on particular aspects, they all highlight the importance of HRD and within that overall umbrella, the importance of training to the process of development. From the perspective of HRM, HRD is central to the adaptability and flexibility of the workforce and for engaging the commitment of employees. This involves not simply training for the skills to be used on the job but a broader notion of employee development in which the enterprise is committed to the career development of employees. HRD, thus, becomes part of the psychological contract which enterprises strike with their employees in return for high levels of commitment, loyalty and adaptability.

Training in Australia

Our knowledge of the practice of HRD in Australia has, until recently, been poor. However, since 1990 the Australian Bureau of Statistics has collected detailed information on training and development in Australian organisations. Three key surveys are published by the ABS. The Employer Training Expenditure Survey (ABS 1990a, 1991, 1994) was originally devised as part of the policy development process that led to the *Training Guarantee Act* and collects figures on how much Australian organisations spend on training their employees. The Training and Education Experience Survey (ABS 1990b, 1998) is a census of a sample of the population and collects information on the extent and type of training received by individuals at work. Finally, the Employer Training Practices Survey (ABS 1994c) is a survey of organisations and collects information on the type of training that organisations provide to their employees and their reasons for doing so.

Expenditure

The Training Expenditure Survey is the most significant of the ABS surveys and provides a series on training expenditure from 1989 to 1996. The most recent survey reveals that in 1996, only 18 per cent of Australian organisations surveyed reported some training expenditure. This represents a significant decrease from the 1993 figure of 25 per cent. The average expenditure on training per employee was $186 over the July–September quarter, representing an annual rate of approximately $744. Employees received an average of 4.9 hours of training over the quarter (19.6 hours, or less than three working days per annum). Australian organisations spent an average of 2.5 per cent of payroll on training. Thus, while the level of training activity appears to have increased since 1989, there has been a significant decrease since 1993. This, perhaps, reflects the suspension of the Training Guarantee Scheme in 1994 and its subsequent abolition in 1996.

Spending on training also varies considerably by sector and industry. In 1996, public sector organisations spent 3.2 per cent of payroll compared with their private sector counterparts who spent 2.3 per cent. However, the increase

Table 4.1 Employer training expenditure (July–September quarter, 1989–96)

	1989	1990	1993	1996	% change 1989–96
Employers reporting training expenditure %	22	24	25	18	-18
Payroll spent (%):					
Private sector	1.7	2.2	2.6	2.3	+35
Public sector	3.3	3.2	3.4	3.2	-3
Total	2.2	2.6	2.9	2.5	+14
Average expenditure per employee (A$)	133	163	191	186	+40
Average training hours per employee	5.5	5.9	5.6	4.9	-11

Source: Australian Bureau of Statistics 1997

from 1989 is almost entirely accounted for by the private sector which improved its performance by over 30 per cent, while public sector spending as a percentage of payroll has remained fairly static. Variation across industry sectors is even more apparent, with air transport, mining and communications spending well over the average while manufacturing, retail and recreation and personal services spent considerably less than the average. These figures, therefore, present a picture of generally modest expenditure on training activities, but with a trend improvement, particularly in the private sector.

Distribution

The Training and Education Experience Survey (ABS 1994) reveals the extent and distribution of training within the Australian workforce. The survey showed that in 1993, 86 per cent of workers received some form of training. On-the-job training was the most common form of training with 82 per cent of workers receiving this type of training. The incidence of in-house training in organisations was far less with only 31 per cent of workers receiving this form of training. About one-fifth of the workforce (19 per cent) was studying for an educational qualification. However, like the figures on training expenditure, figures on the type of training received by employees varied considerably between industries. Employees in the utilities, communications or service industries were more likely to receive training than those in transport, manufacturing or agriculture. Part-time workers were consistently less likely to receive training than full-time workers (Baker & Wooden 1995).

There were also considerable differences in training experiences between employees in different occupations. Thus, professional and para-professional workers were considerably more likely than unskilled and semi-skilled workers to receive training. Females, although slightly more likely to receive training than males overall, were less likely to receive training in sub-professional occupations, particularly in blue-collar occupations. Further analysis of the statistics highlighted the gender difference more clearly. Of those who participated in training in 1990, females received 46 hours of training, compared to 66 hours for males.

Practices

The Training Practices Survey gathered data on the type and extent of training practices within organisations using the same sample frame as the Training Expenditure Survey. Table 4.2 (see p. 74) gives a summary of some of the key findings from this survey. The survey confirms that the major reason for investment in training was the improvement of employee work performance. However, the organisation of training was rather ad hoc and unsystematic. Formal needs analysis methods were not often used, written training plans were not frequently used and most enterprises did not employ qualified trainers. Training expenditure, however, appeared to be increasing, driven by processes of organisational change—investments in new technology, implementation of quality assurance programs and organisational restructuring.

The ABS data is supported by case study research into why Australian organisations provide training to their employees (Smith et al. 1995; Hayton et al. 1996). This study, known as *Industry Training Studies*, shows that although the level of systematic training provision is low in Australian enterprises, there is a growing awareness among managers of the need to train which is being driven by the need to improve quality, invest in new technology and the demands of work re-organisation.

Training practices and approaches in Australian organisations

The *Industry Training Studies*, conducted by Charles Sturt University and the University of Technology Sydney, has explored training practices in Australian enterprises and why organisations adopt different approaches to training (Smith et al. 1995; Hayton et al. 1996). Over a two-year period from 1994–96, the research team studied 42 organisations in-depth and carried out a survey of 1750 studies of Australian private sector organisations. Organisations in five industry sectors were studied:

- building and construction;
- food processing;
- electronics manufacturing;
- retailing;
- finance and banking.

Table 4.2 Enterprise training practices in Australia

Training practices	Employers reporting training (%)
Reason for training:	
Improve work performance	91
Respond to new technology	61
Improve quality	60
Methods to determine training needs:	
Skills audit/TNA	22
Informal	47
None	9
Existence of written training plan:	22
Employ a qualified trainer:	33
Changes in training expenditure (last 12 months):	
Increased	51
Decreased	9
No change	40
Factors for increasing training expenditure:	
Technological change	32
New management practices	25
Quality assurance	21

Source: ABS 1998

The research team developed a model of how training operates at the organisational level (see Figure 4.1). The model focuses on the distinction between those factors that give rise directly to training—training drivers—and those factors that shape the type of training which the organisation eventually adopts—training moderators.

Training drivers are those factors that immediately give rise to a demand for training within the organisation. The operation of one or more of these drivers will produce an impetus to train. However, the creation of a training impetus within an organisation does not explain the vast variety of training arrangements that emerge from organisations that appear to be operating under the influence of the same training drivers. The diversity of the training arrangements that eventually emerge is explained by another set of factors—the training moderators. These factors moderate the training impetus and determine the type of the training which is carried out in each organisation. Because the combination of training moderators tends to be unique to the circumstances of each individual organisation, the operation of only a relatively small number of training drivers can produce an almost infinite variation in the training arrangements that finally emerge.

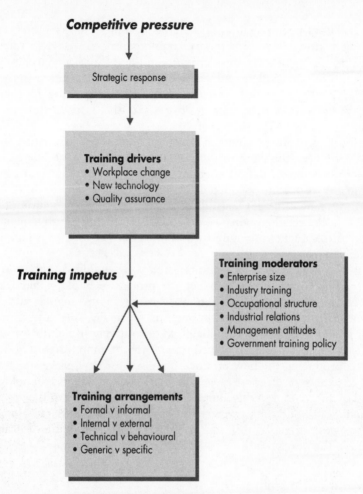

Figure 4.1 Model of enterprise training

The operation of the model starts outside the enterprise with the competitive pressure that is exerted by the business environment. Competition of itself does not directly give rise to training, although it is the force that compels the organisation to take actions which result in the creation of a demand for training.

Drivers of training

Changes that were introduced as part of the strategic response to the new competition were the real drivers of the training effort. These training drivers were remarkably simple and recurred consistently throughout the *Industry Training Studies* research. The first of these drivers was workplace change.

The extent and pace of workplace change varied between enterprises and between industries. The type of training provided to support workplace change also varied considerably. Thus in the food processing industry, organisations were using the industry level training program devised under the award restructuring process, the Certificate in Food Processing, to support the introduction of multiskilling and teamwork at a very broad level. In the retail industry, one large retailer was using on-the-job coaching to support a massive reduction in management levels and the introduction of semi-autonomous teams on the shopfloor.

Quality improvement emerged consistently as a key driver of enterprise training. However, the interpretation of quality improvement differed significantly across industries and between enterprises. In the manufacturing enterprises, quality assurance was linked to accreditation under the International Standards Organisation (ISO) standards and/or the implementation of TQM processes. In the retail and finance organisations, quality improvement rarely involved formal quality programs such as these but was focused on improving customer service.

Most of the organisations in the research were involved in the introduction of various forms of new product and process technology, although the extent of technological innovation was greater in the manufacturing and finance sectors than in construction or retail. Generally, the training implications of investing in new technologies were relatively straightforward. New product technologies often involved on-the-job training for employees who would be producing the new product. Training for new process technology was more extensive. In most cases, training for new process technology was supplied by the vendor of the equipment. Firms would look to the vendor for the training of key personnel, often a mix of engineers and shopfloor employees, who would then, in turn, be responsible for the training of other staff involved in the new process.

Moderators of training

The training moderators were the factors revealed in the research that were strongly associated with enterprise training but that did not automatically produce a demand for training. Instead, the training moderators influenced the type of training arrangements that the organisation eventually put in place. The model of enterprise training identified six training moderators:

1   enterprise size;
2   industry traditions of training;
3   occupational structure;
4   industrial relations;
5   management attitudes;
6   government training policy.

Enterprise size

The effect of the size of the enterprise on training provision was as marked in this study as in other recent Australian research (ABS 1997). Enterprise size was very strongly associated with training. The case studies provided a useful commentary on the reasons for the importance of size. Size is a proxy for variety of other factors that impact on the ability of the organisation to provide training:

- *Resources* The larger the organisation, the greater the economies of scale that can be achieved in training and the greater the ability of the enterprise to provide internal, formal training and to support this training with high investments in training infrastructure.
- *The nature of the workforce* Larger enterprises have more skilled and professional employees who require higher levels of training. In Australia, the percentage of jobs requiring post-school qualifications in enterprises of fewer than 20 employees is 18 per cent; in enterprises with more than 100 employees this figure rises to 32 per cent (ABS 1994). Thus the demand for training is greater in proportional terms in larger enterprises.
- *Networking* Small organisations have particular problems in accessing training providers whereas larger organisations, particularly those employing training specialists, often have well-developed relationships with a network of training providers and with the training authorities.

Industry traditions

The industry sector in which the organisation operates was strongly correlated with training in the *Industry Training Studies* research and was revealed very clearly in the case studies as a major influence on the type of training that was to be found in any individual organisation. Industries clearly have their own traditions of training. Training in the construction industry, for example, is focused tightly on the apprenticeship system and apprentice training is to be found in all the enterprises in this sector. The finance industry has a tradition of expecting employees to undertake finance and banking qualifications in their own time if they wish to progress and the industry has developed close links with the providers of this form of external, accredited training. More recently, as a result of award restructuring, certain industries have established industry-level training arrangements, partly in response to developments in the industrial relations system. A good example of this is the Certificate in Food Processing developed by the food processing industry training bodies. Similar developments were taking place in the electronics, construction and finance industries.

Occupational structure

Occupational structure refers to the mix of occupational groups found in the organisation's workforce. Occupational structure is closely linked to initial vocational training. Different occupations clearly require different qualifications in terms of duration, content and level of post-school qualifications. There is much evidence in Australia to show that workers with initial post-school qualifications are more likely to receive subsequent, formal training than those without (ABS 1998). Seventy-eight per cent of managers and professionals in Australia have a post-school qualification—higher than any other occupational group (Karpin 1995). Those enterprises with higher numbers of managers and professionals in their workforces will tend to provide more training and often this training will be formal and off-job in nature.

Industrial relations

Industrial relations—defined in the research as the number of employees covered by an industrial award and the presence of training provisions in awards or agreements—was correlated with training but the correlation was not very strong. This finding reflects the results from the case studies examined in the *Industry Training Studies* that industrial relations has a strong influence on the climate for training although it is not, in itself, a driver of training. Thus industrial relations processes, particularly award restructuring and enterprise bargaining, have emphasised the importance of training for the operation of the new, restructured awards, without specifying the form that the training should take. In some industries, as we saw above, these processes have led to the implementation of new, wide-ranging, industry-based training programs. The findings of the research confirmed the importance of industrial relations in creating an organisational climate conducive to the improvement of enterprise training.

Management attitudes

As Finegold and others have noted, management attitudes are very important in training decision-making (Finegold 1991; Karpin 1995). However, management attitudes may be fragmented within the enterprise. Many senior managers in the case enterprises pledged their commitment to the training of their employees—but attitudes at the middle and junior management levels were often quite different. Managers at the operational level often preferred training that was short, sharp and tightly focused and, since many of the decisions regarding the implementation of training were taken at this level, operational managers had a significant influence on the form that the training takes.

Government training policy

Few of the organisations studied were engaged with the National Training Reform Agenda and the impact of the Training Guarantee appeared very limited. However, other elements of government training policy could be discerned having an effect on enterprise training decision-making. Thus the availability of grants for innovative training programs had persuaded some enterprises to make substantial investments in training infrastructure. The work of the government-sponsored industry training advisory bodies had been particularly effective in persuading some industries to move to more industry-wide training arrangements. The development of national competency standards had also had an effect in some enterprises, guiding the development of training programs designed to meet these standards. Thus, like industrial relations developments, government training policy seems to create a framework within which certain forms and approaches to training are more likely to occur.

Training arrangements

The outcomes of the processes of interaction between drivers and moderators are the training arrangements that are finally put in place. The diversity of the arrangements in terms of the dimensions of training activity—formal versus informal, external versus internal, technical versus behavioural, generic versus specific—as well as the overall levels of expenditure on training and the distribution of that training between occupational groups in the workforce, is the product of the unique interactions between training drivers and training moderators that take place within each enterprise.

Management development

There are a number of reasons why management development is an increasingly important issue for T&D (training and development) practitioners in the 1990s. Despite the corporate downsizing that thinned out the management ranks of so many organisations in the 1980s, there are still a significant number of managers in Australia. Estimates put the managerial population at about 770 000, requiring about 30 000 new managers to be appointed per year simply to replenish the stock (Dawkins 1991).

Management is becoming an internationalised occupation as increasing numbers of managers are posted overseas to supervise the operations of transnational corporations. In the international context, however, it is clear that Australian managers do not match the educational and training profiles of their overseas counterparts. Only 21 per cent of Australian senior managers possess an undergraduate degree compared with more than 60 per cent of European managers and over 80 per cent of American and Japanese managers (Dawkins 1991). Training for managers in Australia also appears low by international standards, with Australian managers receiving an average of 4 hours training per year compared to an estimated 42 hours for managers in the USA.

The performance of Australian managers has also been criticised. The short-term, profit orientation of management in this country has been unfavourably compared with the longer-term, strategic view adopted by managers in competitor countries (Dawkins 1991). Studies of major change programs such as award restructuring have left little doubt that the performance of local managers is largely responsible for the success or failure of corporate change programs and thus change needs to be predicated upon the development of managers in the enterprise (McKenzie, Milner & Rimmer 1990).

In an attempt to make the mechanics of management development more relevant to the actual practice of management, competency-based approaches have become increasingly popular both overseas and in Australia (Saul 1989; Armstrong 1991). Following the work of Boyatzis (1982), an increasing number of organisations have attempted to define the exact competencies required of their managers. Boyatzis originally identified 19 competencies which he grouped into five clusters:

1 goal and action management;
2 leadership;
3 human resource management;
4 directing subordinates;
5 focus on others.

Boyatzis was careful to state that competencies alone were not a sufficient condition of management effectiveness; they had to operate within a favourable organisational context to result in performance.

The major problem with the development of management competencies is the inherent complexity of the job and the lack of any universally applicable definition of what a manager does. As a result, lists of management competencies often become lists of mere activities or attributes, implying a return to the days of the 'traits' approach to management development when it was assumed that managers were born rather than made (Woodruffe 1991).

Nevertheless, the problem of the relevance of management development programs has continued to influence the development of new techniques in the field. In particular, techniques which emphasise the role of the individual manager in determining his or her own training needs and accepting the responsibility for meeting these needs have become popular.

- *Action learning:* stresses the importance of activity and problem-solving to the development of managerial skills. In an action learning situation, managers taken from different organisational backgrounds work in groups on specific organisational problems. The multi-perspective approach of such a group helps the manager to learn not only about problem-solving but also to question any operating assumptions made which result in less than effective behaviour (Revans 1982).
- *Self-development:* problems of releasing managers for formal training have made the notion of self-development very popular. The title, however, may be misleading. The self refers to the acceptance by the manager of responsibility for his or her own learning. This may involve attendance at formal training programs, but will also involve the formulation of training and a plan for meeting those needs through the use of work situations. The role of the T&D practitioner is very much one of a facilitator/counsellor, helping the manager to work out his own program of development and persisting with it.
- *Outdoor management development:* not a strictly individualised form of development, an outdoor development program makes use of challenges

in the natural environment to encourage individual reflection and team-building. A typical outdoor program offers both individual and group opportunities for development followed by extensive debriefing by a skilled facilitator to encourage learning from the experiences.

• *Development centres*: a refinement of the assessment centre process used in the selection and appraisal of managers in many larger organisations. The construction of the centre remains broadly similar, that is a series of individual and group exercises observed by assessors who meet after the centre activities to produce an individual assessment of each candidate. However, the development centre is specifically geared toward the identification of development needs and the construction of an individualised training program for each candidate. This is considered to be a much less threatening process for those who go through the process.

The Karpin Report

The level of concern about the capabilities of Australian managers and management development practice led the then Minister for Employment, Education and Training, Kim Beazley, in 1992 to establish the Industry Task Force on Leadership and Management Skills, commonly known as the Karpin Committee after its chairman, David Karpin, executive director of resources giant, CRA. The Karpin Committee's research has confirmed the pessimistic picture of Australian management presented above. But the Karpin Committee has also shown how the role of the Australian manager has changed in the last 20 years and how it is likely to change in the next 20 (refer Table 2.1).

Karpin paints a picture of the evolving Australian senior manager as a globe-trotting, corporate executive, managing workforces in several parts of the world. Whether this will be true of all Australian managers or simply the corporate executives that formed the samples for much of the research underpinning Karpin's deliberations is a matter of some debate. However, this is the basis on which Karpin based his main recommendations. These include:

• the development of an 'enterprise culture' starting at the level of primary and secondary schooling;
• capitalising on the talents of diversity and, particularly, those of women;
• measures to improve the management of small business by using, among other things, a system of qualified mentors or advisers to provide advice to small business managers;
• developing a new, frontline management development program for the estimated 180 000 frontline managers in Australia who have not received any formal, management training;
• the development of a framework of management competency standards for use across all industries so that all managers gain a common core of skills;
• measures to improve the standards of management education offered by university business schools including moving away from the traditional,

gendered focus of management education, the accreditation of MBA programs and the establishment of a new, national management school;
- the promotion of best practice in management through measures such as international study tours for up to 1500 Australian managers each year;
- the establishment of the Australian council for management development which would oversee the implementation of many of Karpin's proposals and maintain a national focus on management development.

Karpin's views about the role of the manager have attracted some criticism. In particular, Karpin has been accused of underestimating the changing nature of managerial work as a result of the introduction of teamwork in many organisations (Emery 1995). In many cases, teams are taking over the role of the traditional manager and making many decisions for themselves. In this situation, managers may become facilitators rather than leaders. It is not clear what the final impact of Karpin will be on management education in Australia. Although the report received widespread publicity at the time of its release, most of its recommendations have not been put into practice. The idea of a new national management school, in particular, was quickly dismissed by the federal government for whom this proposal represented an unnecessary increase in public resources. Furthermore, the election of the Coalition federal government in March 1996 considerably reduced the impact of the recommendations.

Organisational learning

Many organisations undergo a number of change programs in an attempt to improve competitiveness. Culture change, quality circles, TQM become fads or fashions which organisations subscribe to, but they have little or no lasting impact on effectiveness (Abrahamson 1996). Over time, however, some organisations continue to change and improve while others find it more difficult. A learning process would therefore appear to take place within some organisations which enables them to survive in changing environments. The concept of organisational learning is not new. It originated with economists who noted that successful organisations became better at what they did, over time. For instance, car manufacturers learnt to make cars cheaply and more quickly; retailers learnt how to keep constant supplies of goods on the shelves. In this way, the organisations became more efficient and more profitable.

What is new is the increasing emphasis being placed on organisational learning as a process. It is now being seen not just as something that happens naturally, but as something that should be made explicit and should be fostered. In other words, in a rapidly changing economic environment, organisations need to learn and adapt quickly and efficiently. As Kim (1993) has said, all organisations learn, but organisational learning does not necessarily imply that what is learned is good for the organisation. Organisations may learn bad habits as well as good. A number of elements assist in creating organisations which effectively learn. These organisations have been labelled 'learning oganisations'.

Systems thinking

Systems thinking forms the basis of many commentators' views on learning organisations. People working within organisations need to know that one part or process within an organisation never functions in isolation; change always leads to effects elsewhere. Therefore people taking actions need to take account of all the possible effects. An organisation does not just form a system of and by itself: it is also part of a wider system (in fact, of many wider systems) or an 'environment'.

Senge et al. (1994) suggest that it is hard for people to think in systems terms, because the way in which language is constructed can only have one (or a few) causes for one effect and vice versa. They also suggest that thinking in systems terms enables managers to avoid seeing organisational change as only a top-down process. Change can be initiated at any level of an organisation and should be participative in nature, because everyone is affected by any change.

Changes to the system, either internally or externally, have wide-ranging effects on the organisation. The organisation reacts and this process is almost involuntary. But the organisation has a choice: it can learn from these changes. Like an individual learner, it notes the experience and reflects on it. Next time, the reaction need not be involuntary and the organisation can anticipate the changes and move to pre-empt them.

Changes in how work is organised

The concept of the learning organisation is gaining popularity because the environment in which organisations operate is seen as becoming increasingly complex and fast-changing. Some of these changes include (Dunphy & Stace 1990)

- decentralisation of operations;
- a move to flatter organisation structures;
- the introduction of cultural change programs;
- technological innovation;
- increased networking between organisations;
- the breakdown of demarcations;
- multiskilling of the workforce;
- the increasing use of casual or otherwise 'loosely attached' workers;
- an increased use of autonomous workteams at many levels of production, working without supervision and making their own decisions.

Individual learning

Organisations can only learn through their individual members. Individuals can undergo learning outside their organisations but organisations do not learn except through individuals. Kim (1993) suggests a model of learning that adds the role of memory to experience. He adds the concept of individual mental models, which are deeply ingrained assumptions, generalisations, or even pictures or images that influence how we understand the world and how we take action. While the models help people to make sense of the world, they can also confine the way in which we understand things, and may be dangerous if we assume they are reality.

The relationship between individual and organisational learning

Organisational learning is the ability of the organisation to adopt changes in response to changes in the marketplace and to learn and improve as time goes on. The ability of the organisation to learn underpins the effective implementation of organisational change.

Organisational learning is not simply the sum of the learning of each of the individuals in the enterprise. Organisational learning implies a capacity to transmit the lessons from one generation of employees to another and to adapt as a result of the learning process. Organisational learning is a much deeper process involving the development of insights and knowledge over a long period of time and the ability to critically assess the assumptions on which the organisation is basing its actions.

For individual learning to become organisational learning, the role of memory is crucial. An organisation's memory is stored in its mental models, which function as individuals' do: there will be frameworks and routines. There will also be written-down materials: databases, reference manuals, personnel procedures, plans, copies of letters, technical manuals, proformas. As Field and Ford (1995, p. 22) suggest: 'it is organisational memory that ensures that lessons learnt are not subsequently forgotten, and that there is continuous improvement (rather than one step forwards, one step backwards)'.

Learning theory for individuals cannot simply be transposed into learning theory for organisations. However, organisations do seem to have the capacity to learn from their experiences.

Barriers to organisational learning

There are many barriers to effective organisational learning. Field and Ford (1995) have identified four critical dimensions within the organisation that have to be co-ordinated if effective organisational learning is to take place. These include employee relations and consultation and agreements, work organisation, skill formation and technology and information systems.

Employee relations: If the employee relations climate is adversarial, every change will be approached with suspicion and no one will be willing to become flexible outside their normal working conditions. Many opportunities for learning—by management and workers—will be lost.

Work organisation: If work is organised in too structured a manner, people will not have the chance to learn anything new or to help other people in other departments.

Skill formation: Training may be carried out in a very conventional manner, e.g. sending employees to a training centre for a course. Their learning is not shared and they feel frustrated because they see no chance of trying out what they've learned. In cases like this training can actually be bad for learning.

Technology/information systems: Knowledge about new technology may be jealously guarded by certain people and training may be inadequate. People cannot access the new technology themselves to make their own work better and more interesting.

Conclusion

The move from personnel management to HRM has seen a shift from a focus on employee relations to HRD. Whereas the personnel manager was primarily concerned with questions of maintenance—recruiting the right people, administering employees correctly and ensuring smooth industrial relations—the human resource manager is concerned with the question of how to improve the performance of the workforce. This involves creating the right organisational conditions in which people can maximise their contribution to the organisation. From this perspective, HRM is vitally concerned with the development of the organisation and its employees. HRM becomes a employee development-led rather than an employee-relations led function. In this context, the activities and responsibilities of the training practitioner are changing significantly. No longer is the training practitioner concerned with training for workforce maintenance—induction, skills training, training leave and so on. The training practitioner becomes an HRD practitioner concerned with organising and brokering opportunities for improvement. This means that the focus of the HRD practitioner is increasingly concerned with learning rather than with training.

However, this does not mean, as some commentators have put it, that training is no longer relevant (Ford 1997). Far from it. Training, as the planned activities of the organisation to foster learning and development in the workforce, is more important than ever. Organisations have to take their training activities more seriously. Organisations need to decide what types of learning they want to take place at work and design their training to ensure that the learning takes place. So a new alliance needs to be forged between training and learning. Fostering and developing that alliance is the new role of the HRD practitioner.

References

Abrahamson, E. 1996, 'Management fashion', *Academy of Management Review*, vol. 21, no. 1, pp. 254–85.

Armstrong, A. 1991, 'Management skills and performance audit', *Asia Pacific HRM*, vol. 29, no. 4, pp. 25–39.

Australian Bureau of Statistics (ABS) 1994, *Training and Education Experience Australia, 1993*, AGPS, Canberra.

—— 1998, *Employer Training Practices, Australia 1997*, AGPS, Canberra.

Baker, M. & Wooden, M. 1995, *Small and Medium Sized Enterprises and Vocational Education and Training*, Monograph no. 1, National Training Markets Research Centre, Adelaide.

Beer, M., Spector, B., Lawrence, P.R., Quinn Mills, D. & Walton, R.E. 1984, *Managing Human Assets*, Free Press, New York.

Boyatzis, R.E. 1982, *The Competent Manager: A Model for Effective Performance*, Wiley, New York.

Dawkins, J.S. 1991, *The Australian Mission on Management Skills: Volume 1: Report*, AGPS, Canberra.

Dunphy, D. & Stace, D. 1990, *Under New Management: Australian Organizations in Transition*, McGraw-Hill, Sydney.

Dyer, L. & Kochan, T.A. 1995, 'Is there a new HRM? Contemporary evidence and future directions', in B.M. Downie and M.L. Coates (eds), *Managing Human Resources in the 1990s and Beyond: Is the Workplace Being Transformed?* IRC Press, Queens University, Ontario.

Emery, F. 1995, 'Managers look past snake-oil for ideas', *Business Review Weekly*, 16 October, p. 76.

Field, L. & Ford, B. 1995, *Managing Organisational Learning: From Rhetoric to Reality*, Longman, Melbourne.

Finegold, D. 1991, 'Institutional incentives and skill creation: Preconditions for a high skills equilibrium', in P. Ryan (ed.), *International Comparisons of Vocational Education and Training for Intermediate Skills*, Falmer Press, London.

Ford, G.W. 1997, 'Journeys of learning enterprises—Integrating people, process and place', paper presented to the Australian Human Resources Institute National Convention, Brisbane, 18–21 May.

Hayton, G., McIntyre, J., Sweet, R., MacDonald, R., Noble, C., Smith, A. & Roberts, P. 1996, *Enterprise Training in Australia*, Office of Training and Further Education, Victoria, Melbourne.

Karpin, D.S. 1995, *Enterprising Nation: Renewing Australia's Managers to Meet the Challenges of the Asia-Pacific Century. Report of the Industry Taskforce on Leadership and Management Skills*, AGPS, Canberra.

Keep, E. 1989, 'Corporate training strategies', in J. Storey (ed.) *New Perspectives on Human Resource Management*, Routledge, London.

Kim, D. 1993, 'The link between individual and organizational learning', *Sloan Management Review*, Fall, pp. 37–50.

Legge, K. 1995, *Human Resource Management: Rhetorics and Realities*, Macmillan, London.

Lepani, B. 1995, *Vocational Education and Training (VET) 2005*. Report prepared for NSW TAFE, November.

McKenzie, D., Milner, S. & Rimmer, M. 1990, 'Award restructuring: The first stage adjustment', *Working Paper no. 3*, National Key Centre in Industrial Relations, Monash University, Melbourne.

Revans, R.W. 1982, *The Origin and Growth of Action Learning*, Chartwell-Bratt, Bickley, Kent.

Saul, P. 1989, 'Using management competencies to improve management performance and stimulate management self-development', *Asia-Pacific HRM*, vol. 27, no. 3, pp. 74–85.

Senge, P., Kleiner, A., Roberts, C., Ross, R. & Smith, B. 1994, *The Fifth Discipline Handbook: Strategies and Tools for Building a Learning Organization*, Doubleday, New York.

Smith, A., Hayton, G., Roberts, P., Thorn, E. & Noble, C. 1995, *Enterprise Training: The Factors that Affect Demand*, Office of Training and Further Education, Melbourne.

Walton, R.E. 1985, 'From control to commitment in the workplace', *Harvard Business Review*, vol. 63, no. 2, March–April, pp. 77–84.

Woodruffe, C. 1991, 'Competent by any other name', *Personnel Management*, September, pp. 30–3.

Case Study

C

Training and development in change management: An energy industry example

Denva Scott

During the last fifteen years the energy industry in Australia has undergone significant transformation as it struggled with the impact of increased competition and other major changes in the environment. Energetics, an Australian energy company involved in the distribution and marketing of energy to industry, commercial premises and to homes, is a company that was caught up in these changes. The company has approximately 1800 employees and a turnover of about $1 billion per annum.

Twenty years ago the company had a monopoly on the distribution of natural gas within its defined distribution area. Despite its original monopoly position, Energetics vigorously pursued a strategy of growth and expansion of its market. It did this by introducing new applications for the use of natural gas and by marketing its technical expertise to industry. The fact that it was capital rich provided ample resources for the development of new applications. In addition, natural gas is pure, easy to distribute and flexible in its uses so that it was viewed as an attractive product. The growth strategy was successful and resulted in Energetics holding over 90 per cent of the market share of sales of energy to industry within its area of distribution by the early 1980s.

The organisational structure was appropriate for this growth strategy at that time. The organisation was vertically integrated, but it was also bureaucratic and hierarchical with eight levels from chief executive to the organisation's frontline. Energetics was a self-sufficient internal labour market with all employees believing they had a job for life.

Human resource policies reflected this structure. Reward schemes provided for awards for 10, 25, 30 and 40 years service. The 'heroes' were the employees who had been employed for more than 40 years. People were actively encouraged to find jobs within the company for their family members and this was honoured in the company magazine with many stories of multiple generations of one family featured. Allied to this, was Energetics' strong technical culture. The majority of managers were trade-qualified or engineers. They had been promoted because of their superior technical knowledge and experience. This culture was reinforced by training that focused on providing greater levels of specialisation within the area of expertise.

Training was functionally based and sought to provide employees with the technical skills necessary to do their jobs. Consequently, training was provided in-house and was teacher-centred and knowledge-based. There was a dedicated training facility with fifteen trainers and a school of over 100 apprentices. The facility also trained non-trade workers and provided supervisory training for foremen and supervisors. Sales training was not introduced until the late 1970s and was located in the sales and marketing department.

During the 1980s and 1990s the nature of training and its provision evolved through four phases. Phase 1 was a period of growth and focused on management development; phase 2 focused on customer service; phase 3 was a period of redirection and restructuring; phase 4 focused on ways of dealing with increased competition by reducing training.

Phase 1: Growth—Management development

During the 1980s there was substantial growth in Australian energy markets. Between the late 1970s and mid-1980s, Energetics' markets grew until it held the majority of the manufacturing industrial market in its licensing area. It had also expanded its coverage of geographic areas through the purchase of other energy distribution companies. This provided the means to pursue new areas of growth in petroleum exploration and production and other non-energy industries such as property development.

A new era of training was developed to support this growth. In the late 1970s the personnel executive predicted the requirement for a new type of manager for the future and designed a management development program to meet this need. The aim of the program was to develop a pool of candidates who could manage multi-disciplinary functions and who could bring new ideas and ways of working into the management functions they would hold.

The program included the active recruitment of graduates from university campuses, a graduate development program, a cadet training scheme, a succession planning system and two management development programs run in-house. One program was for young people with the potential for management, the other for newly appointed managers. A management development co-ordinator was appointed to bring together the various strands of the management development program.

These initiatives were effective in changing the profile of Energetics' managers and by the late 1980s there was a younger and more diverse management profile. The average age had dropped by ten to fifteen years; there were managers with professional qualifications in a variety of disciplines including marketing, science and engineering, and a number of the management team had been recruited externally. The traditional path of promotion into management via technical excellence had been broken.

Phase 2: Business challenges—Customer service

In 1988 Energetics faced significant challenges. Their traditional energy market was mature, competitors were gaining ground, technology was out of date and one of the consequences was the loss of more than 5 per cent of their product through system losses. Significant resources were dedicated to dealing with crisis management. In addition, diversification had produced its own problems: new businesses required different management and professional skills and a substantial amount of executive time not justified by the return on investment.

It was decided to move away from a strategy of diversification to focus on the core business—energy production and distribution. This allowed for consolidation of resources, but it required an improvement in technology and customer service. Both developments had implications for the provision of training.

The company undertook a massive program to improve its technology. Three programs were initiated: one involved replacing a large proportion of their distribution network; the other two involved introducing new electronic technology. This electronic technology enabled the establishment of a customer database and a system to manage the service department. Staff were required to learn how to operate these systems.

The second initiative was designed to provide Energetics with a competitive edge based on excellence in customer service, rather than on technical excellence, the traditional focus. The focus on customer service was the crux of the culture change program and training was regarded as critical for this change process. Two training initiatives were taken as part of this culture change program: an organisation-wide training program on customer service and the introduction of Four Quadrant Leadership.

The organisation-wide training program was developed as a result of learning about customer service organisations in the USA. Fourteen managers spent two weeks on a study tour of organisations in the USA known for their excellence in customer service. This was followed by a customer service 'guru' visiting Energetics for two weeks and speaking to more than 500 employees about the customer service philosophy. An in-house program was developed to teach employees the basic skills and philosophy of a customer-service driven organisation. Two months later this program was introduced for all employees. It was an interactive, fun, learner-centred program run along a vertical slice of the organisation which was not functionally based.

This was a turning point for training in Energetics. Training was regarded as strategically important because it was acknowledged as the basis of the culture change process. This was signalled by two training managers attending the customer service tour in the USA and by the investment in resources required to develop the customer service training program.

At the same time, all managers, supervisors and forepersons were introduced to the concept of leadership using the Four Quadrant Leadership program. All participated in a two-day program to teach them the basic skills involved in leading, as opposed to supervising or managing. This program introduced the concept that the job of the manager involved more than budgeting and resource allocation—it primarily involved leading people.

Phase 3: Potential pitfalls

The third phase emphasised the role of employees as part of Energetics' success. Employees became more focused on customer service as a consequence of the training provided in phase 2; but they also became aware of the inadequacy of existing systems and work processes as a means of delivering high quality customer service. Many employees started asking for resources to meet these expectations and they became aware of their lack of problem-solving techniques. This latter shortcoming was accentuated by cross-functional boundaries. Problems involving more than one business function were difficult to solve because there were no lines of communication between functions and each function was a stand-alone business unit: this meant that there was no incentive for the businesses to assist each other.

In 1991 the executive sought to deal with these issues by adopting ten strategies, three of which related to employees. These three strategies were

1 ensuring employees understand the Energetic's vision;
2 driving leadership harder;
3 providing employees with the skills necessary to do their jobs well.

A document titled *It's Time for Action*, which included a vision statement and a plan for action, was published and personally presented to all employees by the general manager. This document sent a message to employees that they were empowered to take action and were trusted with strategic information enabling them to take the appropriate action using the resources available.

Two years later the organisation's structure was changed in an attempt to improve the company's competitive position. Decision-makers were brought closer to the customers through regionalisation. Three regional centres were set up and located so that within ten years, due to population growth, they would be in the centre of their distribution area. In addition, at least three layers of supervision were removed to provide a flatter organisation structure.

These changes influenced the nature of training provided and the way in which it was provided. The business was now regionalised and vertical business units no longer existed. In addition, the business needed multiskilled and flexible employees, not employees with only one area of specialisation. As a result, the training function was centralised and training courses were developed to teach employees about the total work process rather than their one piece of it. Leadership training was intensified to provide leaders and managers with the skills needed to lead a broad portfolio and a larger number of direct reports. Upward feedback was introduced through employee surveys of leaders' skills in the workplace. A number of quality facilitators were trained and quality teams were established as part of the total quality approach implemented with the new technology.

Training was centralised within the human resource development area. This was done for a number of reasons reflecting internal and external developments:

- to minimise the duplication of resources;
- training was seen as a core culture change tool and it was considered essential that the messages coming from the training area be consistent;
- job functions were blurring, for instance service people with technical trades such as plumbers needed to become salespeople and it was difficult providing separate technical, sales training with such a varied skill mix;
- outside the organisation, training was becoming a profession in its own right, with major improvements in technology and methods such as experiential learning and coaching; centralisation of the function facilitated the application and implementation of new training techniques.

In addition to the training initiatives, changes were made to other human resource policies. A competency-based classification structure was introduced to replace the inflexible and out-of-date award structure which rewarded employees for performing one function and for years of service. The previous award structure conflicted with the new business direction which needed flexible employees who could perform more than one function and who were not constrained by demarcation boundaries. All award employees to mid-level supervisor were now covered by the award which based pay on competencies used. Assessment of competencies was done internally according to standards developed internally and benchmarked against the National Training Board (NTB) standards.

Phase 4: Competition

1995 was a year of further major change. The federal government planned energy utility reform involving the provision for free trade of energy between geographical regions, and the buying and selling of energy in a free market. This development challenged the practice of cross-subsidisation in the industry.

The industry had grown up around the practice of distributing costs of the infrastructure among the various customer sectors. This meant some sectors subsidised others. However, with the opening up of the industry to external scrutiny, cost structures would become more open to scrutiny and increasing competition. Customers could therefore choose whether they were prepared to pay for these costs.

Subsidies would have to be removed so that each customer sector could stand independently. This required a reduction in costs. The company reacted by opening as many activities as possible to external competition, taking measures to cut costs and outsourcing any non-core activities. For instance, meter reading and the servicing of appliances were outsourced. This resulted in the reduction in the number of employees from 3000 to 1800.

The organisation was again restructured to mirror the customer base. All the functions necessary to service a set of customers were together. In addition, due to the federal government energy industry reform agenda, there could no longer be a transfer and sharing of information from areas of the company that were not open to competition (such as the network) to areas that were open to competition (e.g. marketing). Otherwise Energetics' marketing area could be seen to have an unfair advantage over other competing energy marketing companies.

Significant changes were also made in the provision of training. The first major change was the discontinuation of the apprenticeship training program. This decision was taken because of the decreasing demand for these skills as a result of the changes in the structure and technology used in Energetics. It was difficult justifying the training of a large number of apprentices when the company was unable to keep qualified employees fully occupied.

Three other factors hastened the closure of the apprenticeship program: redundancy, cost-cutting and the perception that it was not a core activity. Once some employees were made redundant, the company could no longer guarantee jobs to graduates of the apprentice school. Also, when the company's cost structure came under scrutiny it was difficult to justify the costs of the program. Finally, the apprenticeship program had a reputation as a centre of excellence and trained other people on behalf of TAFE, including TAFE teachers. It was difficult justifying the costs associated with training 'the competition'.

The closure of the apprenticeship program was a major signal for change because apprenticeships had been part of the company for over 50 years. Many managers had begun their careers as apprentices. Similarly, training and human resource development more generally were no longer seen as a core activity. The human resource development area was regarded as an inflexible entrenched empire.

The centralised human resource development function was disbanded and line managers became responsible for training and employee development. In-house training was discontinued and an internal co-ordinator was appointed to each business unit. Their role was to determine training needs and manage the contractors providing the training.

The future

Energetics now has the opportunity to use the competitive environment as a platform for growth. They have diversified into other energy forms and are using technical expertise as a platform for growth into overseas market. In the short term, the company will manage a number of external service providers rather than providing the service itself. The challenge will be to manage an increasingly competitive environment with the potential for growth and expansion. Skill development will be required in new business development, core energy and core management skills.

Training played an important role in the transformation of Energetics. As the energy industry changed so did the skill and competency requirements of managers, supervisors and employees. The strategies, techniques and structures associated with the provision of training changed in response to these changes.

However, just as Energetics was transformed from a bureaucratic, technologically based company to a competitive service company, so the very nature of training was also transformed. It changed from a focus on technical skills to a culture change tool, to a means for adding value to the business through the line. Training was transformed to human resource development, and this cannot be regarded as either a passive spectator or a victim of the change process. In Energetics, human resource development was an integral part of business strategy implementation and, as strategy changed, so did human resource development and its delivery.

Industrial relations and human resource systems

5

Max Ogden with Robin Kramar

Industrial relations arrangements arise out of the objective reality of economic development. Economics is influenced by, and in turn influences, market demands, technological innovations and investment strategies. These in turn require appropriate skills, competencies, business strategies, knowledge, work organisation, management systems, legislative frameworks and government policies.

Economic and social developments usually move ahead of common understandings and these are often at odds with institutional and legislative arrangements. Such lags appear especially true during times of major change, such as the shift towards the post-Fordist paradigm which has been under way since the mid-1980s, which is not yet the dominant form of work organisation in most industries. Prior to the early 1980s work organisation in nearly every industry had been dominated for about 50 years by Taylorism, later to be know as Fordism. This approach was based on standard, high volume, products and services, involving an almost infinite division of labour and strict hierarchies, with high labour content, where price was about the only competitive advantage, requiring little skill, innovation or commitment on the part of employees.

Management, unions, employees and governments worldwide are seeking to make sense of the new post-Fordist paradigm. It manifests itself through the new emphasis on market diversity, customer service, design, warranty, quality, rapid product turnover, enviromentally sound products, with lower volumes and fewer standard products and services. Price, while always important, is no longer the only factor determining competitiveness. The very uniqueness of a company's product or service is often its competitive advantage. This has meant that inevitably there will be a greater focus on the enterprise management systems and industrial relations.

This has led to management practices and standards such as total quality management (TQM), ISO9000 and 14 000 standards, flexible technological systems, quality assurance and organisational restructuring—including outsourcing and work reorganisation. It has become clear that to meet these challenges requires a holistic management system, meaning human resource management and industrial relations strategies must be core operations of the business.

Despite the uneven adoption of new industrial relations and human resource management practices, the adoption of these is widespread (Hegewisch & Brewster 1993; Kramar & Lake 1997). This chapter examines developments in the industrial relations arena and discusses their implications for human resource managers. The first section identifes key elements of the 'new industrial relations' and briefly compares these to traditional practices. The second section identifies some of the issues associated with the implementation of recent developments in industrial relations and the final section identifies the major features of the 1996 *Workplace Relations Act*.

Under the old system, direct labour was often low skilled and cheap, but there was a large labour component which meant it was the major cost. Under the new paradigm for most industries, excepting personal services such as hospitality and health, the direct labour content is becoming very low, and capital/technology, raw materials and distribution are the major costs. The real issue for management, and especially human resource managers, is less about cutting labour costs (even if this is achieved it represents only a small percentage of overall costs) and more about how to organise and motivate employees to make the best use of the technology and capital through their skill, knowledge, innovation and commitment. These forms of labour can be referred to as 'old and new labour', and new labour is increasingly known as 'knowledge work'.

Different organisations and countries respond to these changes in different ways. Some organisations continue to use traditional industrial relations and human resource practices because they are able, at least for the foreseeable future, to compete in their particular market segment. Some companies may be unaware of new systems, managers often resist the introduction of different management practices such as teamwork or the devolution of responsibility because they perceive that it reduces their responsibility, therefore threatens their role. The political, economic and cultural climate of a particular country has a significant effect on management and industrial relations systems.

In *The Seven Cultures of Capitalism*, Charles Hampden-Turner and Fons Tromenaars (1993) examined management and corporate governance practices in twelve countries, by surveying and interviewing 15 000 managers. They concluded that there are seven distinct ways of managing the capitalist system. They observed that in the early days of capitalism in Anglo–Saxon countries, the drive for quick profits was successful and created new capital rapidly. However, in the post-Fordist world, with huge investment requiring longer timeframes and intricate and integrated systems, they suggest that countries with inclusive cultures, and longer cultural horizons and patience, such as Japan, and to a lesser extent Germany, are likely to be more successful.

They note that Anglo–Saxon companies expand mainly by taking over already existing businesses because it is quicker. It is argued managers feel pressured by investors and the stock market to achieve short-term results through take-overs. In countries with inclusive cultures, such as Japan and Germany, the tendency is to generate growth by retaining more profits and self-funding investment in new ventures or expansion. Hampden–Turner and Tromenaars also indicate that a private company is often managed differently from a publicly listed company, with the private company tending to be more patient and long term.

From the perspective of most employees, their companies could and should be much more efficient, and they would assist such improvement but are rarely asked. They usually see things that even the best manager cannot be expected to see. Employees regularly complain that they make suggestions that are ignored, only to be implemented some time later with the manager taking the credit. There are various reasons for this feature, including a concern at perceived loss of power; pressures from outside such as the stock market and investors for short-term gain (despite what at times will be long-term disadvantage); new management ideas and practices including outsourcing; legislative and political climate; economic situation; the particular market or industry the company is in; personal style or even prejudice against individuals and groups.

Elements of the new industrial relations

Recent developments in industrial relations have involved changes in a number of areas including in the focus of negotiations, the roles of the parties and the issues regarded as central for negotiation. Recent legislation has carried these developments further in pressuring managers, employees and trade unions to operate differently in the workplace. These developments have raised a number of issues for concerned parties and the Industrial Relations Commission (IRC).

Focus of negotiations

Since the early 1980s debate has continued about the need for reform of industrial relations practices and outcomes so that they promote efficiency and productivity (Dabscheck 1995). Employers argued the centralised industrial relations system produced inefficiencies through the existence of multiple award coverage in many workplaces (Business Council of Australia 1989; Hilmer 1989), the proliferation of occupationally based unions, the 'flow on' of increases through an industry or occupation, creation of narrow inflexible job structures and disorderly workplace negotiations (Drago, Wooden & Sloan 1992). It was asserted Australian business could be made more efficient and competitive by reforming industrial relations through deregulation and reducing the roles of third parties, including industrial tribunals and trade unions (Callus 1997, p. 17).

Unions, while acknowledging that elements of awards were outdated and impeded efficiency, argued that there was ample scope for change and a greater focus on the workplace within the existing centralised national system. This system provided for equity within the wage structure and a safety net for low paid workers. The unions also argued that the centralised system prevented some companies from using low wages as a substitute for better management, and protected those employers who were prepared to pay the more attractive wage rates. There is evidence that unionised workplaces pursuing better wages and conditions require managers to respond by being more efficient.

In 1987 the focus in federal industrial relations began to shift to enhance the level of enterprise bargaining and productivity-based wage increases. In March 1987 the Australian Industrial Relations Commission (AIRC) introduced the Structural Efficiency Principle (SEP). This principle provided for wage increases on the basis of efficiency improvements resulting from changes in work and management practices, the reduction of demarcation barriers and improvements in training (Deery 1995). Subsequent decisions of the AIRC further supported the achievement of enterprise improvements in productivity and efficiency through formal union–management agreements. In April 1991, the AIRC refused to endorse the call from the ACTU and the federal Labor government for a new form of enterprise bargaining on a number of grounds, including:

- lack of a clear definition of the 'enterprise';
- unresolved question of how increases in productivity (and profitability) would be measured and translated into wage increases; and
- difficulties involved in prescribing a ceiling for negotiated wage increases (Deery 1995, p. 61).

However, the AIRC doubted that increased enterprise bargaining would improve economic performance and it emphasised the need for preparing the ground before moving to greater use of enterprise bargaining (Kramar, McGraw & Schuler 1997, p. 109). This need was demonstrated by the lack of detailed provisions for implementation in existing enterprise agreements. The failure to include these provisions for implementation was the consequence of a number of factors. Many participants on both sides did not understand or have the considerable time and resources required to implement change. In addition many change provisions were resisted by middle managers, and sections of the workforce, perhaps indicating that they did not understand the ramifications when first agreed. As a result many agreements which looked good on paper, when reviewed a year later were found to have only been partly implemented or in some cases not implemented at all. Enterprise bargaining was often wrongly interpreted by employers as a means of trading-off employment conditions for wage increases. Consequently, many negotiations focused mistakenly on minor issues with little overall impact on real efficiency outcomes. For example, managers tended to concentrate on such things as tea breaks, annual leave loading, penalty rates and washing time. These provide minimal efficiency improvements, but upset most employees because these are hard-won conditions that make work a little more bearable. The real issue is how to get employees and management committed to high quality products and services, delivered promptly and cost effectively to the customer, through new work systems and skills.

Devolution of bargaining to the enterprise was in fact not new. Over-award campaigning had been a characteristic first in the metal industry from the late 1950s, and then in many other industries. The strategy ultimately supported by the ACTU was to establish new standards in wages and conditions through bargaining and industrial activity at the enterprise or industry level, and then to use those results in national test cases in the IRC (under its various titles) to argue that these new standards should apply to all awards. Many important gains—the third week of annual leave, wage increases, the 38-hour week, Melbourne Cup holiday—'flowed on' to most workers.

What is new about enterprise bargaining is

- the range of issues encompassed by the negotiations;
- the possibility of modifying the award; and
- the new agreements need a proactive, co-operative, and detailed implementation phase (over-award agreements simply required the parties to ensure the award and agreement were being adhered to).

The enterprise bargaining process allowed employment conditions to be more closely linked to the needs of the organisation. Some of the matters included in the more proactive enterprise agreements included consultation and information sharing, redesign of work including work teams and breaking down demarcation, national competency skill standards, commitments to training, skills-based pay and career paths, commitments to best practice management systems based on a holistic approach, achieving key performance indicators, gainsharing, flexible working time systems, annualised salaries, and various other local issues. The rewriting of the influential Metal Industry Award was supported by the enterprise bargaining process. The Award was simplified from its classical Taylorist format with 348 classifications detailing minute divisions of labour to a document which provides 14 pay and career levels setting out the required technical, social and responsibility competences for each level, but does not provide descriptions of work. Such new awards and enterprise agreements are characteristic of work that is no longer, 'defined by content, but by intent' as Melbourne company and union adviser Hugh McBride so succinctly put it. These changes began to be implemented in enterprises in 1996, and have continued in the era of award simplification and allowable matters under the Australian *Workplace Relations Act 1996* where the parties in the metal industry agreed to maintain the national competency-based skills system, despite opposition from the federal government.

In October 1991 the AIRC introduced the Enterprise Bargaining Principle and its decisions made provisions for the use of sections of the *Industrial Relations Act* that related to consent awards and certified agreements. In 1992, the federal government further encouraged enterprise bargaining through amendments to the Act reducing the power of the AIRC to prevent agreements that it did not consider of benefit to the parties and the community. The commission was now obliged to certify agreements if six tests were met:

1   employees must not be disadvantaged by the agreement;
2   a disputes settlement procedure must be included;
3   a term of operation must be specified;
4   in a single enterprise agreement, at least one union with members at the workplace must be party to the agreement;
5   unions must consult their members about the terms of the agreement;
6   unions must report the outcomes to the commission (s. 134 E(1)).

The making of agreements at the enterprise level was further encouraged through the *Industrial Relations Act 1993*. This Act provided for collective agreements to be made by trade unions, and for enterprise flexibility agreements to be made by non-union employees. The ability of employees to register agreements without trade union involvement was a major shift in the federal system of industrial relations. The two types of agreements provided for greater flexibility in terms of meeting award conditions, such as by doing off-sets. The 'no net disadvantage test' continued to be applied to all types of agreements. Under that test, the AIRC could withhold approval of agreements that were regarded as contrary to the public interest or that reduced employee entitlements below those of an award or Commonwealth, state or territory law (Quinlan 1996, p. 5).

The *Workplace Relations Act 1996* further encouraged enterprise bargaining and a reduced role for third parties such as trade unions. This Act:

•   requires the simplification of awards by restricting them to only 20 'allowable matters' by 30 June 1998;
•   gives agreements negotiated between individuals or non-union collectivities and employers the same status as those negotiated with trade unions; and
•   reduces the arbitral role of the IRC.

The Act strengthened enterprise agreements as an alternative to awards. The legislation was strongly opposed by the unions, and significantly amended in the Senate by the Australian Democrat and Labor members.

There was also a move to enterprise bargaining in the various state jurisdictions. However, the frameworks regulating enterprise bargaining in the states differ from that of the Commonwealth. Major differences also exist between the two jurisdictions in a number of specific areas, such as the way minimum standards are established, the scope of individual contracts and the vetting of non-union agreements (Quinlan 1996, pp. 6–8).

The roles of the parties

Throughout Australia's history the roles of trade unions, employers, industrial tribunals and employees have both influenced and been influenced by the nature of industrial relations legislation. The Constitution conferred powers on the federal government to legislate on industrial matters. Section 52 (xxxv) provided the most important power: allowing the federal government to make laws with respect to 'conciliation and arbitration for the prevention and settlement of industrial disputes extending beyond the limits of any one state'. The federal government is unable to legislate generally about the terms and conditions of employees; however, it is able to establish tribunals to deal with industrial matters.

The Commission in its various forms (Commonwealth Court of Conciliation and Arbitration; Commonwealth Conciliation and Arbitration Commission, AIRC, IRC) has been important for several reasons. It regularly establishes social minimum standards in wages and other conditions, it is an important medium for settling disputes and provides an organised basis for the introduction of new concepts and standards. It was established as part of a social contract, which on one hand involved a tariff regime to protect the growing manufacturing industry, and on the other protected living standards, and legalised trade unions. Part of this contract protected management's prerogative to determine many employment policies without the involvement of trade unions or the industrial tribunals.

The IRC became an important vehicle for the implementation of forms of work organisation which reflected Taylor's objective of taking the thinking out of jobs to ensure greater management control, through the strict division of labour between management and labour, and between different skills. The old Metal Industry Award was a classic example.When management first began adopting Taylor's system with its strict demarcations, it was often opposed by unions because of the deskilling effects.

This division of labour and fragmentation was reinforced by the registration of a large number of trade unions, many of which had legal coverage for different occupations or job classifications. Awards tended to follow 'the contours of union jurisdictional coverage much more closely than they did the nature of the firm's business' (Deery 1995, p. 58). Consequently, a multiplicity of awards operated in an organisation. In 1989 the average number of awards operating in each workplace was four, while in workplaces employing between 1000 and 2000 employees an average of nearly seven awards operated (Business Council of Australia 1989, p. 51).

The Commission rarely makes decisions which totally break new ground. Its decisions usually reflect what already substantially exists. For instance, its first decision on the basic wage in the Harvester Judgement established a wage rate of 42 shillings for a six-day week for an unskilled male worker. The judgement discussed the amount required to support two adults and two or three children in a frugal existence and the 42 shillings was what a fair and reasonable employer already paid. Similarly, the tribunals' decisions about women's wages reflected the social and economic values of the time. In 1949 the decision to increase women's basic wages to 75 per cent of the male basic wage reflected prevailing market and social norms. Trade unions, therefore adopted a strategy of changing market and social norms through overaward campaigns for all employees. The Commission rarely departed from this approach until the early 1980s when it handed down a decision about the introduction of technological change. This decision was 'probably the most significant decision for Australian workers since the Harvester decision' (Nolan 1988, p. 255). On 2 August 1984 the Commission ruled in the Termination, Change and Redundancy Case that employees were entitled to job protection benefits including redundancy payments, protection against unfair dismissal, increased notice of termination and consultation on change at the workplace. Employers challenged the decision in the High Court, claiming it interfered with management prerogative. The employers argued that, when it was established in 1904, the commission was expressly prevented from making decisions that impinged on management's right to make all decisions pertaining to the management of the enterprise. The High Court upheld the commission's decision. The decision was significant because it allowed the commission to play a constructive role in the negotiation of issues that emerged in enterprise agreements and that dealt with matters tradition-ally regarded as management prerogatives such as work systems, information sharing through consultative mechanisms and the introduction of new technology. This is now being expressly excluded in the award allowable matters process.

Between 1983 and 1996 a series of agreements between the ALP/ACTU (known as the Accords) were influential in shaping industrial relations and other economic and social policies. These Accords influenced trade union activity and shaped industrial relations outcomes so they assisted national eco-nomic goals. Initially, there was an understanding that the government would pursue policies for faster economic growth and reduced unemployment, and the unions would not use the outcomes from these policies as the basis for increased pay because the social wage provided equity and a safety net. Later Accords emphasised improving performance in the workplace (Kramar, McGraw & Schuler 1997, p. 94).

The Accords provided a framework for dealing with broad economic and social issues. The matters considered as part of the Accords included:

- safety net increases;
- the social wage as an integral part of living standards;
- skill formation systems, including changes in the education system;
- consultation and democratic workplace arrangements;
- strategic plans for some industries;

- regular meetings of the representatives from unions, employers and government;
- funding for a range of initiatives involved with workplace reform such as industrial democracy, the Best Practice Demonstration Program;
- occupational health and safety;
- discrimination and equity in the workplace.

The Accords provided an opportunity for parties involved in industrial relations to understand each other's position. They enabled the development of an understanding that industrial relations arrangements were an integral part of, and a significant influence on economic and social outcomes. They also facilitated an understanding that the performance of an organisation is dependent on more than just the operation of industrial relations at the workplace.

The Accords had a significant effect on the union movement. Unions were required to think more strategically. One consequence of the broader timeframe and scope they adopted was that unions became involved in super-annuation in the 1980s, following their increased awareness of the anticipated problems providing pension payments. Another consequence was the development of a proactive approach to a number of economic and employment issues. The most obvious example of this new approach was the European study tour undertaken by a number of union officials and the subsequent publication of the strategic document *Australia Reconstructed*. This document provided a union blueprint for the redevelopment of the economy into high skill, high value-added areas, in order to compete in the new global marketplace.

Australia Reconstructed, which was highly regarded in many quarters including international unions, examined a number of disparate policies and developed them into a coherent strategy. It integrated policies such as wages, industrial democracy, national and job skill formation, industry policy, social policies and a new 'strategic unionism'. Unions were then able to respond to the industrial problems at the enterprise level in a way that better fitted within a national vision of value adding. For several years, a number of unions such as the AMWU, CPSU, FSU, argued for improved company performance by promoting best practice policies. They often came forth before the company did. These unions sought improvements in skills and training systems, industry strategies, a rationalisation of the number of unions, fewer industrial disputes and a greater commitment to value-added export industries.

The term 'best practice' would probably not have become common parlance without the Accords. The term 'best practice' appeared in many agreements and was promoted by the Best Practice Demonstration Program funded by the federal government. The notion of best practice reflects an approach to management that acknowledges the interrelationship between customer service, quality, cost, work design, competent management, information sharing and consultation, equity, training, industrial relations, and overall strategy. Case study E on organisational change refers to some initiatives undertaken under this Best Practice Demonstration Program.

Despite the change of government, the influence of the various Accords will continue to be experienced for a number of years. They assisted the Commission to play a more proactive role. They also facilitated an understanding, between organisations and within companies, of the value of building an industrial relations environment on consensus rather than conflict and antagonism, at national, industry and local level.

The Accords enabled the ACTU to act with more authority and one voice because of the consensus among the unions. The employers, on the other hand, often had difficulty reaching consensus as their plethora of organisations tended to represent different interests. During the period of the Labor government, large companies and people actually running businesses were the ones listened to by the government. Under the Coalition, employer associations, primary producers and employers in the mining industry have more influence, and, with amalgamations, the employer organisations are tending to have a wider consensus, while the union movement perhaps has less of a consensus than previously.

One interpretation could be that the Labor government was attempting to strengthen high value–added export industries and therefore attracted representatives from these industries into consultation. On the other hand, the Coalition government appears to be committed to the commodities industries and less to value adding and a Coalition government is always perceived to be more pro-business. These differences influence the approaches to industrial relations under the two governments.

It is significant that the Metal Trades Industry Association at one stage in the late 1980s sought to join the Accord. This industry probably had the most co-operative approach to implementing the new skills agenda, despite tough negotiations. The metal industry is at the forefront of global competition in terms of skills, technological change, new work and management systems, and revised industrial relations practices.

Issues for negotiation

In the context of registered enterprise agreements, the most common issue dealt with has been enhancing flexibility of arrangements regarding hours of work. Between 1992 and 1996 almost two-thirds of the agreements dealt with hours of work issues such as the number of hours worked each week, the span of ordinary hours, averaging hours over a month, quarter or year, and meal breaks (Callus 1997, p. 19). Increasing casualisation and subcontracting, however, can undermine the commitment of employees and result in a lack of organisational knowledge. Some employers are commited to less casualisation in enterprise agreements (e.g. the Sheraton Hotels agreement and quite a number in the metals, food, steel, aluminium, construction industries and some in the finance industry).

The issue of career paths has also become more important in the industrial relations arena. The SEP and the restructuring of organisations into flatter and less hierarchical structures have encouraged the consideration of career structures within the industrial relations context. Neil Watson a Melbourne consultant puts it well: 'We are unhinging pay from structure', so that employees will not get their promotion by moving up the structure, but by extending their skills, knowledge, responsibility and accountability, no matter where they actually work. This trend is reflected in the introduction of pay for skill and responsibility.

However, this issue has often caused conflict as many managers, while requiring the new skills, are reluctant to pay for them immediately. Interest in productivity indicators in agreements increased between 1992 and 1996, and more than a third of agreements included provisions relating to productivity measures. Training provisions were included less often: in 1992 they were contained in 59 per cent of agreements, in 1996 in only 37 per cent of agreements. This decline may be explained in two ways. First, having reached an agreement once, there is no need to repeat it in subsequent agreements, and second, if it is included in awards it is less necessary, especially for smaller companies, to have it in the agreement. During 1996, agreements provided for wage increases of, on average, between 4 and 6 per cent per annum (Callus 1997, pp. 19–20).

Conflict has been central to an understanding and the practice of industrial relations. Conflict is always present in the workplace, but it manifests itself in different ways, depending on a variety of factors such as the economic situation, attitudes of governments, philosophy guiding a particular union or the union movement, management philosophy, and the overall social and political climate. Conflict is inevitable in organisations where managers are required to obtain the highest profits for shareholders and owners, while employees seek to get the best wages and conditions. Conflict is also often an expression of not only demands for improved economic conditions, but also for improved work design, involvement in decision-making, a reduction in alienation and better management practices, although these issues may not be the explicit basis for the conflict.

There has been a significant fall in the expression of open conflict since 1981. Working days lost in 1995 were one-tenth of those in 1981 and only one-quarter of the number of employees were involved directly or indirectly in these disputes. In 1981 the number of disputes was almost five times the number of disputes in 1995 (Kramar, McGraw & Schuler 1997, p. 107). Traditionally, industrial conflict is most likely to occur in public sector and larger workplaces, rather than smaller and medium size organisations (Callus et al. 1991, p. 63).

Open conflict is only one expression of conflict in the workplace. However, conflict is often expressed in an unorganised and fragmented way such as low morale, poor quality work and absenteeism. For instance, voluntary annual turnover across Australian workplaces was found to be 19 per cent, while 4.5 per cent of employees were absent from work in an average week. Davis states that 'the cost of high turnover rates dwarf the costs and time lost through strike action, yet strikes and industrial action have retained a much stronger hold on public interest and imagination' (Kramar, McGraw &

Schuler 1997, p. 106). The expression of conflict can also have positive effects on the workplace. It provides unions and management with the opportunity to deal with differences between managers and employees and to work constructively on developing policies which satisfy both the organisation's and employees' needs. Unions can help channel conflict and feelings of alientation into disciplined, negotiable and constructive resolution. Also some strikes, depending on their length and outcome, can result in employees returning to work with better morale and improved productivity. The benefits of union involvement has been demonstrated by Paula Voos and Lawrence Michell (1992). They reported that union enterprises displayed characteristics which were indicative of well managed organisations. They found union enterprises tended to be more productive, had more training, introduced technological change more quickly and smoothly, had less employee turnover, had higher wages, and had more competent management. In these enterprises, union representatives usually worked in the company much longer than management, and therefore tended to have greater commitment to its success. The reasons cited for these benefits included that unions got conflict into the open and channelled it into more constructive directions, the better wages and conditions attracted employees to stay in the enterprise, unions are more aware of skill developments and technological change occurring across their industry, and the higher wages challenged managers to be more competent. A skilled human resource manager understanding these processes could get excellent results for the company. A point that is often not understood by theorists of industrial relations is that shop stewards, as elected workplace union representatives, spend the bulk of their time fixing problems before they reach the stage of crisis and industrial action, and can do this precisely because they are close to, and trusted by their members.

A problem for unions and management is some of those officials and managers who have won their reputation and power as a result of conflict are often suspicious of, and reluctant to participate in co-operative industrial relations practices. A culture of open conflict prevails even where it may not be necessary. Their reaction suggests that sophisticated industrial relations practice requires both unions and management to exercise appropriate power and independent positions, using co-operative, even consensual processes so that benefits are delivered to both the business and the employees. The focus must be on outcomes, short and long term.

Implementation and outcomes of the new industrial relations

Because implementation is such an important part of the new enterprise bargaining, human resource managers have a major role to play not only in securing the enterprise agreement but ensuring that it becomes a reality. In the more successful companies, implementation has involved some of the following:

- proper training of the parties involved in the consultative committees;
- working with unions to ensure that the whole workforce, including

managers and administration, is thoroughly familiar with the agreement and its likely effect on their work;

- appointment and training of in-house facilitators and trainers;
- engaging appropriate consultants with expertise in such things as work redesign, information systems, skill formation, strategic planning, etc; and
- the appointment of an internal full-time facilitator (usually someone from the unionised employees), whose job is to drive the process, be on the spot to solve problems, and generally be a champion of the change process.

Because of the vagaries of the implementation phase, it is not easy to assess the outcomes in terms of the provisions of the agreements. A survey of over 2000 workplaces and 19 000 employees conducted by the federal Department of Industrial Relations examines the reported effects of enterprise agreements. However, these results need to be accepted with caution because it is difficult to isolate the specific effects of the agreements from other organisational or structural changes occurring at the same time (Callus 1997, p. 20). Table 5.1 shows that a consistently high percentage of managers report 'no change' on most indicators, particularly quality of product/service, absenteeism, skills; and in the case of profits a high percentage reported 'no change' or a decrease. Callus considers that these results should 'caution us against expecting too much too soon from the enterprise bargaining system' (Callus 1997, p. 21). Experience suggests that it takes about five years to move a company from its traditional mode of operation to a new one approaching and maintaining best practice. Commitment to this goal and tenacity by all parties are required.

The Workplace Relations Act 1996

The Workplace Relations Act 1996 (the Act) sets a new direction for industrial relations through the strengthening of non-union collective bargaining and the process of enterprise bargaining. The stated objects of the Act place greater emphasis on the responsibility of employers and employees to manage employment relationships, on the economic impact of employment conditions and wages, and on conciliation.

Table 5.1 Percentage of managers reporting effects of agreements

Indicator	Increased a lot	Increased a little	No change	Decreased a little	Decreased a lot
Labour productivity	9	53	38	1	0
Quality of product/service	6	40	53	0	0
Profits	6	38	40	12	3
Skills	5	41	54	0	0
Absenteeism	3	13	68	9	8

Source: DIR 1996, pp. 130–3

The Act provides for the continuation of awards. However, as mentioned previously, these awards are simplified to 20 allowable matters which include classifications and skill-based career paths, hours of work, rates of pay, leave, including annual leave and carers' leave and allowances. The AIRC has the power to make an award dealing with these allowable matters, but it is limited to making a minimum rates award. Non-allowable matters, except in exceptional circumstances, will be regulated on the basis of agreement reached between the parties or where no agreement is reached by management. Awards will therefore assume safety net status. There is also scope to make non-union collective agreements—Certified Agreements, which replace Enterprise Flexibility Agreements—even when unions have members present. These agreements need to be approved by the majority of employees. The AIRC can certify the agreement (s. 170LT) if it meets a number of conditions, including that it satisfies the no disadvantage test, it has been genuinely approved by a majority of employees and it was made without coercion. The Act recognises the direct, individual employment relationships in the form of Australian Workplace Agreements (AWAs). These are written agreements made between an employer and an employee dealing with matters pertaining to their employment relationship. They must be scrutinised by the Employment Advocate to ensure that they satisfy the no-disadvantage test and include minimum requirements such as anti-discrimination provisions and dispute resolution procedures. Unions are very critical of this process because the contents of AWAs remain secret so unions do not know to what extent the employee has been forced to concede important pay and conditions. If the Employment Advocate has concerns about the AWA passing the no-disadvantage test, and the employer and other parties are unable to resolve the issue, the AWA must be referred to the AIRC. The AWA wholly displaces any federal or state award or state agreement. Twelve months after the Act came into force, it was estimated that only about 3000 employees were covered by AWAs.

Unions are not necessarily excluded from the bargaining process. Employees have the right to nominate a bargaining agent, which could be a union. It could be expected that the requirement for employers to offer the same terms to all employees in similar jobs will encourage employers to pursue pattern bargaining on an individual basis and limit 'their capacity to strike genuinely individual contracts of employment' (Callus 1997, p. 24).

The government argues that the Act will give employees a choice:

- between a variety of employment relationships both collective and individual;
- whether to be union members;
- of which union they prefer to join;
- whether to appoint a bargaining agent and whether the agent is a union (Angwin 1996, p. 37–8).

Unions argue that such choices are not 'free choices' because they do not take account of the uneven power relations between an individual and his or her employer. Employers have the power to hire and fire, and victimise a person. The overwhelming power—and its abuse—of the employer over the individual worker was, of course why workers banded together to form unions in the first place. Unions therefore see these terms in the Act as a blatant attempt to weaken the bargaining power of employees by undermining their collective and union strength.

Various predictions about the new legislation have been made. Callus (1997, p. 24) believes that the legislation will lead to the marginalisation of 'unions in bargaining to a degree not seen in Australia this century'. On the basis of the outcomes of the movement to enterprise bargaining during the 1990s, now furthered by the Act, the legislation could also increase the gap between male and female wages and have a detrimental effect on ocupational health and safety outcomes (Quinlan 1996).

In the post-Fordist era, unions worldwide are facing crisis. Empirical evidence suggests that in those countries which have chosen a more consensus relationship, the unions remain important and the outcomes in terms of competitiveness, employment and equity are better than in countries that have not worked through the change process in a less co-operative manner.

Conclusion

During the 1990s significant changes have occurred in the issues and processes involved in managing industrial relations. The federal legislation represents a 'new reform agenda directed at a reconfiguration of industrial relations through a dismantling of the collective apparatus of industrial regulation' (MacDermott 1997, p. 52). States have also brought in changes, though their legislation tends to take a less controversial approach, one known as 'managed decentralism'.

It is important not to be overwhelmed by the legislation. While important and influential, in the end industrial relations are sorted out at the enterprise or industry level. If union/s and employer/s decide that they want a constructive relationship, they can establish that. The legislation, particularly the *Workplace Relations Act* becomes central when some of the parties, usually the employer/s, decides to exclude the union, and then both sides seek to use all legal loopholes to pursue their objective. In numerous companies however, relations are sufficiently positive that both sides prefer to sit down and negotiate agreements, with the legislation playing a minimal role. What is interesting, and arguably unprecedented, is the number of companies preferring to continue a constructive relationship in a legal framework so conducive to excluding unions. This constructive relationship is not because these companies have suddenly become enamoured with unions, but the challenge of the new global economy requiring skilled, innovative, committed employees can best be met through consensus and co-operation, and not the conflict ridden, top-down command structures so characteristic of Fordism and old industrial relations.

The problem for most governments is to achieve an in-depth understanding of the dynamics driving enterprises in the post-Fordist era, and to stengthen them through framework legislation and policies that promote co-operation between management, unions, and employees. The roles of tribunals, trade unions, governments and managers have developed in response to changes in industrial relations during the last ten years. These roles will continue to change and the parties will need to develop a variety of skills to operate effectively under the legislation. They will also need to balance a desire for increased efficiency and productivity in the short term with the need to consider the impact of changes in the workplace on employees and on the development of long-term growth.

The challenge for human resource managers is to develop a thorough understanding of the underlying dynamics of the changing world, and from there to pursue a strategy that ensures they are integral to the business plan, and even at its very core. Industrial relations in all businesses, whether union or non-union, will increasingly determine a company's success or failure.

References

Angwin, M. 1996, 'The Workplace Relations Bill: Implications for leadership', *Employee Relations Brief*, vol. 1, no. 3, July, pp. 37–8.

Business Council of Australia 1989, *Enterprise Bargaining Units: A better way of working*. BCA, Melbourne.

Callus, R. 1997, 'Enterprise Bargaining and the Transformation of Australian Industrial Relations', *Asia Pacific Journal of Human Resources*, vol. 35, no. 2, pp. 16–25.

Callus, R., Morehead A., Cully M. & Buchanan, J. 1991, *Industrial Relations at Work: The Australian industrial relations survey*, AGPS, Canberra.

Dabscheck, B. 1995, *The Struggle for Australian Industrial Relations*, Oxford University Press, Melbourne.

Deery, S. 1995, 'Industrial Relations', in G. O'Neill and R. Kramar eds, *Australian Human Resources Management: Current trends in management practice*, Pitman, Melbourne.

Drago R., Wooden, M. & Sloan, J. 1992, *Productive Relations?*, Allen & Unwin, Sydney.

Hampton-Turner, C. & Tromenaars, F. 1993, *The Seven Cultures of Capitalism*, Doubleday, New York.

Hegewisch, A. & Brewster, C. 1993, *European Developments in Human Resource Management*, Kogan Page, London.

Hilmer, F. 1989, *New Games, New Rules*, Angus & Robertson, North Ryde, NSW.

Kramar, R. & Lake, N. 1997, *International Strategic Human Resource Management: Report,* Australasian Centre for Human Resource Management, Sydney.

Kramar, R., McGraw, P. & Schuler, R. 1997, *Human Resource Management in Australia*, Addison Wesley Longman, Melbourne.

MacDermott, T. 1997, 'Industrial legislation in 1996: The reform agenda', *Journal of Industrial Relations*, vol. 39, no. 1, pp. 52–76.

Nolan, J. 1988, 'Recent Developments in Employment Law', in G. Palmer ed., *Australian Personnel Management: A Reader*, Macmillan, Melbourne.

Quinlan, M. 1996, 'The reform of Australian industrial relations: Contemporary trends and issues', *Asia Pacific Journal of Human Resources*, vol. 34, no. 2, pp. 3–27.

Voos, P. & Michell, L. 1992, *Unions and Competiveness*, Economic Policy Institute, Washington, DC.

Transforming employee relations from adversarial to problem-solving: ICI Botany

Tony Mealor

ICI was the largest chemical manufacturer in Australia with much of its production coming from the complex of factories located on its Botany site. This case deals with the large-scale transformation of the organisation at the Botany site between 1986 and 1996 and the transition from a traditional adversarial industrial relations culture to one based on sophisticated employee relations and strategic human resource management.[1]

Context of change

ICI commenced its Australian operations in 1874 as Jones, Scott and Company, a Victorian-based explosives maker. The company grew by diversification and merger until the incorporation of the Imperial Chemical Industries Australia and New Zealand Ltd in 1928. The company changed its name to ICI Australia Ltd in 1971 and, until the 1997 sell-down, was 62.5 per cent owned by the UK-based Imperial Chemical Industries plc. The company has some 9500 employees spread across 110 locations around Australia. ICI was a confirmed leader in the Australasian industrial chemicals, plastics, paints, commercial explosives and fertiliser markets.

The chemical manufacturing industry worldwide generally operates on a six-year 'boom and bust' investment and rationalisation cycle. Following a collapse and rationalisation in 1982, demand in the industry peaked in 1988 with prolific investment being made in new plant. This overcapacity for production came on stream in the early 1990s and coincided with the worst recession the industry had experienced since the 1930s great depression. Like other operators in the chemical industry, ICI was forced to dramatically reduce costs from 1990 to 1994, and some 30 sites across Australasia were either divested or shut down

The first wave

Major change was initiated at ICI's New South Wales Botany site in December 1986 when a set of demands was presented to the workforce by management. These demands targeted the hourly paid workforce and addressed the restructuring issues of downsizing, restrictive work practices and organisational change. The workforce rejected management's directives and the next three years saw what could justifiably be described as a period of industrial anarchy. Botany became a battleground where management and the unionised workforce fought for supremacy. The industrial issues were being fought against a background dominated by sheer corporate survival as a series of tariff reductions began to threaten the company's livelihood.

The $27 billion Australian plastics industry was at the top of its cycle in the late 1980s. There was a world shortage of ethylene, the basic plastics raw material, and ICI had commissioned a new ethylene cracker plant at Botany. In such a buoyant market it was difficult to make a decision to shut the site down in a lock-out response to strike action, even in an extreme industrial relations confrontation. Nevertheless, this decision was made after a major strike in February 1989 saw customers being forced to lay-off their own workforces, and negotiations between ICI management and unions had ground to a halt.

ICI sued key union delegates personally for damages of $26 million; the unions remained adamant that there would be a 'war of attrition' should the writs be enforced. This confrontation provided a catalyst for change. The stand-off was broken by a spill in both management and union ranks. Company negotiators steeped in the previous adversarial culture were replaced by human resource professionals; at the same time union representatives took on a more accommodating and pragmatic approach. This led to an uneasy truce in which a new culture emerged based on a participative employee relations strategy aimed at negotiating a radical enterprise agreement.

The enterprise bargaining model

Elements of the enterprise bargaining model that emerged are shown in Figure D1. Ideally, senior management would begin the change process by scanning the environment, benchmarking and setting its strategy and goals against the challenges identified. These findings would then be communicated to the workforce. Concurrently, management would ensure that its employee relations process would provide a successfully negotiated agreement. Investment in new technology would be used to introduce changes in work organisation and to introduce more extensive training and education. All of this would be incorporated in the enterprise agreement, and out of the entire process would come world-class products and services. Such a strategic path appears logical and straightforward: however, large-scale change rarely happens in this way, particularly in organisations with well-established, traditional corporate structures.

From confrontation to collaboration

Ultimately, the change process at ICI's Botany site was driven by crisis, desperation and opportunism. Employee relations were so poor they had to be tackled first. Protracted negotiations with the Federated Engine Drivers' & Firemen's Association (FEDFA) over the first agreement built a minimum level of trust between the participants (Mealor 1992). Both sides had taken risks and left themselves vulnerable to betrayal. When this did not occur, further risks were taken; gradually the negotiators found themselves working

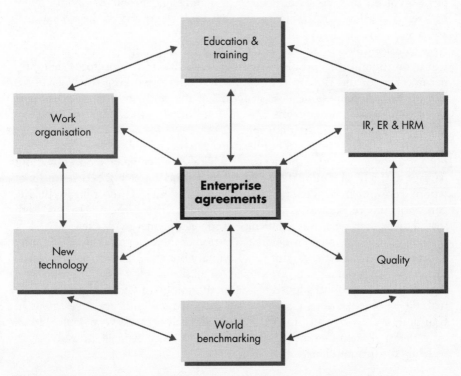

Figure D1   Elements of a best practice enterprise agreement

conjointly on problems in a process similar to that outlined by Walton and McKersie (1965). The bundle of interventions that emerged were subject to a process of tough-minded debate and a growing commitment to keep the plant operational, and increasingly operating to standards of world's best. The key issues to be tackled were work organisation and the shift roster, governance and teams and the reward system—including training and pay for skills.

The model agreement developed with the FEDFA had spread throughout the site by 1993 when the three remaining unions on the site, the Amalgamated Metal Workers Union (AMWU), the Communications, Electrical, Electronic, Energy, Information, Postal, Plumbing and Allied Services Union of Australia (CEPU) and the Federated Iron, Manufacturing and Engineering Employees Union (FIME) entered into a combined site agreement. This agreement was ratified by Commissioner Palmer under section 134 of the *Industrial Relations Reform Act 1993* and ran for two years. This marked the plateau which followed the turbulence of the first wave of change.

Incremental change

A new spirit of co-operation came with the new agreements and the high levels of trust engendered. By the end of 1992, senior workforce delegates had been involved in years of difficult negotiations and problem-solving. They had reached a level of sophistication that took them out of the operational arena and allowed them to collaborate with management on strategic initiatives (Mealor 1996). The focus of attention for all groups on site had moved from confrontation to problem-solving. In 1992 senior workforce delegates became part of the Botany Improvement Team, a working party set up to address the uncompetitive cost structure of the site. Over the next twelve months they pared down some $14 million dollars in fixed and variable costs while maintaining production levels.

In 1993, a team comprised of HR management and union convenors carried out a manpower review of the site to see where labour could be reduced without damage to the organisation. This resulted in a reduction of 112 people, many of whom were employed as temporaries and on staff contracts. According to the site convenor, this marked a turning point in union/management relations: both shared the pain in what was a difficult but strategically necessary exercise.

These years may be considered as a period of incremental change (Dunphy & Stace 1990). Change was not revolutionary but the organisation was learning. A quality program was introduced for all site employees, and production personnel were also introduced to the methodology of statistical process control. These were serious exercises and involved a significant investment in time and money. By this time the Botany site had become very stable. However, the market is inherently unstable, and by the end of 1994, pressures were building for further change.

The second wave

The catalyst for the second wave of change was the introduction of a chemical engineer with a PhD from Cambridge. Originally appointed to commission a new plastics plant, he was appointed site manager in May 1995. In this role he undertook a world tour to benchmark the industry and determine the nature of future competition. What he found was disturbing. Even with all of the improvements and the dramatic change in culture, the site's productivity was well below world's best—especially in terms of labour costs per tonne of product and plant reliability. This profile needed dramatic improvement if the Botany site was to attract the necessary reinvestment to underwrite ICI Australia's planned thrust into Asia. Another wave of change had to wash over the site, but how to generate it without risking the loss of the substantial benefits already gained?

The new site manager brought a continuity of managerial philosophy. He eschewed coercive or directive control strategies and took the need for transformative change to the senior management team and the site union convenors. They decided to spend a weekend away from the site to think strategically about the future. By the time the weekend was over, a new strategy had been formulated. The catalyst for change would be a reduction in labour costs, but the negative impact of the intervention would be minimised. The site manager communicated the strategy in an employee newsletter in October 1995:

> As you may be aware, a group from the site camped at Myall Lakes to discuss the challenges facing the site. Despite the variety of backgrounds, we strongly agreed on what we want the site to be and how we shall achieve it. We want the site to be special: our level of performance should be awesome.
>
> We want the site to have a confident 'can do' atmosphere. We want to act with unity and common purpose.
>
> The first step to achieving these goals will be to talk to everyone on site, inviting them to join our quest for something special or leave with dignity and our best wishes. The invitation to stay will explain what is expected of employees on Botany. This will include personal accountabilities for safety, a willingness to work flexibly, a desire for excellence and a thirst for knowledge.
>
> Those who wish to leave will have to work to make their role redundant and pass on their skills and knowledge to the relevant people. Their workgroup will be expected to support them. This process has been chosen because it should remove fear. It will require involvement of everyone and it will force us to look at new ways of doing things. In conjunction with this initiative, three others were chosen:
>
> 1 A site leadership team (called the 'White Team') has been formed. It comprises the Section Heads and three senior union officials. The remit of this team is to revise the site's consultative and management framework. The aim will be to collapse as many groups as possible and stop as many meetings as possible.

2   A thorough review will be performed of the contractors used on site and our method of interacting with them.

3   A communication team has been formed which will keep people fully informed of progress and gather advice about the sort of information people want to hear.

All in all, while not without some anxiety, the next 12 months promise to be exciting and stimulating as we regain our position as the supreme site in Australia and beyond. We have a tremendous opportunity to do something of importance to ourselves, the Company and Australia. If we are willing, we will do it.

The major intervention and catalyst for the second wave of change was a downsizing exercise with dignity. Previous attempts at labour rationalisation on the site had been expensive in terms of capital costs, loss of skills and experience, and emotional damage among survivors. This new strategy for downsizing was high risk, but one which senior management and trade unionists felt was worthwhile for the future of the site and the workers who depended upon it for a living. It would send a signal to the ICI Australia Board and the workforce that all site employees were serious about fighting for Botany's long-term future.

Over the next year the strategy was operationalised and 186 people left the site as their skills and knowledge were passed to their work teams. The collaborative initiative seems to have worked and there is little evidence of damage from post-downsizing trauma (Littler et al. 1994; Cascio 1993).

Perceptions of success

To conclude, it is worth revisiting the case study from the perspectives of the major actors—management, the trade union and the workforce. In doing so, three separate viewpoints emerge with one common focus: the ICI Botany case was a successful experiment in employee relations for those involved.

Management perspective

Over the decade of change ICI Australia led the industry in workplace reform; furthermore, corporate productivity indicators such as sales per employee improved from $176 000 in 1985 to $376 000 in 1996. Since the first wave of change began to take effect, returns on equity trended upward from 7.1 per cent in 1990 to 15.6 per cent in 1996. In the same period, profit after tax has increased from $74 million to $220 million. The company climbed out of the recession in 1995 with its highest ever profits of $269 million at a time when many competitors were hurting deeply. The continuity of vision and strategy that top management pursued paid off in 'bottom line' results; much of that strategy involved the creation of an empowered, highly trained and committed workforce as a competitive advantage. Gurner (1995, p. 31) comments:

> Management at ICI Australia has carried the banner for workplace reform in the industry during the 1990's, relentlessly pursuing world standards of productivity while absorbing reductions in tariff protection … undergoing a company-wide rationalisation that has produced one of the leanest corporate entities in the country.

In strategic human resource management terms, the Botany site provides a model where innovations never before seen in the corporation (and in Australia) were trialled and implemented. Employee relations on the site were recognised as the best in ICI Australia, and senior visitors from the parent have voiced the opinion that they are the best they have seen in their corporate world. Confidence is such that the site has attracted $379 million in reinvestment over the decade of change.

It is essential, however, for the survival of the program that performance continues to improve and is captured by rigorous indicators. Corporate history also needs to be kept alive. Few now remember, for instance, the management/union confrontation prior to the first wave of change. Like the holocaust, its memory should be preserved as an object lesson for future generations of managers and trade unionists. The challenge is now to maintain and extend the collaborative working relationships between management and the workforce and to ensure that the rhetoric of human relations does not become a substitute for productive reality.

Union's perspective

ICI Botany was widely seen in the union movement as a model of strategic trade unionism. Those unions who have lost their membership on the site to the AWU, however, do not necessarily share this view. Although some of the interventions over the decade of change caused concern, most unions now include them in enterprise bargaining. For example, twelve-hour shift systems, annualised salaries, self-managed teams and payment-for-skills are now quite widespread. The Australian Council of Trade Unions (ACTU) claims that many innovations in the Botany model were generated by the unions and the workforce, and reacted to by management: this view has some substance for the period of the early negotiations and also helps maintain union support for the innovations. However, later outcomes in second order change were arrived at through collaboration. To idealogues in the unions and in the workforce this has been tantamount to 'sleeping with the enemy', and is equated to class treachery. Much of this kind of rhetoric was heard early in the decade when the craft unions strongly opposed enterprise bargaining. Such views are seldom voiced now, but the vexed questions which collaboration raises in terms of governance are still largely unaddressed. The debate on industrial democracy in Australia has wilted through trade union and governmental inaction over the Accord years, and, with some notable exceptions

(Davis & Lansbury 1996; Ford & Tilley 1986), there is no rigorous examination or developed literature in the area for Australia.

'Approaching the twenty-first century, trade unions appear to have been a phenomenon of the twentieth century to which we are prepared to say good-bye' (Guest 1995, p. 137). Strategic trade unionism differs from classical trade unionism—it is proactive rather than reactive. Technological change is welcomed as an opportunity for wealth-creation, the corollary being that there will also be job creation in the long run. Downsizing is acceptable if it contributes to the survival of the firm and ensures job security for those left in the core workforce. Members are regarded as 'customers' to be served rather than 'rank and file' troops in the class war over distributive issues and ownership of the means of production. Integrative rather than distributive bargaining is the mode of interaction with employers (Walton & McKersie 1965). In that the ICI Botany experience embodies all of these notions in visible practice, it was lauded by many in the movement as a model of strategic trade unionism. It seems that where strategic HRM meets strategic unionism, the outcomes can be truly win/win in nature. However, where either negotiating party rejects a collaborative approach, the resulting agreement is likely to be win/lose and, ultimately, lose/lose for both parties. A high trust system is very vulnerable. To survive in the future, unions will have to provide wins for the membership, and the Botany model has shown how this can occur.

Worker's perspective

The unionised workers on Botany site enjoyed a quality of work and social life with little parallel in the industry anywhere in the world. Released from the insecurity of hourly pay and overtime and working humane rosters designed by themselves, they looked forward to fulfilling careers which were the envy of their peers. A shift in demographic profile (researched by the author over the decade of change) saw blue-collar workers move up a social notch into middle-class status, although few other middle-class employees would enjoy the following:

- annual salaries including all allowances and overtime;
- shift rosters averaging four shifts on, followed by four shifts off;
- maintenance work rosters providing every weekend a long weekend;
- self-management in a team environment;
- payment for skills rather than job description;
- same superannuation scheme as that enjoyed by the directors;
- paid training and education;
- subsidised health scheme;
- unlimited sick pay;
- security of tenure;
- interest-free loans to buy company shares;
- protection and representation of the unionised workforce at all organisational levels.

'I don't talk about the job in the pub. If they don't believe me I look like a dickhead; if they do, it makes them jealous and they get dirty on me' (Botany process technician). With condensed working hours and little pressure for over-time, workers' lives are no longer centred on Botany. Their social sphere has expanded as their standard of living and lifestyles have improved. Where previously the tyranny of shiftwork had narrowed the scope for social interaction, the workforce now enjoys more leisure time than most other comparable workforces in the community. Friendships are no longer limited to (mainly) fellow shift workers. Off-site activity has become the centre of attention rather than, as in the past, the on-site political conflict and the daily machinations which surrounded income enhancement through increasing overtime. Some argue that energy has been lost from the site in this process. But it can also be argued that it was negative energy which brought the site to crisis point.

From the workers' perspective, the decade of change at Botany has produced a quality of life for themselves and their families which was beyond imagination in the 1980s. Data from formal and informal interviews and focus groups suggest that they will go to great lengths to preserve that lifestyle. It is this energy that will have to be channelled into further change.

Where to now?

What can be learned from the Botany case? It seems that a bundle of mutually-supporting interventions was the prime factor of success in the first wave of change at Botany. In moving from a traditional industrial relations environment to an organisation driven by strategic human resource management, the pace of change slowed to the extent that the process itself came under threat. After a plateau was reached, and with a change in senior management, second order change was launched with a major downsizing intervention taking a year to implement. The collaborative process that had been maturing over a decade on the site would normally have been destroyed by a downsizing exercise. However, the joint planning and implementation of the downsizing prevented this happening; and this collaborative approach was structurally and strategically formalised in the enterprise agreement. Interventions to support second order change such as investment in technology, information systems, training and development and a gainsharing system have been put in place.

The way forward will now be determined by the efficacy of these systems in supporting and continuing to drive the change process into third order change where the enterprise truly becomes a learning organisation. Further longitudinal analysis of the case will reveal if this occurs. What can be said now is that a decade of change at ICI Botany has informed politicians and legislators, inspired a plethora of change agents and provided a model for industry and the union movement. Whether or not the program lives up to the promise of the second decade, nothing can detract from the significant achievement to date.

References

Cascio, W. 1993, 'Downsizing: what do we know? What have we learned?', *Academy of Management Executive*, vol. 7, no. 1, February, pp. 95–104.

Davis, E.M. & Lansbury, R.D. 1996, *Managing Together,* Addison Wesley Longman, Melbourne.

Dunphy, D. & Stace, D. 1990, *Under New Management*, McGraw-Hill, Sydney.

Ford, W. & Tilley, L. (eds) 1986, *Diversity, Change and Tradition*, Department of Industrial Relations/AGPS, Canberra.

Guest, D. 1995, 'Human resource management, trade unions and industrial relations', in J. Storey (ed.), *Human Resource Management: A Critical Text*, Routledge, London.

Gurner, H. 1995, 'ICI Australia seeks its own way ahead', *Business Review Weekly*, 28 August, p. 31.

Littler, C., Bramble, T. & McDonald, J. 1994, *Organisational Restructuring: Downsizing, Delayering and Managing Change at Work*, Industrial Relations Research Series 15, Department of Industrial Relations, December.

Mealor, A. 1996, 'From confrontation to collaboration at ICI Botany', in E.M. Davis & R.D. Lansbury (eds), *Managing Together*, Addison Wesley Longman, Melbourne.

Mealor, A. 1992, 'ICI Australia: The Botany experience', Industrial Relations Research Centre, University of New South Wales, Kensington.

Walton, R.E. & McKersie, R.B. 1965, *A Behavioural Theory of Labor Relations*, McGraw-Hill, New York.

Note

[1] There is a fuzzy and changing overlap between these areas and the terminology can be confusing. The term *employee relations* was introduced to Australia through the publications of the Business Council of Australia (BCA) as a largely successful attempt to soften the pluralist and conflicting connotations surrounding *industrial relations*. *Employee relations* has unitarist overtones and is used solely in the context of the organisation. The term is not to be confused with *employment relations* which has been coined to cover the nexus and overlap of human resource management and industrial relations. At the societal level *industrial relations* is universally used to describe the relationships between capital, labour and the state.

Understanding the process of organisational change

Patrick Dawson

As we enter the twenty-first century, changes in the world economic order have influenced the ongoing process of organisational adaptation to rapidly changing global demands. The emergence of China as a growing economic power, the development of industries in Eastern Europe, the globalisation of financial markets, the rapid expansion of commercial activity within the Asia-Pacific region, developments in technology and the liberalisation of trade, have all contributed to a climate of change and transformation.

Companies have sought solutions within this context of global competition, often seeking to emulate other successful organisations through adopting the latest market-driven panacea. In the 1990s, business process re-engineering emerged as a fashionable management technique offering a technology-based method of reorganising an organisation's business processes to give it a competitive edge. The term 're-engineering' was made fashionable by the marketing hype and success of Michael Hammer and James Champy's (1995) best-selling book *Reengineering the Corporation: A Manifesto for Business*. These management consultants advocated that there was a need to adopt a radical and fundamentally new approach to business: they promoted the concept of re-engineering as 'the fundamental rethinking and radical redesign of business process to achieve dramatic improvements in critical contemporary measures of performance, such as cost, quality, service and speed' (1993, p. 32). Although they continually stressed that their approach was novel, their study largely mirrored many of the claims of other writers in this area and in practical terms, their approach simply provided a list of changes that companies should either implement or suffer the consequences (for a critique, see Taylor 1995; Willmott 1995, p. 96).

The rhetoric and hype of consultants re-badging old ideas to sell 'new' products can often confuse the uninitiated and promote myths about mutual, all-encompassing benefits of workplace change (Buchanan 1997). Similar and additional myths have also been promoted by academic debates, partly due to the fragmented and diverse literatures currently surrounding discussions on new organisational arrangements (see Storey 1994, pp. 1–21), and partly due to academic adherence in research and teaching to conventional approaches to planned change.

This chapter opens by questioning the extent to which company initiatives simply represent a series of management fads or real innovations in the world of work, and by identifying current trends in workplace change. This is followed by an examination of the different approaches to understanding organisational change, with a focus on organisational development, contingency theory and the newly emerging processual approach. The chapter concludes by claiming that conventional change models should be replaced by processual frameworks which are better able to explain the complex ongoing dynamic of organisational change.

Management fad or workplace innovation?

A host of change initiatives, such as total quality management (TQM); just-in-time (JIT); cellular manufacture (CM) and best practice management (BPM), have been developed, used, extolled and rejected by a vast array of companies searching for state-of-the-art solutions to organisational problems. For example, within the automotive industry the publication of *The Machine that Changed the World* (Womack, Jones & Roos 1990) promoted the view that companies should discard conventional organisation structures with 'lean' yet flexible multiskilled forms of production. Similarly, Rosabeth Moss Kanter, in her popular book *When Giants Learn to Dance*, claimed that competitive corporations of the future should develop a strategic business action agenda towards 'flatter, more focused organisations stressing synergies; entrepreneurial enclaves pushing new stream businesses for the future; and strategic alliances or stakeholder partnerships stretching capacity by combining the strength of several organisations' (1990, p. 344). The common view deriving from these studies is that change should be treated as the norm rather than a series of one-off exercises and that managers and organisations need to break with tradition. This has resulted in the proliferation of popular articles and books on proactive management in the design and implementation of change for competitive advantage.

Within the academic community, this focus has generated a number of debates. For example, are the new production and service concepts being introduced by organisations resulting in a proliferation of management fads (Mitroff & Mohrman 1987, p. 69), real innovations (Dunphy & Stace 1990), or simply an increased tendency to imitate other organisations (DiMaggio & Powell 1983)? On these issues, Abrahamson has argued that 'fads and fashions may constitute vital processes that animate random variations from which increasingly efficient innovation can evolve' (1991, p. 609). While there may be some truth in this claim, the degree to which these changes are bringing about a radical change in the organisation and control of work remains open to debate. For example, Pollert (1988) has suggested that these changes are mainly ideological with no substantive basis; others have been more concerned with the degree to which current transitions in work are generally enhancing or eroding the quality of working life and employee involvement (Argyris, 1998; Francis & Southern 1995; Storey 1994; Willcocks & Grint 1997).

The position taken here is that real innovations in the organisation of work are occurring (Dawson & Webb 1989). However, these changes do not reflect a simple movement towards some ideal-type flexible firm; nor do they hold a utopian vision of a new world order (Atkinson & Meager 1986), or the simple repackaging of old wine in new bottles (Pollert 1988). Some of the common threads that can be discerned from the various strategies for workplace change include:

- movement from a union-based system of collective bargaining to a more individual contract-based system of employee relations;
- focus on cultural change strategies to secure total employee participation and commitment;
- delayering and downsizing of organisations with a concomitant devolution of control and responsibility to employees for aspects of industrial engineering;
- redefinition of supervisory management from a directive and overseer type control function to one centred on communication, liaison, and motivation (often referred to as a movement from a policing role to coach); and,
- elimination of demarcated single operator tasks with multiskilled teamwork activities (Dawson 1996, p. 18).

The general push is for a movement away from a system based on a detailed division of labour—where employees are closely observed and directed by supervisors, and a union-based collective bargaining system of industrial relations is the norm. The direction is towards a system where individual tasks are replaced by group activities—although in some cases reliance on existing plant and equipment has severely constrained group work—where employees take control responsibilities previously carried out by higher ranking personnel, and a more individual 'staff-based' system of employee relations is encouraged through the use of customised employment contracts. As indicated elsewhere (Dawson 1994, p. 166), these transitions can be located along three continua consisting of the following dimensions:

- *work organisation*: ranging along a continuum from individual based tasks to group work;
- *workplace control*: ranging from tight transparent control mechanisms (direct control) to autonomous self-directing systems (responsible autonomy); and
- *workplace relations*: varying from traditional union-based ('implied adversarial') system to the individual contract-based ('implied collaborative') system of employee relations.

In short, it is argued here that the current schemes for company change can have both positive and negative effects. It is only through a detailed analysis of change in each individual workplace that we can start to explore what this means for employees and the future of work.

'Triggers' for change: Organisations in context

There are a number of external 'triggers' to change arising from the competitive contextual conditions that companies operating in a global marketplace increasingly face. These shifting external forces include technological developments, government laws and regulations, major political and social events, and changes in international agreements on tariffs and trade: each of these can necessitate the need for change within an organisation.

Apart from these external factors, there are also a number of internal triggers to change. These comprise: technology, people, task, and administrative structures (see Vecchio et al. 1992, pp. 591–3). A change in an organisation's technology may involve the installation of a single piece of equipment or the complete redesign of a production process. The option of revising administrative structures involves redesigning organisational structures and modifying other processes such as communication and reward systems. Changing the human aspect of an organisation is a popular change strategy and involves modifying attitudes, beliefs, values, technical skills and behaviours. The task of an organisation refers to the primary product or service of a firm, whether it is concerned with the manufacture of washing machines or the provision of hospitality services. Consequently, a change in the task of an organisation generally requires fundamental organisational transformation to produce and market different types of goods or services. In practice, these four areas often overlap and a change in one area will often require change in another.

Internal and external triggers to change are often interdependent. For example, a push for a change in technology may result from competitive pressure, or from the exposure of local engineering personnel to the benefits of new developments in capital equipment. Similarly, changing employee attitudes at work may be the result of a complex interplay between a change in management style and a general shift in attitude within the community. Moreover, it should be stressed that employees, particularly those in management and senior management positions, are often able to influence environmental factors rather than simply respond to them. Agreements between major competitors, lobbying key politicians and the use of the media to influence public opinion, can all be used to facilitate proactive strategies for change. Furthermore, because a change in one factor is likely to result in significant changes to others, it is often difficult to anticipate and plan for every eventuality. For example, a change in technology may result in significant restructuring and bring about an unintended and/or undesirable reaction from the workforce. In fact, resistance to change is a subject receiving considerable attention in the management literature (Aldag & Stearns 1991, pp. 716–19; Buchanan & Huczynski 1985, pp. 419–23; Dunford 1992, pp. 300–3).

Organisational development: The use of external change agents

Strategies for overcoming resistance to change are a central concern of the organisational development (OD) approach to managing planned change (see, for example, Aldag & Stearns 1991; Gray & Starke 1988). Although there are many different OD models, the general approach has been described by Huse as 'the application of behavioural science knowledge in a long-range effort to improve an organisation's ability to cope with changes in its external environment and increase its internal problem-solving capabilities' (1982, p. 555). It is based on a human relations perspective that stresses the importance of collaborative management. According to French and Bell, this can be defined as 'a long-range effort to improve an organisation's problem-solving and renewal processes ... with the assistance of a change agent or catalyst and the use of the theory and technology of applied behavioural science, including action research' (1983, p. 15).

Typically, the OD approach is planned: it attempts to consider and include all members of an organisation; the proposed change is supported by top management; the objectives of change are to improve working conditions and organisational effectiveness; and an emphasis is placed on behavioural science techniques which facilitates communication and problem solving among members (Beckhard 1969). According to French (French 1969; French & Bell 1983), the nine distinguishing characteristics of modern OD approaches are as follows:

1 The focus of the change effort is on the whole system (whether an organisation or a divisional department) and can be used with healthy and unhealthy organisations.

2   The change program involves planned interventions introduced systematically to improve an organisation's health and effectiveness.

3   Top-down strategies are applied where change begins at the top and is gradually applied downward throughout the organisation.

4   The approach takes the view that employees at all levels of an organisation must be committed to the change (in other words, change must never be forced).

5   Change should be made slowly, allowing for the continual assessment of change strategies.

6   Specialist change agents should be used to guide OD programs.

7   The approach should be interdisciplinary, drawing on behavioural science knowledge.

8   OD programs should be based on data, so that choices are made on the basis of objective information rather than on assumptions about what constitutes the 'real' issues.

9   The objective should be to achieve lasting rather than temporary change within an organisation.

Generally, the OD approach involves a number of steps commencing with the appointment of a change agent (usually an individual outside the organisation) who intervenes to start the change process. The six major steps in an OD program comprise identifying a need for change; selecting an intervention technique; gaining top management support; planning the change process; overcoming resistance to change; and evaluating the change process (Aldag & Stearns 1991, pp. 724–8). However, the main problem with this approach is that it adopts a normative framework and assumes that there is one best way to manage change that will increase both organisational effectiveness and employee well-being. The professional consultants engaged in OD are generally not concerned with the development of theory or with the design of systematic programs of research but, rather, with a set of normative prescriptions that guide their practice in managing change (Ledford et al. 1990, pp. 4–6). The OD camp has also been criticised for failing to account for the increasing incidence of revolutionary change which, according to Dunphy and Stace, may more effectively be achieved by coercive top-down strategies of change (1990, p. 67).

Lewin's planned approach to change: Unfreezing employee attitudes

Kurt Lewin's three-phase model of change set the scene for much of what we know as OD today (Weisbord 1988, p. 175). Although similar arguments can be levelled against Lewin's model, it remains an influential theory and a common approach advocated by consultants and management educationalists (see, for example, Gray & Starke 1988; Robbins 1988). The main thrust of Lewin's theory is that an understanding of the critical steps in the change process will increase the likelihood of the successful management of change. The three general steps identified by Lewin (1951) comprise unfreezing, changing, and refreezing. Unfreezing is the stage in which there is a recognised need for change and action is taken to unfreeze existing attitudes and behaviour. This preparatory stage is deemed essential to the generation of employee support and the minimisation of employee resistance. According to Lewin's technique of force-field analysis (1947, pp. 5–42), there are two sets of forces in operation within any social system; namely, driving forces that operate for change and restraining forces that attempt to maintain the status quo. The example of smoking illustrates this: there are strong driving forces to stop smoking (e.g. social pressure, cost, fear of cancer, new laws, disapproval of children and the concern of others); nevertheless, restraining forces (e.g. habit, camaraderie, relief of tension, spouse smoking and the dislike of coercive methods) may act to maintain the status quo (Weisbord 1988, p. 79). If these two opposing forces are equal in strength, then they are in a state of equilibrium. Thus, to bring about change you either need to increase the strength of the driving forces or decrease the strength of the resisting forces. Furthermore, as these two sets of forces are qualitatively different, it is possible to modify elements of both sets in the management of change. In practice, however, the emphasis of change consultants have been on providing data that would unfreeze the system through reducing the resisting forces rather than increasing the driving forces (Gray & Starke 1988, pp. 596–629; Weisbord 1988, p. 94). Once these negative forces have been reduced, then the consultant embarks on moving the organisation towards the desired state. The second stage of the change process involves the implementation of new systems of operation. Once the new systems are in place, then the final stage of refreezing occurs. The process of refreezing involves the positive reinforcement of desired outcomes to promote the internalisation of new attitudes and behaviours. An appraisal of the effectiveness of the change program is the final element used in the last step to ensure that the new way of doing things becomes habitualised.

Lewin's three-phase model of change is still widely used throughout the business world. The strength of the model lies in its simple representation making it easier to use and understand; however, its simplicity is also its major weakness as it presents an unidirectional model of change. Moreover, by creating an image of a need to design in stability (refreezing), the model has a tendency to solidify what is a dynamic and complex process. It may also result in the creation of cultures and structures not conducive to continuous change. On this point, Weisbord has argued that Lewin's concept begins to fall apart as the rate of market and technological change enters a state of perpetual transition, rather than 'quasi-stationary equilibrium' (1988, p. 94). In short, Lewin's theory although largely inappropriate to organisations operating in rapidly changing environments, remains part of the textbook orthodoxy on change management.

A typology of change strategies: The use of contingency models

Proponents of the contingency approach reject the search for a universal change model in their aim to develop useful generalisations about appropriate strategies and structures under different typical conditions. The contingent factors deemed to be of primary significance include either single variables, such as technology (Perrow 1970; Thompson 1967; Woodward 1980) or the environment (Burns & Stalker 1961; Lawrence & Lorsch 1969), or range of variables, such as in the ambitious study by Pugh et al. (Pugh & Hickson 1976) which examined the relationship between contextual factors and structural variables (see also Wood 1979). As Daft notes:

> Most research in organization theory is a search for contingencies. Investigators try to understand the relationships among variables so they can recommend which strategies and structures are appropriate in each situation. Because organisations are open systems, one important contingency is the environment. Organisation theorists attempt to determine which organisation characteristics allow firms to deal effectively with different kinds and rates of environmental change. (Daft 1986, p. 22)

Dunphy and Stace (1990, 1994) have developed a contingency model of organisational change that adopts this approach. The two dimensions of their model are the scale of change and the style of leadership required to bring about change. The authors identify four types of change: 'fine tuning' and 'incremental adjustment' refer to small-scale changes ranging from the refining and clarification of existing procedures through to the actual adjustment of organisational structures; 'modular transformation' and 'corporate transformation' refer to large-scale changes from divisional restructuring to revolutionary changes throughout the whole organisation. The appropriate style of leadership is seen to range along a continuum from participative to autocratic, namely: 'collaborative', 'consultative', 'directive' and 'coercive'. By using these dimensions, Dunphy and Stace identify four types of change strategies. 'Participative evolution' and 'forced evolution' refer to incremental change through collaborating and directive change respectively. 'Charismatic transformation' is described as large-scale discontinuous change achieved by collaborative means; and, finally, 'dictatorial transformation', which describes major coercive change programs.

Dunphy and Stace argue that the model provides a framework for planned change strategies which challenges the personal value preference of managers and consultants. They suggest that 'appropriate' change strategies are generally determined by the change agent and not by the needs of the organisation. For example, they point out that OD practitioners have tended to focus on collaborative models, whereas corporate strategy consultants have tended to select dictatorial transformation as the appropriate strategy for managing large-scale discontinuous change. The authors argue that, while there is a place for each strategy, selection should be made on the basis of dominant contingencies (Dunphy & Stace 1990).

There are three major weaknesses with this contingency approach to change. First, the model does not tackle the political dimensions of change. There is a surprising lack of reference to notions of power (Pfeffer 1981) and the political character of organisational change (see for example, Mangham 1979; Pettigrew 1973). As Dunford (1990) has pointed out, 'managers are portrayed as neutral conduits' who ignore their own self-interests in making rational decisions that seek to promote organizational effectiveness and survival.' Second, their notion of the environment as 'an entity out there' that imposes its will (Dunford 1990, p. 132) discards the importance of perceptions in shaping organisational decision-making and the way that members of organisations may exert their own influence on the environment through various activities, such as lobbying, holding positions on pertinent committees, and social involvement with key politicians. Third, no attempt is made to provide a typology of change strategies and conditions for their use under different periods during the process of change. In short, the models suggest that there is an appropriate strategy, given that you can identify the context and purpose of change, and that this strategy will see you through the entire process of regaining internal fit with the external environment.

In their more recent book *Beyond the Boundaries*, Stace and Dunphy (1994) further develop their model using the same leadership and scale of change dimensions. Apart from the additional category of Taylorism (used to refer to change avoidance), they have renamed three of their change strategies in accepting less clear divisions between various approaches to change. 'Participative evolution' has become 'developmental transitions' and 'forced evolution' has become 'task focused transition', both refer to incremental change (with partial overlap with modular transformation) through largely consultative and directive change respectively. 'Charismatic transformation' continues to refer to inspirational change achieved through consultation; while 'dictatorial transformation' has been redefined as 'turnarounds' to account for major coercive change programs (overlapping with the more modular-directive type). This refined model is an improvement on their previous categorisation and they do appropriately advocate the benefits of a more eclectic approach. Their situational strategies for change continue to ignore critical aspects associated with power relationships and organisational politics (under their subject index there is no mention of politics, power or conflict). In evaluating the appropriateness of particular strategies to contingent conditions, the focus is on the strategic fit between a company and the business environment. While the external environment is a central contextual condition (situation), it is not the only contextual factor (take for example, the contextual influence of the history and culture of an organisation), nor should it be used to side-step analyses of political considerations in understanding the management of change (see Dawson 1998).

The apolitical character of their proposed situational model for managing change is surprising given their discussion of the BHP change program. Here they show how David Rice (senior executive) encountered major resistance from the unions to his directive change strategies; following early retirement he was replaced by John Prescott who developed a participative approach to change that involved union representatives (Stace & Dunphy 1994, pp. 126–9). This need to develop and adapt implementation strategies to both the internal and external contextual environment, and to accommodate political dimensions and unforseen contingencies arising from the substance of change, is central to the contextual research on change that has emerged from Europe over the last decade. Frameworks being developed under this relatively new movement offer an alternative to conventional approaches to understanding change.

An emerging contextualist movement: The European experience

Currently, there is a growing body of research seeking to examine processes of change within an historical and organisational context (Johnson 1987, p. 58). Many of the foundational studies were multi-disciplinary (Clark et al. 1988), drawing on a range of perspectives and methods such as the business historian, the corporate strategist and organisation theorist (Whipp et al. 1987). These have been concerned with detailed examinations of the process of organisational transition (Child & Smith 1987). Moreover, through examining the context and content of processes of change, advocates of this perspective generally focus on a particular type of research strategy and meth-odology (Pettigrew 1990). In contrast to the dominant approach in organisa-tion theory which emphasises the importance of sophisticated quantitative analyses (Ledford et al 1990, pp. 6–8), the focus of contextualists is on longi-tudinal qualitative data. For example, Clark et al. (1988), in their study of the changeover from electro-mechanical to semi-electronic telephone exchanges, use a compendium of different methods, including semi-structured inter-views, non-participant observation, work diaries and group discussions. These methods are employed to examine technological change as a process, and overcome problems associated with the aprocessual and apolitical contingency approaches of writers such as Woodward (1980):

> Writers such as Woodward tend to see technology in a static fashion as having 'impact' or 'imposing itself' on organisational behaviour. Such an approach neglects the processes through which new technologies are implemented and operated and outcomes of change established and modified. (Clark et al. 1988, p. 30)

Jon Clark and his colleagues develop a framework for analysing the process of technological change based on three main elements: the stages of techno-logical change; issues arising during change; and critical junctures in the process of change (Clark et al. 1988, p. 31). They note that technology, as an engineering system that embodies certain social choices, may define the 'design space' of outcomes shaped by organisational actors at critical junctures during the process of technological change (1988, pp. 29–32). In the detailed accounts of change, their research clearly demonstrates the importance of managers, trade unionists and workgroups in shaping the process of technological change in the workplace. The study not only identifies the independent influence of engineering systems on work, but also the important influence of individuals and groups during the unfolding of 'radical' (major) change programs. In tackling the temporal dimension of transformative change, detailing the substance of the change (in this case, technology in the form of telephone exchange modernisation), and incorporating an analysis of the politics of change, the research can be identified as being part of a broader international 'contextualist movement' that seeks systematic and detailed analyses of processes of change.

Similarly, the work of Child and Smith (1987) and Pettigrew (1987) can be defined as contextualist research, the former, in their case study of organisational change at Cadbury Limited, where they were particularly interested in the sectoral influence (context) on the process of transition; and the latter, in examining leadership and transformational change. Although there are noticeable differences between these studies (for example, whether the focus is on technology or 'firm-in-sector' perspective), there is a common methodology and research strategy linking them. Each study has placed a high premium on longitudinal case studies and the collection of in-depth qualitative data (Child & Smith 1987, p. 584; Clark et al. 1988, pp. 224–8; Pettigrew 1990, pp. 267–92). There is also a conceptual and theoretical overlap in their concern for the context in which changes are occurring, the substance or content of the change program, and the process (rather than snapshot analyses) of change. In short, the grouping of research under the contextualist approach includes those seeking to combine a fully historical perspective with emerging organisational dramas (Pettigrew 1985), and those concerned with more specific processual research (Clark et al. 1988).

Making sense of organisational change: A processual approach

The approach taken here is that organisations undergoing transition should be studied 'as-it-happens' so that processes associated with change can reveal themselves over time and in context. By so doing, past reconstructions and future expectations become important data to understanding the current contextual conditions under which change unfolds. Within organisations, there are often a number of competing histories on the process of organisational transition; these may be further refined, replaced and developed over time. The dominant or 'official version' of change may largely reflect the political positioning of certain key individuals or groups within an organisation, rather than serving as an accurate account of the change process. These oral, and sometimes documented histories, may also act to shape, constrain and promote the direction and content of future change programs. During the complex dynamic of workplace change a company may move in and out of a number of states—sometimes concurrently—as the process of change is continuously influenced by the interplay and conflict between historical reconstructions, current contextual conditions and future expectations.

Throughout the process of workplace transition, a range of different factors can shape the speed and direction of change and influence the longer-term outcomes on workplace arrangements. Under the framework the author has developed elsewhere (see Dawson 1994; 1996), there are three main groups of determinants used to explain the process of organisational change, namely, the politics, context and substance of change.

The *politics of change* category is used to refer to the political processes associated with the conception, implementation and operation of new workplace arrangements. It includes elements of conflict and resistance, decision- and non-decision-making activities, processes of negotiation and consultation, and the multi-level and external individual and group influence on the substance, transition and outcomes of change. It is concerned with ongoing power-plays and political activity, as well as with the reconstruction of rational linear accounts. For example, after-the-fact histories can provide powerful justifications for current courses of action, making the 'legitimate' reconstruction of past events an important political means to promote future possible change outcomes. In this respect, politics is assumed to be endemic to organisations and central to processes of workplace change.

The *context of change* is taken to refer to the changing internal and external contextual conditions that inform the historical setting, current operations and future company expectations. It is composed of an interrelationship between elements internal to the organisation and those present in the external environment. External contextual factors include: changes in market conditions and level of competition, availability of new technologies and management techniques, competitor change strategies, changing social expectations, promotion and access to government supported initiatives, and changing international trade agreements. Internal contextual factors can be subdivided into five main groups: human resources; primary product and/or service; technology; administrative structures, and the history and culture of an organisation. For the most part, these follow Leavitt's (1964) classification already discussed. However, the additional category of history and culture has been included to refer to organisational history (which is dynamic and may comprise of a number of competing histories) and organisational culture. Following Schein (1985), this category comprises surface and deeper level elements that continually interact in the contextual evolution of shared beliefs and in the creation, revision and reconstruction of common histories and formalised accounts (for a further elaboration of these contextual elements see Dawson 1994, pp. 41–5).

The *substance of change* is taken to refer to the core elements of particular workplace change initiatives. The first of three main dimensions is the scale and scope of change, ranging from small-scale discrete change to a more 'radical' large-scale transformation. A distinction can be made between change at the level of the unit, plant/branch, division and corporation. Second is the defining characteristics and timeframe of the change program; this dimension refers to the labels attached to change projects and the actual content of the change in question. The speed of change can vary: programs may evolve incrementally over a number of years only to be followed by a fairly rapid and specified period of implementation. Thus, the longer-term nature of these changes can go unnoticed in studies that focus on only one critical period in the process of workplace change. It is also worth noting that organisational timeframes rarely reflect a commitment to a longer-term strategic plan, but generally emerge during the unfolding of change programs (see also Quinn 1980). The third, and final dimension, relates to the perceived centrality of the change to the survival of the organisation. If the transition is viewed as central to the continued operation and competitive position of the company, then it can have major implications for the timescale, resource support and overall employee commitment to change (see for example, Dawson 1994, pp. 104–22).

This group of determinants categorised under the substance of change are not static; they change over time and overlap with contextual and political elements. For example, it is not uncommon for definitional confusion to surround the introduction of new management techniques and for the content of change to be redefined during the process of organisational adaptation. Moreover, knowledge of the substance of change and clarification of what the change means for a particular organisation can in itself become a political process, influenced by external contextual views and the setting of internal agendas around the management of change. In this sense, there is a continual interplay between these three groups of determinants during the process of organisational change.

This comprises the main elements of Dawson's (1994) processual approach, which has been formulated to further our understanding of the change process and to aid analysis of complex change data. With regard to the latter, the perspective facilitates data analysis by providing a flexible, adaptable framework that can both inform and be informed by the design requirements of case study research (for further discussion, see Dawson 1996, pp. 79–91). Unlike the contextual research of Pettigrew (1990), the processual approach outlined above can also be used to formulate data-generated guidelines for practitioners of organisational change (for an example of the type of practical guidelines that can be generated from this approach see Dawson 1994, pp. 172–80). Taken as a whole, it is argued here that a processual approach can be used to explore the realities of organisational restructuring and question popular myths about the change process and consequent outcomes for the work of employees.

Conclusion

This chapter set out to introduce some of the main themes, debates, and approaches to the study of organisational change. It argues that the rhetoric behind market-driven panaceas should be treated with extreme caution as there are no simple solutions to the complex dynamic of competition and change. The superficiality of some change initiatives may do little to improve the competitive position of a company; however, the general uptake of change programs among business is bringing about real innovations in the world of work. Some of the common threads centred around:

- *work organisation*—movement from individual based tasks to group work;
- *workplace control*—shifts from a system based on close supervision and the direct control of work to one where employees take control of their responsibilities and exhibit a form of responsible autonomy);
- *workplace relations*—situations where conventional union-based collective bargaining system of industrial relations are being promoted and replaced, by more individual, 'staff-based', systems of employee relations.

The chapter then examined different approaches to studying and managing workplace change. Particular attention was given to organisational development (OD), contingency theory and processual research. The OD approach was shown to be based on a human relations perspective that seeks to improve an organisation's health and effectiveness by using an OD change consultant to operationalise a series of normative prescriptions to guide and plan the practice of managing change. Top-down strategies are applied and change is achieved through involving employees at all levels of an organisation (coercive strategies are deemed inappropriate to the OD philosophy). The Lewin three-step model of unfreezing, changing and refreezing was outlined and the applicability of notions of 'refreezing' under periods of rapid change was called into question.

The Dunphy and Stace situational model was the focus of analysis for examining contingency theory. Their model offered a choice of strategies for planned change under different conditions by using a scale of change dimension and a style of leadership dimension. This model allowed for the appropriateness of a broader range of change strategies but ignored some very important elements associated with power-relationships and organisational politics. In contrast it was then shown how this political dimension has been incorporated into the more contextualist research developed in Europe. The work of Jon Clark and Andrew Pettigrew was discussed and the author's own processual framework was outlined. These advocate the merits of longitudinal research and argue that the three main groups of determinants to be accounted for in any study of organisational change are the politics, substance and context of change. Although it is not surprising that an author should forward his/her own framework as being the most appropriate (illustrating the importance of politics) from the perspective of the reader, they should familiarise themselves with the range of different approaches and make their own critical judgement. Understanding the process of organisational change remains an important and contentious issue in need of further investigation, analysis and study.

References

Abrahamson, E. 1991,'Managerial fads and fashions: The diffusion and rejection of innovations', *Academy Management Review*, vol. 16, no. 3, pp. 586–612.

Aldag, R.J. & Stearns, T.M. 1991, *Management*, Cincinnati, South-Western.

Argyris, C. 1998, 'Empowerment: the emperor's new clothes', *Harvard Business Review*, vol. 76, no. 3, pp. 98–105.

Atkinson, J. & Meager, N. 1986, *New Forms of Work Organization*, Institute of Manpower Studies Report no. 121, University of Sussex.

Beckhard, R. 1969, *Organization Development: Strategies and Models*, Addison-Wesley Reading, MA.

Buchanan, D. 1997, 'The limitations and opportunities of business process re-engineering in a politicized organizational climate', *Human Relations*, vol. 50, no. 1, pp. 51–72.

Buchanan, D. & Huczynski, A. 1985, *Organizational Behaviour*, Prentice-Hall, London.

Burns, T. & Stalker, R. 1961, *The Management of Innovation*, Tavistock, London.

Child, T. & Smith, C. 1987, 'The context and process of organizational transformation', *Journal of Management Studies*, vol. 24, no. 6, pp. 565–93.

Clark, J., McLoughlin, I., Rose H. & King, R. 1988, *The Process of Technological Change: New Technology and Social Choice in the Workplace*, Cambridge University Press, Cambridge.

Daft, R.L. 1986, *Organization Theory and Design*, West Publishing Company, New York.

Dawson, P. 1998, 'Cellular manufacturing at General Motors: Applying a processual framework' in Karwowski, W. & Goonetilleke, R., (eds) *Manufacturing Agility and Hybrid Automation II*, Louisville, Kentucky: IEA Press.

Dawson, P. 1996, *Technology and Quality: Change in the Workplace*. London: International Thomson Publishing.

Dawson, P. 1994, *Organizational Change: A Processual Approach*. London: Paul Chapman Publishing.

Dawson, P. & Webb, J. 1989, 'New production arrangements: The totally flexible cage?', *Work, Employment & Society*, 3, no. 2, pp. 221–38.

DiMaggio, P.J. & Powell, W.W. 1983, 'The iron cage revisted: Institutional isomorphism and collective rationality in organizational fields', *American Sociology Review*, 48, pp. 147–56.

Dunford, R.W. 1992, *Organizational Behaviour: An Organizational Analysis Perspective*. Sydney: Addison-Wesley.

Dunford, R.W. 1990, 'A reply to Dunphy and Stace', *Organization Studies*, vol. 11, no. 1, pp. 131–4.

Dunphy, D. & Stace, D. 1990, *Under New Management: Australian Organizations in Transition*, McGraw-Hill, Sydney.

Francis, A. & Southern, G. (1995) 'Epochs and institutions: Contextualising BPR', *New Technology, Work and Employment*, vol. 10, no. 2, pp. 110–20.

French, W. 1969, 'Organization development: Objectives, assumptions and strategies', *California Management Review*, vol. 12, pp. 23–46.

French, W. & Bell, C. 1983, *Organization Development: Behavioural Science Interventions for Organization Improvement*, Prentice-Hall, Englewood Cliffs, NJ.

Gray, J.L. & Starke, F.A. 1988, *Organizational Behavior: Concepts and Applications*, Merrill, Columbus, Ohio.

Hammer, M. & Champy, J. 1993, *Reengineering the Corporation: A Manifesto for Business Revolution*, HarperBusiness, New York.

Huse, E.F. 1982, *Management*, West Publishing Company, New York.

Johnson, G. 1987, 'Commentary on Chapter 1', in A. Pettigrew (ed.), *The Management of Strategic Change*, Basil Blackwell, Oxford.

Kanter, R.M. 1990, *When Giants Learn to Dance: Mastering the Challenges of Strategy, Management, and Careers in the 1990s*, Unwin Hyman, London.

Lawrence, P. & Lorsch, J. 1969, *Organization and Environment*, Harvard University Press, Harvard, MA.

Leavitt, H.J., 1964, 'Applied organizational change in industry: structural, technical and human approaches', in W.W. Cooper, H.J. Leavitt & M.W. Shelly (eds), *New Perspectives in Organizations Research*, New York, John Wiley.

Ledford, G.E., Mohram, S.A., Mohrman, A.M., & Lawler, E.E. 1990, 'The phenomenon of large-scale organizational change' in A.M. Mohrman, S.A. Mohram, G.E. Ledford, T.G. Cummings, & E.E. Lawler, *Large-Scale Organizational Change*, Jossey-Bass, San Francisco, CA.

Lewin, K. 1947, 'Frontiers in group dynamics', *Human Relations*, vol. 1, pp. 5–42.

—— 1951, *Field Theory in Social Science*, Harper & Row, New York.

Mangham, I. 1979, *The Politics of Organizational Change*, Westport, Greenwood Press.

Mitroff, I. & Mohrman, S. 1987, 'The slack is gone: How the United States lost its competitive edge in the world economy', *Academy of Management Executive*, vol. 1, pp. 65–70.

Perrow, C. 1970, *Organizational Analysis*, Wadsworth, Belmont, CA.

Pettigrew, A. 1990, 'Longitudinal field research on change: Theory and practice', *Organization Science*, vol. 1, no. 3, pp. 267–92.

Pettigrew, A. 1987, 'Context and action in the transformation of the firm', *Journal of Management Studies*, vol. 24, no. 6, pp. 649–70.

Pettigrew, A.M. 1985, 'Examining change in the long-term context of culture and politics', in J.M. Pennings (ed.), *Organizational Strategy and Change*, Jossey Bass, San Francisco, CA.

Pettigrew, A.M. 1973, *The Politics of Organizational Decision-Making*, Tavistock, London.

Pfeffer, J. 1981, *Power in Organizations*, Pitman, Boston.

Pollert, A. 1988, 'The "flexible firm": Fixation or fact?', *Work, Employment & Society*, vol. 2, no. 3, pp. 218–316.

Pugh, D.S. & Hickson, D.J. 1976, *Organizational Structure in its Context: The Aston Programme I*, Saxon House, London.

Quinn, J.B. 1980, *Strategies for Change: Logical Incrementalism*, Irwin, Homewood, Illinois.

Robbins, S.P. 1988, *Management: Concepts and Applications*, Prentice-Hall, Englewood Cliffs, NJ.

Schein, E.H. 1985, *Organizational Culture and Leadership*, Jossey-Bass, San Francisco, CA.

Stace, D. & Dunphy, D. 1994, *Beyond the Boundaries: Leading and Re-Creating the Successful Enterprise*, McGraw-Hill, Sydney.

Steers, R.M. 1991, *Introduction to Organizational Behavior*, HarperCollins, New York.

Storey, J. (ed.) 1994, *New Wave Manufacturing Strategies. Organizational and Human Resource Management Dimensions*, Paul Chapman Publishing, London.

Taylor, J.A. 1995, 'Don't obliterate, informate: BPR for the information age', *New Technology, Work and Employment*, vol. 10, no. 2, pp. 82–8.

Thompson, J.D. 1967, *Organizations in Action*. New York: McGraw-Hill.

Vecchio, R.P., Hearn, G. & Southey, G. 1992, *Organizational Behaviour: Life at Work in Australia*, Harcourt Brace Jovanovich, Sydney.

Weisbord, M.R. 1988, *Productive Workplaces: Organizing and Managing for Dignity, Meaning and Community*, Jossey-Bass, San Francisco, CA..

Whipp, R., Rosenfeld, R. & Pettigrew, A. 1987, 'Understanding strategic change processes: Some preliminary British findings', in A. Pettigrew (ed.), *The Management of Strategic Change*, Basil Blackwell, Oxford.

Willcocks, L. & Grint, K. 1997, 'Re-inventing the organization? Towards a critique of business process re-engineering', in McLoughlin, I. & Harris, M. (eds), *Innovation, Organizational Change and Technology*, International Thomson Business Press, London.

Willmott, H. 1995, 'The odd couple? Re-engineering business processes, managing human resources', *New Technology, Work and Employment*, vol. 10, no. 2, pp. 89–98.

Womack, J.P., Jones, D.T. & Roos, D. 1990, *The Machine that Changed the World*, Rawson Associates, New York.

Wood, S. 1979, 'A reappraisal of the contingency approach to organization', *Journal of Management Studies* 16, no. 3, pp. 334–54.

Woodward, J. 1980, *Industrial Organization: Theory and Practice*, 2nd edn, Oxford: Oxford University Press.

Managing change: Culture building at Texicom

Robin Kramar

Texicom Ltd is a major manufacturer and supplier of products and services in the telecommunications industry. Services include telephones, and telecommunications, power and information technology equipment. The company was incorporated in October 1986 and listed on the Australian Stock Exchange in December 1987. At the end of 1988 it acquired a vertically integrated telephone business.

The new business provided Texicom with a metal operation and extensive plastic moulding equipment. However, the company inherited a number of problems with this acquisition: outdated production technology meant that the business of manufacturing telephone handsets in high volumes had been run into the ground; there was an adversarial 'them and us' workplace culture; and complex industrial relations arrangements involved four main trade unions and one support union. With regard to this latter issue, there was often little consultation between union officials and the members of the workforce.

During its first six years of operation, Texicom faced a rapidly changing and turbulent environment. The telecommunications industry was deregulated, the economic recession continued, competition from other manufacturers increased and interest rates changed. The company developed a variety of marketing, business, investment and employee relations strategies to adapt to these changes to compete successfully in the world telecommunications market.

Human resource strategies were designed to build a culture that encouraged continuous improvement in the product quality, acceptance of change and an alignment of individual and company objectives. The strategies included changes in organisation and work structures, a revised management style, attempts to create a sense of shared values and the development of employee skills and career paths. An enterprise agreement formally recognised and codified these changes and also provided for a wage increase.

The context of change

The market

In 1989 Texicom's future looked bright. The telecommunications industry was growing at a rate of 30 per cent per annum worldwide. Texicom aspired to reach a position of market leadership in Australia and produce world-class technology for export. Australia represented 3–4 per cent of the world telecommunications market and this was considered sufficient to provide Texicom with a critical mass for local production and export.

Overseas market opportunities were opening up. There was a growing demand for telecommunications infrastructure in the Asia-Pacific region, and the prospect of a deregulated single European Market provided significant potential. The growth in sales from $150 000 in 1987 to $133 662 000 in 1990 reflected this optimism.

The company

Texicom is a worldwide operation with more than 1000 employees. Its operations are spread over five countries—Australia, Germany, Hong Kong, Taiwan and New Zealand. The company's head office is in Melbourne and its manufacturing operation in Sydney. The Australian company constitutes the major component of Texicom, with more than 600 employees.

The workforce is diverse in terms of skills and ethnic background. About 40 per cent are highly skilled, with some 60 engineers involved in the development of new products and another 30 engaged in product support. However, many of the other employees were in less skilled jobs. More than two-thirds of the male workforce and some 80 per cent of female employees were plant and machine operators. Employees were drawn from Europe, Asia, South America and Middle Eastern countries.

The managing director reported that '[Texicom's] sound cash position and the halving of debt during the year just ended, plus an aggressive marketing program to accompany the planned introduction of exciting new products in

1989/90, auger well for continuing improvements in performance'. These expectations were not met. Although sales grew between 1989 and 1990, the value in 1992 was lower than in 1990. In addition, operating profit before and after tax was negative in all but two years between 1987 and 1992. Texicom faced loss of sales, demands from customers for higher quality products and increased competition.

Technology

Substantial technological developments in the industry resulted in the introduction of a variety of new products. Texicom provided many of these, including products for the integrated services digital network (ISDN). However, like most suppliers it had difficulty providing stable and suitable product offerings for the ISDN service.

A further development was provided in such value-added services (VAS) as basic switching and transmission functions delivered by telecommunications. These result in the addition of significant value to manual intervention for telephone answering services and the provision of visual services. By 1991 the total domestic market for VAS was estimated at $350 million.

The nature of manufacturing technology changed markedly during the 1980s. Robotic production lines enhanced quality production and introduced such changes as:

- cheaper cost of production;
- designing products to suit specific customer needs rather than assembly of standard products;
- the nature of the value-added chain with value being added at the stage of software development rather than assembly;
- provision of traditional services as a result of the merging of computer and communication technologies.

These developments required changes in the marketing of products, the skills required of employees, the quality of the products and the extent of co-operation between manufacturers in the industry, as well as enhanced co-operation between equipment manufacturers and suppliers of the services.

Industrial relations

Developments in industrial relations and in government policy encouraged reform in Texicom. Decisions of industrial tribunals and the federal industrial relations legislation encouraged the determination of enterprise wages and conditions within the framework of a centralised system of industrial relations. Since 1987 the Industrial Relations Commission encouraged granting wage increases in exchange for productivity increases. The October 1991 National

Wage Decision included principles that encouraged enterprise bargaining and the continued revision of awards. These decisions facilitated:

- involvement of employees in the management process through joint consultative arrangements at the workplace;
- determination of wages and working conditions to suit enterprise conditions;
- simplification of union involvement and representation in the process of determining wages and working conditions;
- work re-organisation and development of career opportunities.

This approach to industrial relations was supported by the Metal Trade Industry Association (MTIA)—the employer association supported by Texicom—and trade unions representing their employees. Developments in the industrial relations arena provided opportunities for rewriting some employment policies.

Government policy

The Australian government sought to make Australian companies more internationally competitive by reforming employment practices. It encouraged workplace reform through initiatives administered by Departments of Education and Employment, Department of Industry, Technology and Commerce, and Industrial Relations. These initiatives included the Best Practice Demonstration Program which provided organisations with funds to assist in the development and implementation of workplace reform and the Workplace English Language and Literacy Program.

Another major change was the deregulation of the telecommunications industry and the removal of tariffs. In November 1990, the federal government announced its decision to adopt AUSTEL's recommendations. These included the removal of restrictions on resale of domestic and international telecommunications capacity. Optus Communications was successful in securing the licence to compete with Telecom. It was predicted that Australian telecommunications companies, including Texicom, would benefit from Optus operating as a second carrier.

Deregulation and a reduction in tariffs resulted in:

- increased competition among manufacturers, ultimately leading to an increased need for quality products;
- the role of the telecommunications industry changing from a public utility to a provider of service activities, which led to consumer demand to meet their special needs.

Texicom faced many threats and opportunities between 1988 and 1992. The company needed to improve product quality, improve sales and market opportunities, manage a variety of stakeholders (including suppliers, customers and employees) in different ways and utilise developing industrial relations and workplace reform possibilities.

The transformation

The board and senior management of Texicom sought to transform the company to provide the quality products and services required in the telecommunications industry. Major changes were made in business, marketing, investment and human resource strategies. New process technologies were introduced, executive and managerial appointments were made and measures taken to build a culture suited to the needs of the business. The board and the senior executives provided a clear direction and strategy developed through top-down business planning. Within this framework, a number of recently appointed managers implemented policies designed to build a continuous improvement culture based on quality, teamwork, consultation and company identification.

The main levers for the creation of the culture were:

- a clear statement of the organisational purpose as a basis for policies, including employee relations;
- relocation to a newly constructed manufacturing plant;
- development of more open consultative methods of communication;
- development of a continual improvement program.

Business philosophy and mission

A mission statement and business philosophy were developed by the corporate office in Melbourne and disseminated through the annual report. The business philosophy and mission stated:

> [Texicom's] business philosophy is based on utilising state-of-the-art technology combined with economically-priced production and efficient sourcing of components, materials, to deliver products that are of required customer quality.
>
> Our mission is to be the leading Australian-owned designer, manufacturer and supplier of telecommunications products, systems and services and to grow strongly in an increasingly competitive world market.

The strategies implemented to follow this mission included:

- reorienting Texicom's export market from the domestic to the international market;
- increasing investment in research and development activities so products could be specifically designed for overseas customers, particularly in the Arabian Gulf region, the Pacific and Asia;
- use of vertical integration to acquire companies that contributed to the manufacture of products;
- development of strategic alliances, including association with a Canadian company, a joint venture with a Chinese power supply company, and agreement to become the Australian distributor for a Canadian company;
- development of closer relationships with suppliers and distributors and the introduction of a supplier quality assessment program to improve pricing, quality, lead times and flexible scheduling;

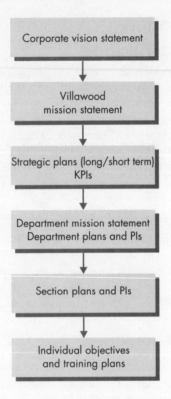

Figure E1   Strategic planning

- investment in technological innovation and a new manufacturing plant;
- restructuring of the organisation to remove four layers in production and one level of management, abolition of the positions of foreman and charge hand and the creation of the position of team leader.

Senior management at the manufacturing plant used the company mission and vision as a basis for the change program and its human resources plan. Figure E1 identifies the strategic planning process and the way the corporate vision determined the mission of the manufacturing plant, individual employee plans and training plan. The human resource plan identified a number of employee relations issues critical to the achievement of the company's mission. These included building the culture, establishing quality systems and continuous improvement programs, establishing structures for consultation, improving communication, developing training and development and managing the Best Practice Demonstration Program.

Relocation to a new plant

The process of relocation was understood to be an important first stage in building a culture with more direct communication between employees and management. A range of initiatives designed to improve communication included establishment of consultative mechanisms, encouraging employees to learn better communication skills, changing organisational structures to facilitate easier communication, informing employees and trade union representatives about issues associated with the move, and using ceremonies to mark stages of progress.

Negotiations and consultations began with the planning of the new manufacturing plant. The planning stage was used to start changing the focus of negotiations from issues associated with broader national, industry or occupational matters to company-specific issues. Employees and union delegates at the site negotiated matters associated with the move. The union organisers from all five trade unions formalised the terms of the move in the Relocation Agreement.

Direct communication with employees was fostered by a discussion group established by the operations manager. This group consisted of nine employees from eight different locations of the old manufacturing plant. It met for one hour every Thursday morning for the three months it took for the move to be completed. Its purpose was to channel and communicate information through to other employees on progress of the relocation and related issues, and to bring back any queries and concerns.

Many employees expressed concern about transport to the new site. As a result, Texicom chartered a bus service to operate between the old and new sites for the starting and finishing of shifts. The service was operated for nine months and for most of this time was subsidised by the company.

A number of ceremonies were used to mark the move to the new manufacturing plant. These included:

- a luncheon at which the executive general manager of Texicom received the key to the plant from the developers;
- a free 'housewarming' luncheon in the new building for all employees;
- an official opening attended by senior federal government ministers and advisers.

All the ceremonies were thoroughly covered in the in-house newsletter and the official opening was widely covered in the print and electronic media.

Consultation and communication

The managers at the manufacturing plant sought to develop more effective communication between a variety of stakeholders of Texicom. Texicom staff developed closer relationships with suppliers and distributors to improve the supply chain; and marketing, and research and development staff worked more closely with customers to design products more specific to their needs. The human resource manager and operations manager sought to improve communication between employees and managers at the manufacturing plant. Open, direct communication and consultation with staff was regarded as an essential component of building a less adversarial culture and improving the quality of production.

The steps taken to improve communication included:

- removing levels of management and introducing team-based workgroups in some production areas;
- establishing a joint consultative committee to contribute to operational and strategic issues;
- informing employees about a variety of company matters through an in-house newsletter and through informal meetings with the human resources manager;
- using whiteboards to identify production problems;
- providing English classes to employees assessed below the prescribed minimum English comprehension levels.

Teams

Improved communication was also sought through the establishment of teams. Pilot target teams were established in the modem assembly area, where quality and reliability needed to be improved. The area operated on a make-to-order basis. Management chose this area because it involved using resources from a variety of separate departments in Texicom, tangible results could be observed and the area was not considered 'bread and butter' business. The operations and human resources manager chose long-serving employees as members of the team—most had been with Texicom for more than eight years. The team members undertook two weeks training on process analysis at the workplace resource centre and as a consequence were able to identify the barriers to reliable and high-quality production and to develop solutions to these barriers.

Team members and management believed vertical communication improved as a result of working in a team. They found the team provided a safe forum for discussions about poor quality components provided by other parts of the company, and an avenue for identifying and addressing the issue of store security. The security provided by membership of the team stimulated team members to make suggestions about the way process analysis and target teams could be used in other areas of the plant. In the words of one team member, 'Target teams are proving to be useful and successful in ever-increasing aspects of production because they tackle any barrier to production by studying problems and formulating recommendations, many of which have been evaluated and implemented by the company with positive results, both in practical and measurable results'.

Joint consultative committee

Similarly, the formation of a joint consultative committee sought to enhance employee involvement in workplace decisions and improve communication. A National Wage Case decision required the establishment of joint consultative committees (JCC) as a basis for receiving the productivity element of the wage increase. Of the eight members of the JCC, four were drawn from management and four represented the unions on the site. One union representative was drawn from the trades, two from production and the technical and stores had a combined position. Management representatives were the human resources, production, precision and metal fabrication and new products managers.

The JCC was involved in the process of work re-organisation. The committee:

- monitored the results of skills audits and the training required as a result of these audits;
- discussed wage and classification matters resulting from the revised Metal Trades Award;
- developed criteria for membership of pilot target teams and the areas in which they would operate;
- initiated and applied successfully to the Best Practice Demonstration Program for $323 000 and monitored the benchmarking, training and quality improvement projects undertaken as part of this funding.

The JCC reported:

Through actively increasing employee involvement and revamping communication processes, staff support for a broad range of change issues has been central to overcoming inevitable organisational resistance to change … Evidence that employee participation is gaining momentum was the recent overwhelming turnout for a lunchtime video on training needs assessment and our skills audit program.

Other initiatives

Improvements in communication were also sought by raising the literacy of the workforce using regular English classes. Initially management believed the literacy problems could be addressed in one year; however, when more than 200 employees expressed an interest in improving their English, they realised it would probably take four to five years. A teacher from the Adult Migrant Education Service was based in the plant and provided classes for three hours four days a week. The public course material provided by AMES was supplemented by Texicom work-based examples.

The bi-weekly in-house newsletter included information about changes in the industry, the company and policies. It also communicated work and non-work achievements by individuals and members of their families. The newsletter was considered an important vehicle means for demonstrating the a more open communication pattern in the new manufacturing plant.

Continual improvement program

The continual improvement program was developed by the JCC in response to the federal government's Best Practice Demonstration Program. The three key aspects of this program were benchmarking, establishment of quality systems and training.

The benchmarking process was central to building the new culture. It encouraged attitude change by opening employees' minds to the need for improvement and provided methods that could be used to achieve improvement. The process was undertaken in two phases. In the first phase 41 employees—including 21 award-covered—were selected by the JCC and divided into 9 crews. These crews were responsible for one of the following key performance indicator areas:

- manufacturing (including such areas as inventory accuracy, calibration, production scheduling, preventative maintenance systems and production reporting);
- human resources (training, problem-solving teams, occupational health and safety, and work organisation structures);
- design (design cycle to market).

Each crew was responsible for identifying Texicom's current performance standard, collecting information about national and international best practice companies and developing action plans. The same process was used in phase two which examined the following employment and production issues:

- manufacturing (planning systems and shopfloor scheduling);
- work organisation (integration of support activities, production and cellular work groups);
- training (job induction, needs analysis and competency assessments);
- design (design for manufacturability).

The workplace resource centre assisted by arranging schedules for external visits, identifying the members of the crews and advising on report format. Reports were made to the JCC and to the employee communication sessions.

Quality systems

Australian and international customers required Texicom products to meet certain quality standards. The quality management systems were overhauled to achieve AS3901 (ISO 9000 series accreditation). Quality control moved to the shopfloor as employees became accountable for the quality of their individual production. Quality assurance performed audits of internal systems as well as of supplier quality standards, and documentation was developed with shopfloor employees. In addition, four total quality management principles were developed as part of the strategic planning process.

Training

Training and development policies were formulated as a way of overcoming individual skill gaps and identifying potential skill gaps. The training and development co-ordinator was responsible for allocating budgets to managers and supervisors and for developing individual training plans with the managers and supervisors. A variety of training arrangements were used, but on-the-job instruction was given emphasis on the basis that most people 'learn by doing'. Sixty-one training modules in areas such as electronic, mechanical assembly, quality assurance and telephones were prepared for on-the-job and classroom instruction.

The change facilitators

Board and managers

The changes at Texicom were supported and enhanced by some key Board members and managers, by emphasising the company's needs through strategic planning and by government policy and industrial tribunal decisions. Three new board members, bringing significant experience in public and private companies and with strong engineering and science backgrounds, were appointed at the end of 1989. One of these became chairman in 1992 and instigated reviews of the business, divested activities that did not focus on key activities and developed strategic alliances.

Three managers drove the changes at Texicom. The executive general manager strongly supported the development of a new culture at the new site and was regarded as the symbol of the change. The human resources manager, appointed in 1989, believed strongly in consultation and involving employees in the change process. The operations manager was also appointed in 1989 and brought with him experience in successfully implementing changes in a previous engineering environment. These individuals were committed to developing a new culture at Texicom.

Enterprise-based focus

The initiatives focused on improving product quality and reliability. This focus was supported by the development of the business philosophy and mission and the Enterprise Award. The Texicom Australia Ltd Western Sydney (Enterprise Bargaining) Award 1992 granted employees a 4.5 per cent wage increase in exchange for the implementation of measures designed to improve productivity, efficiency and flexibility. The enterprise agreement was a formal recognition and codification of the changes which management had introduced at Texicom. Four trade unions were parties to it.

Government and external support

The changes at Texicom were supported by government and industrial tribunal policy and legislation. The decisions of the Industrial Relations Commission facilitated the formulation of an enterprise agreement, the trade-off between wage and productivity increases, the provision of training and the establishment of joint consultative arrangements. The federal government encouraged expenditure on training through the Training Guarantee Scheme and on workplace reform through a variety of schemes such as the Best Practice Demonstration Program. This latter program provided the necessary funds to implement many of the initiatives at Texicom.

Conclusion

Competitive pressures stimulated Texicom to develop its marketing, business, investment and employee relations strategies. The change process at Texicom was shaped by developments in the internal and external environments and the views and skills of key managers. The primary purpose of the employee relations strategies was to build a culture that encouraged continuous improvement, an acceptance of change and an identification of individuals with the company needs.

Initiatives included encouraging more direct relationships with employees through teams, joint consultative arrangements and benchmarking crews. Developing new performance standards through a benchmarking process and target teams. The achievement of these standards was encouraged by equipping employees with the skills necessary to improve their performance through training courses.

7 Issues in the design and structure of executive remuneration

Graham L. O'Neill

Executive remuneration refers to the fixed pay, bonuses (including shares and options) and related benefits awarded to those men and women who occupy the most senior decision-making positions in our public and private sector enterprises. Typically, this includes the chief executive officer and the direct reports: in larger organisations, the executive group may include two or even three levels below the chief executive. The total remuneration paid to people at these levels is required to meet several objectives: first and foremost, it must recognise the individual contribution that they make to their respective organisations; it needs to reflect their personal worth in the general managerial marketplace; and it must take account of the difficult and onerous job demands that all too frequently invade their personal lives.

The design and management of executive remuneration is a unique and sensitive area. At an overall level, executives—together with other senior managers—have the potential to impact on their organisation very broadly because they are the dominant group in shaping the work culture, climate and performance objectives (see Lawler & Jenkins 1992, p. 1043). More specifically, it is this senior group of employees who are accountable for safeguarding and growing the funds that shareholders invest in the firm. In this respect, there is an expectation that their own remuneration will, in some significant way, reflect the financial outcomes due to the owners.

The rewards for such senior people are far greater than those paid to the average wage and salary earner. If one assumes that the average earnings for a CEO of a medium-sized Australian firm totals $500 000, and average weekly earnings are of the order of $30 000, this gives a ratio of approximately 16 to 1. Corresponding data from the US is 35 to 1, Japan 15 to 1 and Europe 20 to 1 (Gerhart & Milkovich 1992, p. 542). Political and social sensitivities about the levels of executive pay are often expressed in media headlines following announcements of large amounts negotiated at times of hiring or departure. The potential bonus of some $12 million dollars through a share options arrangement for AMP CEO George Trumbull and the $2.875 million package paid in 1996 to Peter Bartels as he left Coles Myer are cases in point. The significant issue is that although Australian executive remuneration levels lag those of other developed western economies, we are increasingly influenced by international remuneration trends. In this respect, executive remuneration levels can be expected to continue to rise, especially as the market for talented and capable senior management becomes more of an international—rather than purely domestic—pool.

For these reasons, executive remuneration is frequently the subject of public scrutiny. On the other hand, there appears to be unanimous agreement that if Australian organisations are to compete in a global marketplace, we need to provide remuneration levels for our corporate leaders that are internationally competitive. This is reinforced by the growing practice of various companies—ANZ Banking Group, AMP, Telstra and Westpac, now joined, the press reports, by Amcor and BHP—to conduct international searches to fill vacant senior positions. International recruitment brings with it the necessity to meet expectations of a broader and substantially different reward design and structure than has been traditional in Australia. These pressures and influences present challenges and opportunities to those engaged in the planning, design and management of executive reward systems.

The debate about executive remuneration

Government legislation and Stock Exchange requirements in Australia, as with most other western economies, provide for disclosure of executive remuneration as part of the annual reporting requirements of listed companies. This places executive pay clearly in the public domain and guarantees media attention, especially where a corporation's remuneration appears to run counter to its financial performance.

Table 7.1 is taken from an *Australian Financial Review* article naming a prominent Australian corporate followed by the headline 'A bosses' gravy train: earnings down, but rewards up' (*Australian Financial Review* 14 November 1995). The inconsistency between growth in director and executive remuneration, compared with financial performance as measured by earnings before interest and tax (EBIT), over the five-year period shown in Table 7.1 is typical of the apparent mismatch between pay and performance noted by the business press.

The debate about executive remuneration began in the USA in the mid-1980s as more and more executives exceeded $1 million in annual payments. The original sensitivity of the issue was less related to the actual amounts of pay, and more to the fact that these payments were being made at a time when employees were being asked to change existing working conditions and take pay cuts, and many traditional industries were seeking government protection from imports. This led to a spate of criticism, perhaps best summarised by the title of an article in the June 1988 issue of *Fortune* magazine—'The wacky, wacky world of CEO pay' (Crystal 1988). Subsequent critics claim that the level of executive rewards in the US is distorted relative to the past, other employees, and other countries (see Foulkes 1991, p. xiii).

In the early 1990s four influences in the USA combined to change executive pay as a consequence of this debate (see Kay, Lawson & Lerner 1995). First, the Securities and Exchange Commission (SEC) switched to a standardised, tabular format for reporting executive pay in public company proxy statements. The aim of using this format was to make it easier for shareholders to understand executive pay levels, and make comparisons with other companies. In addition, the SEC required companies to include a performance graph showing the relationship between corporate performance and pay, and a report from the board compensation committee detailing the company's executive pay philosophy and specific pay decisions related to the CEO role.

Second, a 1993 federal tax bill capped deductible remuneration for executives at $1 million, unless the additional pay resulted from a qualified performance-based plan. Under the legislation, a plan needs three conditions to qualify:

- it must be approved by a committee of outside directors;
- it must subsequently gain shareholder approval; and
- it must be formula-based, such that an external third party can calculate the amounts at the end of the year.

The third and fourth influences were essentially different perspectives of public scrutiny. Institutional investors began to take great interest in the pay

Table 7.1 Comparison of executive remuneration and company performance[1]

Remuneration ($m)	1990	1991	1992	1993	1994	1995	% change
Non-executive directors	2.169	2.455	3.664	6.93	7.012	10.896	+402
Executives	22.294	24.593	33.948	48.56	63.152	76.907	+244
Total remuneration	24.463	27.048	37.612	55.49	70.164	87.803	+258
EBIT	748.4	736.3	658.9	643.3	671.9	729.9	-2.5

1 Data compiled from annual reports of the company cited

practices of underperforming companies and responded in two ways: by voicing their concerns at shareholder meetings and to board members; and, as a last resort, by shifting their funds to companies that demonstrated more consistency between shareholder returns and executive rewards. At the same time, the business press—and the media in general—increased its coverage of executive pay issues, bringing the more sensationalist aspects in particular into the public domain.

The debate was not confined to the USA: as a result of the privatisation of UK public utilities in the late 1980s, executives demanded—and received—significant private sector style pay increases, including significant share option grants. This led to public outcries of 'fat cat utility bosses', confrontational annual general meetings, and Labour Party threats of increased taxation on utilities to pay for these excesses (Rhoads 1996).

The Confederation of British Industry (CBI) appointed a committee headed by Sir Richard Greenbury to review executive pay. Among its recommendations, later adopted as stock exchange requirements for all listed companies, were the following shareholder safeguards:

- companies must have a remuneration committee consisting exclusively of non-executive directors;
- the chair of the remuneration committee must publish an annual report to shareholders detailing the company's policy on executive pay, and must attend the annual general meeting to answer shareholders' questions;
- full disclosure of executive pay, including bonuses, shares and options, benefits and pension details; and
- specific guidelines for the design of long-term incentive schemes, with particular reference to share options.

There appear to be three central issues at the heart of this debate. First, do executives deserve the amounts they are paid? Second, is performance-related pay sufficiently linked to appropriate measures of performance? Finally, is executive pay structured in a way that is defensible and credible to shareholders, the media and the community in general?

Do executives deserve the amounts they are paid?

There are two perspectives to answering the question of whether executives are worth the high levels of remuneration they attract. The first concerns the essential issue of supply and demand. The available pool of talent capable of successfully filling senior executive roles is relatively small; not only is the total pool small but, as Gerstein and Reisman (1987) argue, various business situations require executives that bring highly specific management competencies. Thus, the start-up phase of a business is likely to require different leadership skills and characteristics than do other stages such as dynamic growth, turnaround or divestiture. It is important therefore to match executive selection to business strategy, and this requires a sound appreciation of which skills and characteristics are essential to performance in the role. This matching of person to context is consistent with Wolfe's (1996) findings where 'qualifications and experience' (including individual attributes, skills and reputation) was the second-ranked factor in perceived value that CEOs bring to their companies.

The logical consequence of these approaches suggests an executive labour market segmentation based on the supply and demand of specific experience, skills and management competencies. Thus, the individual market value of an executive is determined within the parameters of this specialist—but ill-defined—market.

The second perspective has to do with whether or not executives have a measurable impact on business performance. Certainly, in the mind of some commentators, the emphasis on executives and the directness of their impact on a firm's performance is sometimes exaggerated (e.g. McLaughlin 1991, p. 23). Gomez-Mejia and Balkin (1992, p. 172) addressed this issue by asking 'Do top executives matter?'. They reviewed some 30 research-based investigations published between 1960 to 1992, looking at the nature and extent of senior executives' influence on firm performance. Overall, their conclusion is that managerial decisions and environmental forces (i.e. factors outside management's direct control) are both important: the weight of evidence suggests that short-term performance is dominated by external circumstances, while managerial actions (such as strategic planning) are important for the longer term.

However, they also cite evidence of some managerial decisions that do have immediate impact on cash flow, profitability, revenue results and ultimately, market value of the company. In particular, these include:

- the choice of accounting methods for stock inventory (e.g. last–in–first-out versus first–in–first-out), depreciation (e.g. straight line versus accelerated) and amortisation periods;
- investment decisions (including research and development expenditure); and
- acquisition and diversification actions.

Overall, Gomez-Mejia and Balkin conclude that performance is 'highly responsive to managerial behaviours and decisions. Furthermore, there are many situations where the policy choices confronting managers are such that what is better for a firm's shareholders and what may further management's interests are at odds with each other' (1992, p. 176).

Is performance-related pay linked to appropriate measures of performance?

There is an overwhelming belief that the key issue in executive remuneration is to ensure a strong and explicit link between pay and organisational performance. Yet, there is no empirical data to support the notion that linking pay to organisational performance at management and executive levels actually increases the required outcomes (O'Neill 1995). If anything, the objective is to ensure that executive rewards correlate with company (and therefore, shareholder) outcomes. However, even achieving this objective is difficult. McLaughlin (1991, p. 70) comments that 'Pay for performance is the most widely advocated and imperfectly delivered dictum in the land. Failure to deliver often erodes motivation.' Similarly, Flannery, Hofrichter and Platten (1996, p. 194) state: 'Whatever the measures, recent history has shown that merely linking pay to performance or increasing the mix of performance-based, at-risk variable compensation provides no guarantee that an organisation's performance will improve, especially over the long haul.'

Nevertheless, there are strong demands to make some significant proportion of executive pay contingent on performance. But which performance measures best relate to executive reward? Survey data published by consulting firms consistently show more than 70 per cent of major companies operating in Australia have annual bonus schemes for senior executives and managers (e.g. Hay Group 1997a). The overwhelming majority of these plans are based on traditional financial performance measures such as achievement against budgets, profit, revenue, return on investment and the like. Clearly, these are each important in tracking an organisation's success; however, they tend to emphasise singular aspects of performance and, particularly in the case of performance to budget, may be open to 'gaming the system'. If an executive's bonus is dependent on meeting or exceeding an agreed budget, it is a fair bet that the budget setting process is likely to be compromised by significant negotiations predicated on a potential remuneration outcome, rather than genuine longer term corporate performance issues.

The investment community, strongly supported by the business press, see the primary role of management as the creation of wealth for shareholders. In this respect, the focus is more on gaining a more direct correlation between shareholder returns and executive rewards. This emphasis leads to designing remuneration plans that link bonuses more directly with some aspect of shareholder wealth, which could be gains in share price or total shareholder returns (i.e. increase in share price plus dividends) over a baseline period. With a little more sophistication, share price or total shareholder returns may be indexed relative to a select comparator group of companies, as done by leading Australian industrial firm Amcor Limited for its executive bonus system. These approaches certainly align the interests of executives with those of shareholders, but they still have inherent limitations. First, share prices are open to a range of very direct influences other than management decisions and actions. Such influences include cyclical economic swings, the general business environment, government legislation and international influences. Second, share price targets measured over a specific period are a relatively static measure, and do not necessarily reflect sustained increases in fundamental share-holder value. Similarly, where share price gains against an industry comparison group are used, the end result is a relative, rather than absolute, measure of performance. That is, if Company A's share price falls, but the decline is less that the industry benchmark, the target is met. However, from a shareholder's perspective, absolute value may have declined, thus defeating the purpose of providing a direct link between executive pay and shareholder returns.

Many internationally based companies are seeking a more comprehensive measure of overall business performance as a basis for executive and management bonus systems. While recognising that no one measure is perfect, the concept of economic value added, commonly referred to as EVA, has gained some acceptance with major US corporates such as Coca-Cola, AT & T and Quaker Oats. In Australia and New Zealand, EVA has been used by the ANZ Banking Group, Fletcher Challenge and New Zealand Telecom, and is being explored by other large companies.

Put simply, EVA is a measure of economic profit outcomes after deducting the cost of equity capital. Thus it allows for the opportunity cost of shareholder capital employed in the business in calculating a measure of shareholder wealth creation. Despite the growing support for EVA, it is subject to the criticism that its sole focus is on the measurement of outcomes as valued by the external capital market. The issue is that executive incentive plans need to have an equal focus on the development and execution of strategy, not just measuring annual financial or economic outcomes (Marquardt 1996).

Kilroy (1996) argues that the EVA-style value measurement approaches are secondary issues. While shareholder value is *measured* in capital markets, it is *created* in product markets: To create value for shareholders, the focus first needs to be on creating value for customers. His value-based management approach places the executive performance emphasis on the allocation of capital to agreed strategic initiative action plans, translating those plans into key performance indicators with clear, measurable goals, and assessing performance against those value creation accountabilities. Thus, executive rewards are linked to the creation of customer value which in turn increases the value of the business. Creating this chain requires, by necessity, strategic planning attention to markets, customers, asset utilisation and capital. This approach is consistent with the growing adoption of Kaplan and Norton's (1996) concept of the 'balanced scorecard' approach to planning, managing and measuring firm performance.

The issue is whether the variable component of executive remuneration is linked to appropriate measures of performance. The entire process of remuneration design remains more of an art than a science. Nevertheless, there is an undeniable logic to the practice of linking some significant part of executive rewards to increases in the value of the business, if for no other reason than to reinforce the accountability that senior executives have to protect and grow the investment entrusted to them by the owners. However, there is no one answer; the design of variable, performance-based pay plans is by necessity unique to each organisation. The best that can be proposed is that there are certain basic design features required of performance-related pay plans for senior executives:

- the variable component represents a significant portion of remuneration (in today's environment, at least 30 per cent of total 'target' pay for the role);
- payments are contingent upon increases in overall business value;

- potential rewards are truly at risk;
- there are short- and long-term components, where the long-term component remains at risk against maintained performance over time (e.g. 3–5 years).

Design and structure of executive pay

Executive pay is generally structured around three components: 1) fixed annual pay comprising base salary and benefits, 2) short-term incentive and 3) long-term incentive. The way in which an individual company structures the total package available to its executives, particularly the mix of these components, reflects its own desired positioning in the labour market and how it chooses to link remuneration to business objectives. Illustrating this very point, is the different approach that organisations take to the provision of benefits to executives. Table 7.2 summarises the policy approach to the provision of benefits taken by 51 of Australia's leading companies that subscribed to the Hay Group's *Executive Reward Service* in 1997. The table shows that 44 per cent of the companies provide a total cost approach to benefits; that is, the company determines the total amount of fixed annual remuneration it is willing to pay the executive, and he or she can allocate this amount to suit their own needs and lifestyle within the ruling taxation regime. Companies that provide fixed benefits prescribe what executives are permitted to have within the given policy, whereas those with flexible benefits allow some degree of negotiation. Due to the large proportion of companies using the total cost approach, it is common to refer to fixed annual remuneration (FAR) comprising base salary plus the annualised cost of benefits (including fringe benefit taxation and gross-up for non-deductible superannuation contributions).

From the organisation's perspective, the design and structure of executive pay needs to meet three objectives: first and foremost, it must be sufficiently competitive to attract and retain the calibre of person necessary to plan and manage the business; second, it must encourage management to take appropriate risks to increase the net value of shareholder investment; and finally, it must be consistent with the interests and returns generated to shareholders in

Table 7.2 Remuneration policy approach to provision of benefits

Policy approach	% of organisations
Total cost	44
Base salary & fixed benefits	26
Base salary & flexible benefits	20
Other	8
Total remuneration	2
Total	**100**

the medium and longer term. Following is a brief description and commentary on the key components of total executive remuneration.

Fixed annual remuneration

Fixed annual remuneration is the fixed, not-at-risk component of remuneration. Based on data from the Hay Group's 1997 *Executive Reward Service* report, in Australia this part of pay represents an average 66 per cent of the total rewards for CEOs and 78 per cent for other executives. In comparison, American CEOs receive an estimated average of 23 per cent of their remuneration as fixed pay (Meyer 1996). There is every reason to believe that Australian practices will become more aligned with those of American companies as boards seek to put more and more remuneration at risk against performance, with a particular emphasis on long-term incentives for executives.

This guaranteed portion of pay is used in large measure to reflect the complexity of the role, the level of responsibility and the size of the organisation. Recent research by Iob and O'Neill (1998) shows correlations of 0.77 between CEO base salary and job size and 0.78 for other senior executives. It is common practice to review executive salaries annually and average percentage increases reported by consulting firms tend usually to be in line with general business performance. Table 7.3 shows average fixed annual remuneration movements for the 5 years to 1997 according to the Hay Group data base.

Short-term incentives

Short-term performance payments are typically awarded on the basis of achievements measured over the previous year with payments usually made in cash at the end of the performance period. The number of organisations in Australia using short-term incentive plans has almost doubled over the past decade. In 1987 some 38 per cent of companies had short-term incentive plans in place; by 1990 55 per cent of companies had these plans, and in 1996 the proportion had grown to 68 per cent (Hay Group 1997a). As the number of firms using short-term plans has increased, so too has the use of specific, target-based criteria taken over from the allocation of discretionary bonus payments; 38 per cent of all plans require achievement of specific business objectives to trigger payments. The Hay Group's *Short Term Incentives Report 1996–1997* indicates that the average target reward for CEOs is 28 per cent of FAR and 20 per cent for executives. Targets commonly relate to net profit

Table 7.3 Average fixed annual remuneration movements 1993–97

	1993	1994	1995	1996	1997
CEOs	7.7%	10.7%	8.8%	6.2%	9.6%
Senior executives	4.6%	11.5%	10.0%	6.0%	7.9%

relative to budget, comparison with previous year or a specific formula (29 per cent of plans), cost control (12 per cent) and sales revenue and return on capital (both 10 per cent).

Data from the Hay Group's *Short Term Incentives Report 1996–1997* indicates that Australia (together with Canada) appears to fall midway between American and British practices. Short-term payments in the UK still consist predominantly of discretionary bonus awards, whereas practice in the US is overwhelmingly based on specific targets and formula-driven plans. Target payout levels in the US for achieving objectives average 30 per cent of base salary for executives and around 40 per cent for CEOs. Internationally, the most notable example of short-term incentives is the plan provided to Michael Eisner, CEO of the Walt Disney organisation. Eisner, a regular in the US top pay lists, receives 2 per cent of Disney's net income once the return on shareholder equity exceeds 11 per cent (Paulin 1997). In this respect, it is of interest to note that Australian Stock Exchange Listing Rules expressly prohibit performance-based pay plans for CEOs that are based on revenue.

Long-term incentives

Long-term incentives are awarded for two reasons: first, as an inducement to maintain or increase performance over a given period; and second, as a device to retain key executives over time. Long-term incentives are most often provided as share options or some form of share award (e.g. share purchase loans, partly paid shares or restricted share awards). Share options are the most common vehicle, with 51 per cent of long-term plans utilising options. Share options involve providing the right to acquire shares in the company, at a nominated price and time, providing specific performance hurdles are satisfied. The exercise price is usually the market value at the time the options are granted, and the exercise period is usually four or five years out. Performance hurdles vary but typical measures include earnings per share, share price growth or percentage increase in the Accumulation Index. Long-term incentives represent an average 23 per cent of CEO remuneration and 13.5 per cent of senior executive remuneration according to the Hay Group *Executive Reward Service*.

There are two ways to value the long-term incentive component of executive rewards. One is to determine a theoretical value at the time of the grant that represents the current value of the reward to be realised in the future. While this approach does provide a notional value at the time the grant is made, it ignores the actual amount that executives receive from the options. The other approach is to take the actual amount delivered to the executive when the options are exercised. This second approach allows comparison of actual amounts delivered. The disadvantage is that the remuneration value is attributed to the year payment is made and neglects the fact that it is attributable to performance over the preceding years. This discrepancy becomes an issue if the year that the shares are realised is a year of poor performance in comparison with the previous high performance years that triggered the delivery of shares.

The relative merits of using shares versus options for long-term incentive purposes have attracted some debate. Godfrey (1997) argues that if the aim is to provide a closer alignment with shareholder interests, then share purchase plans should be used in place of options. An executive holding options is not in the same position as a shareholder: option holders do not receive dividends and they do not suffer if the share price falls. Furthermore, it is common practice to sell the shares acquired immediately after exercising options. On this basis, Godfrey promotes the use of share purchase plans as providing a closer link with total shareholder returns (as measured by share price growth and dividends), as well as providing voting rights to the executive as a shareholder.

Long-term incentives are by far the fastest growing component of executive pay in the US, with the present value of average annual long-term option and share grants to CEOs growing at 10 per cent to 15 per cent (Paulin 1997). As Paulin comments, if the growth in the value of long-term incentives was eliminated, much of the criticism of executive pay levels would disappear and overall rewards would be more in line with those paid by other industrial economies.

Corporate governance and disclosure of executive pay

Schedule 5 of the Corporations Regulations refers to the requirements for disclosure of executive remuneration by listed companies in their annual reports. The requirements are very broad, including the very definition of an 'executive'. In essence, public companies are required to list total cash and non-cash remuneration received or due to executives from the company for the period in bands of $10 000 commencing at $100 000. Individual executives are not required to be identified, simply the number of executives in each pay band.

Prior to the passage of the *Company Law Review Act* in June 1998, there was significant concern that the disclosure requirements do not provide shareholders with sufficient information to understand the rationale behind executive pay, what their actual reward structure is, and how it might compare with remuneration levels paid by other listed companies. In late 1996 a federal parliamentary committee made a series of recommendations affecting disclosure of executive pay. In particular, the committee suggested that:

- companies be required to include full details of remuneration components, together with the board policies related to determination of the amounts;
- background rationale and explanation of the relationship between board policies, company performance and remuneration paid be provided;
- details regarding service agreements, and the basis of shares or options issued to executives be set out; and
- disclosure should identify the individuals concerned.

The 1998 *Company Law Review Act* met most—but not all—of the parliamentary committee requirements. In particular, greater detail is required for the components of directors' remuneration and for the five highest paid executives. The legislation also requires an explanation in the company's annual report that explains the linkage between company performance and executive remuneration.

While opinions are divided on the issue of identification of individual executives, it is hard to fault the recommendations that provide for further detail of the determination of executive remuneration policies and practices. The outcome provides for greater transparency regarding executive remuneration, its relationship to corporate performance and the underlying philosophy that determined the amounts paid. This level of disclosure cannot be expected to silence all criticism of executive remuneration levels, but it will do two things: it will help shift the focus to understanding the rationale behind remuneration packages, rather than just the amounts being paid; and in doing this, it will make for a more informed debate about remuneration issues and the differences in the remuneration levels and structure across companies.

Although the legislation did not take effect until 1 July 1998, the boards of several leading corporates had already been considering increasing the degree of information provided in their annual reports. Westpac had already expanded its information to shareholders in their 1997 annual report, as shown in Table 7.4.

Likely future trends in executive rewards

The components of executive pay are essentially the same for all commercial organisations. The most significant differences are in the public sector where rewards comprise base salary and benefits (the latter usually restricted to superannuation and a vehicle), and a growing incidence of annual cash bonuses. It is the levels of fixed pay and incentive amounts, and their relative proportions to the total reward package that make one company's remuneration different from another. The challenge for an organisation is to design reward strategies that enable it to compete in the executive labour market for senior people of the calibre required to achieve the business objectives and ensure management continuity for the firm. Devising such strategies requires an approach to executive reward planning that treats pay, benefits and performance-based payments as an important business variable, an approach similar to the way that product and service lines and prices are determined in the overall business strategy.

In Australian business we are likely to see continuation of the changes to executive reward structures that began in the early 1990s. Attention will be given to the following issues:

- more specific positioning of total reward structures against comparable reference groups such as industry leaders, similarly performing companies

Table 7.4 Westpac top 5 executive disclosure

Position	Year	Base pay $	Bonus $	Total cash compensation $	Other compensation $(1)	Total compensation $(2)	Option grant (3)	Exercise price $	Date first exercisable
Managing director & CEO (a)	1997	750 000	750 000	1 500 000	428 745	1 928 745	-	-	-
	1996	750 000	700 000	1 450 000	448 692	1 898 692	-	-	-
Group executive & Chief financial officer (b)	1997	574 270	350 000	924 270	65 525	989 795	500 000	7.89	29/9/00
	1996	500 600	250 000	750 600	259 134	1 009 734	200 000	5.51	29/1/99
Group executive (c)	1997	509 603	375 000	884 603	7 402	892 005	500 000	7.89	29/9/00
							175 000	7.10	28/1/00
	1996	500 000	350 000	850 000	47 953	897 953	200 000	5.51	29/1/99
Executive director & Group executive (d)	1997	550 000	425 000	975 000	6 824	981 824	-	-	-
	1996	550 000	325 000	875 000	6 693	881 693	600 000	5.12	25/1/99
Group executive & Chief credit officer (e)	1997	439 210	180 000	673 210	110 169	783 379	360 000	7.10	28/1/00
	1996	356 000	170 000	526 000	158 807	684 807	100 000	5.51	29/1/99

1 Other compensation includes (in either or both years) contractual obligations

a Superannuation, personal and family travel, health insurance and housing (executive unreimbursed housing expenses for a foreign residence).

b Superannuation, motor vehicles, health insurance, personal and family travel and housing allowance incurs reimbursed housing expenses for a foreign residence).

c FBT on concessional lending and housing allowance.

d Car parking.

e Superannuation, FBT on concessional lending, motor vehicle and housing allowance.

2 Figures do not include fringe benefits tax, other than those individuals whose remuneration is calculated on a 'total cost' basis.

3 Option grants are a right to buy ordinary shares at an exercise price equal to the market value at the date of grant. They have a minimum term of five years and are exercisable after three years.

Source: *Annual Report to Shareholders 1997*

and selected 'benchmark' firms, rather than broader based all-industry or all-organisation comparisons;
- recognition that global competition for senior executives means a shift to global pay levels and structures, particularly with reference to long-term incentives;
- greater manipulation of reward components to suit the differential maturity of businesses, such that the fixed component of pay may be higher in a mature product company while there will be greater emphasis on variable pay in a rapidly growing firm;
- growing demand from boards (and executives) for access to long-term incentives as a means of providing direct alignment between executive rewards and shareholder returns;
- ensuring a closer relationship between granting rewards and the achievement of company performance targets with respect to visible achievements against the overall business strategy, objectives and related performance indicators; and
- a strong likelihood of more stringent analysis of the board remuneration philosophy, the rationale for performance payments and provision of shares and options, and explanation regarding the link between actual remuneration and company performance.

References

Crystal, G. 1988, 'The wacky, wacky world of CEO pay', *Fortune*, 6 June, pp. 68–78.

Flannery, T., Hofrichter, D. & Platten, P. 1996, *People, Performance and Pay*, Free Press, New York.

Foulkes, F. (ed.), 1991, *Executive Compensation: A Strategic Guide for the 1990s*, Harvard Business School Press, Boston.

Fuehrer, V. 1994, 'Total reward strategy: A prescription for organizational survival', *Compensation and Benefits Review*, vol. 26, no. 1, pp. 44–53.

Gerhart, B. & Milkovich, G. 1992, 'Employee compensation: Research and practice', in M. Dunnette & L. Hough (eds), *Handbook of Industrial and Organizational Psychology*, 2nd edn, vol. 3, Consulting Psychologists Press, Palo Alto.

Gerstein M. & Reisman H. 1987, 'Strategic selection: Matching executives to business conditions', in Schien, E. (ed.), *The Art of Managing Human Resources* Oxford University Press, New York.

Godfrey, D. 1997, 'Why shares are replacing options as executive long-term incentives', *Reward Management Bulletin*, vol. 1, no. 7, pp. 115–17.

Gomez-Mejia, L. & Balkin, D. 1992, *Compensation, Organizational Strategy and Firm Performance*, South Western Publishing, Cincinatti, Ohio.

Hay Group 1997a, *Short Term Incentives Report—1996–1997*, Melbourne.

—— 1997b, *Executive Reward Service—1997 Report*, Melbourne.

Iob, M. & O'Neill, G. 1998, 'Determinants of CEO and senior executive reward in Australian organisations', *Reward Management Bulletin*, vol. 2, no. 2, pp. 181–3.

Kaplan, R. & Norton, D. 1996 *Translating Strategy into Action: The Balanced Scorecard*, Harvard Business School Press, Cambridge, MA.

Kay, I., Lawson, G. & Lerner, D. 1995, 'Executive pay under attack', in Cook, M. (ed.), *The Human Resources Handbook 1995–96*, Prentice-Hall, Englewood Cliffs, NJ.

Kilroy, D. 1996, 'Measuring value: equity spread, EVA or CFROI—what's all the fuss about?', *CFO*, November, pp. 62–4.

Lawler, E. & Jenkins, G. 1992, 'Strategic reward systems', in M. Dunnette & L. Hough (eds), *Handbook of Industrial and Organizational Psychology*, 2nd edn, vol. 3, Consulting Psychologists Press, Palo Alto.

McLaughlin, D. 1991, 'The rise of a strategic approach to executive compensation', in Foulkes, F. (ed.), *Executive Compensation: A Strategic Guide for the 1990s*, Harvard Business School Press, Boston.

Marquardt, E. 1996, 'Executive incentive plans: sharpening the focus on strategy execution', *American Compensation Association Journal*, vol. 5, no. 1, pp. 32–9.

Meyer, P. 1996, 'Executive pay trends: where have we been ... where are we going?', *American Compensation Association News*, June, pp. 16–18.

O'Neill, G. 1995, 'Linking pay to performance: Conflicting views and conflicting evidence', *Asia Pacific Journal of Human Resources*, vol. 33, no. 2, pp. 20–35.

Paulin, G. 1997, 'The components of CEO pay', *CEO Pay: A Comprehensive Look*, American Compensation Association, Scottsdale, Arizona.

Rhoads, D. 1996, 'Implications of the Greenbury Report on executive remuneration', paper presented at the American Compensation Association National Conference, Las Vegas.

Wolfe, M. 1996, 'CEO perceptions of their value', *American Compensation Association News*, January, pp. 16–18.

Changing reward and recognition processes in SGS Australia

Cynthia Mundy

SGS Australia, a wholly owned subsidiary of Switzerland's Société Générale de Surveillance, commenced operations in Australia in 1949. The SGS group is the largest independent inspection, testing and verification group in the world. Until the 1980s the company was primarily involved in inspection and testing in the coal industry. SGS expanded into government services in the 1980s and then later into health care and product and systems certification.

SGS Australia employs some 450 people across four divisions spread over 27 branch offices and laboratories. The business units are grouped into four sectors: resources industry and energy, government services, systems/product certification and health-care services. The business units are headed by sector managers who report to the executive committee. The sector business units are supported by the corporate services division providing financial, information and human resource management services.

In the early 1990s the company went through a period of consolidation and restructuring to improve profitability. As a result of this process, a change program was implemented to gain ISO 9002 certification by April 1996. This objective led to a review of other key areas such as leadership, strategy policy and planning, information and analysis, customer focus, quality of processes, product and service and organisation performance. The executive committee launched a program called Towards 2000 to be the driving force behind the change strategy in 1996 and beyond. National improvement teams headed by general managers from across the company were established to take up the lead in the various change initiatives. At the launch, the executive committee stated:

> As a service company SGS recognises that its employees are the only basis for sustainable competitive advantage. The Towards 2000 program aims to make all employees partners within SGS in changing its culture to meet the demands of the 21st century. This program is focusing strongly on the human resource systems implementing systems to support the business objectives.

The reward and recognition team, led by two members of the executive committee, was established under the banner of human resource management planning actions. In May 1996 the team invited a group of consultants to tender for the project. The guidelines were that the company wanted to work in conjunction with external consultants to develop a national reward and recognition strategy.

Initial data gathering and assessment

The first phase of the project was a detailed consultant briefing session with two members of the reward and recognition team and the human resource manager so that the consultants could gain a better understanding of the company structure, culture and history behind the development of the Towards 2000 program. It was apparent that, with the exception of the health-care divisions, the company did not have a formal system of reward and recognition in place. As a result, the employees perceived that issues of reward and recognition were not a corporate priority; in turn, this communicated a lack of commitment to employees. The performance appraisal process, also under review, emphasised a revenue-based approach and was accordingly budget driven with existing rewards tied to dollar outcomes. The bonus structure in place provided opportunity for recognition of high performance to a select level of management and the health-care divisions. Overall, the situation was perceived to be inequitable by the majority of employees.

The comprehensive assessment phase included gathering data and reporting on a range of issues including:

- meetings with various managers to identify key business strategies and corporate priorities;
- site visits to various locations across the company;
- a series of focus groups with staff to gain an understanding of their attitudes and concerns with the Towards 2000 program and the existing reward and recognition structure;
- evidence of change in work habits and performance as a result of the corporate strategy;

- employee perceptions of opportunity for career development and/or promotion within SGS;
- a reward and recognition survey designed to supplement the data drawn from the focus groups;
- data from a climate survey held earlier in the year;
- benchmarking data against competitors;
- level of pay-outs in existing forms of reward and recognition;
- differences in employee needs and concerns from sector to sector.

Throughout the data collection phase the reward and recognition team met and disseminated the results, which were used to shape the reward and recognition strategy. Team members also distributed internal 'press' releases designed to inform employees of significant milestones and to report back on the data gathering process. The general manager and financial controller also presented the team's findings and progress to the national chief executive steering committee.

Findings

Culture and communication

Reactions to the Towards 2000 program showed some initial disappointments. This appeared to reflect a feeling that it is 'all talk and no action' with employees looking for positive examples of how Towards 2000 would make a difference to them. In addition, some significant cultural issues were emerging: a feeling of 'us and them' combined with an element of cynicism about changes within the company and promises made; perceptions that certain sectors were given preferential treatment by management; and that the sales orientation in health care provided a quantifiable measurement process that facilitated a more creative approach to remuneration management than was possible in other sectors.

Another issue that surfaced concerned the lack of communication across the company. In particular, employees felt that they needed more information about reward and recognition processes such as:

- the relationship between performance levels and salary increments;
- who made the decisions in respect to salary as managers did not explain their role in the review process with staff;
- explanation of bonus payments with regard to before or after tax amounts;
- clarification of the performance evaluation system and what individuals needed to do to receive a salary increase;
- information about the reward and recognition system within each division and at the various employee levels.

The diversity of business activity would itself provided a significant challenge in the redesign of the human resource policies and procedures. However, the tension between the sectors and competitive attitudes added a new dimension to take into account in the design strategy .

Reward and recognition

On an employee survey, the average satisfaction rating for SGS's reward and recognition was 6 on a scale of 1–10. This suggests that some elements in the structure were satisfying to employees, while still leaving room for improvement. In particular, 77 per cent of employees rated variable pay in the top five preferred reward and recognition options. While this provided evidence that employees valued performance-based pay, it was also symptomatic of a perceived inequity: many felt that they did not have the same opportunity for performance increments as others and that base salaries were inconsistent across job classifications.

Employees generally emphasised the need for recognition by their immediate manager in addition to other forms of monetary and non-monetary reward. Table F1 reports the results of an employee brainstorming session which developed a list of preferred reward and recognition options.

Employees were asked to rank a list of items from one to ten and then to distribute 50 points between the top five choices. The results, shown in Table F2, revealed that no one option was favoured. However, it was interesting to note that the top three preferred options were monetary. The results of this survey and the focus groups suggested that the employees favoured a performance-based approach to pay.

Although the general response supported performance-based pay, employees had concerns about their manager's authority to make decisions about pay increases. Furthermore, employees were questioned whether managers, if given such authority, would have the capacity to make fair and equitable decisions. Interestingly, while managers had the scope to determine annual merit increases, employees perceived that these were head office decisions.

Table F1   Employee list of suggested reward and recognition options

No shift work for good workers	Mystery flight
Site visit to the head office in Geneva	A rostered day off
Periodic bonus payments	Gift voucher
Training	Profit-share system
Improved superannuation (i.e. aligned with current management structure)	Promotion
	Success—achievement
Time off	Spontaneous, spot rewards
Christmas bonus	Appreciation
Time off with pay for casual staff	Input—'a say'
Money	New equipment
Massage/health spa visit	Respect from co-workers, customers
A fair day's pay for a fair day's work	and management

Table F2   Top five reward and recognition options

Item	Average ranking from 1 to 10	% of respondents who ranked the item in the top 5 preferred options
Individual variable pay	3.6	77
Profit sharing	3.7	69
Group variable pay	5.4	44
Special recognition award	5.5	41
Stock options	5.6	39

An issue raised by management and non-management employees was the lack of consistency of the current reward and recognition system. While sector level managers had responsibility to make recommendations for pay increases, they had few processes and tools to guide them. In addition, managers and non-managers considered the existing performance appraisal process ineffective in identifying and managing high and low performers. Clearly, any changes to the performance review process needed to be consistent with the proposed reward and recognition model.

A final complication related to remuneration administration. Although the human resource department was responsible for the collation and analysis of remuneration records, much of the data was simply not available. In many instances managers had not forwarded the information to head office, and no follow-up had been undertaken. The consequence of poor recordkeeping was compounded by the broad ranging nature of the company's business units. With no formal administration and recording system in place, managers often kept their own records. This led to the use of inconsistent criteria and questionable judgments regarding employee entitlements to salary increases. Indications were that some employees, whose performance was regarded as superior, were missing out on increases. Overall, there appeared to be a general lack of appreciation of the value of remuneration administration and its role in a well-designed reward and recognition strategy.

Design

The need to develop a reward and recognition strategy arose from the Towards 2000 program; it was therefore natural that the design would follow a systems approach commencing with consideration of the business requirements. The design model is outlined in Figure F1 (see p. 176).

It was freely acknowledged that the company's future success was attributable to the work and achievements of the employees. Having a reward and recognition strategy that would recognise their contribution now and in the future was therefore a necessity. The overall objective was to deliver a process that directly supported SGS's business objectives, plans for future growth and

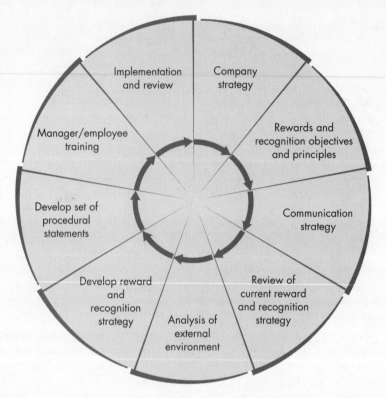

Figure F1   Reward design model

its cultural values. This required an understanding of the business direction, the current readiness of SGS to adopt new processes, and the attitudes and values of staff at all levels.

Early analysis identified that SGS was facing a number of challenges in areas of human resource planning and the evolution of Towards 2000. Some of these were some short-term needs that required immediate attention while more complex, and longer-term challenges could be addressed over the following 18 months. This planned and systematic approach was seen as providing greater control and direction over reward and recognition processes as Towards 2000 continued to evolve. It also ensured that changes in the business objectives, and corporate culture and values were directly linked to the reward and recognition processes.

An overview of the reward and recognition strategy is shown in Figure F2. The model allows for two phases, with the short-term strategy being implemented in January 1997 and the long-term in approximately 18 months. The design team were mindful that the long-term elements might be modified as a result of changes to the corporate strategy or work undertaken by other human resource teams. The initial goal of the process was to implement a comprehensive framework that would maintain and build on the momentum

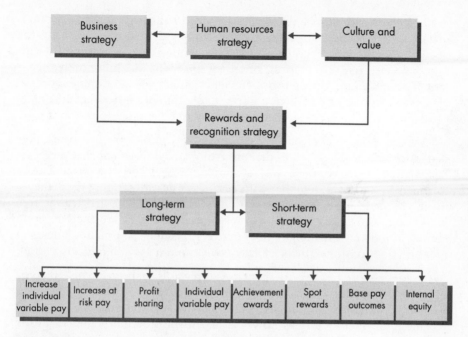

Figure F2 Reward and recognition strategy design

established by the Towards 2000 program. This allowed for significant emphasis to be placed on employee feedback and demonstration of change in behaviour to support the corporate goals.

Reward elements and their positioning

The design team wanted to ensure that there were tangible returns to employees who demonstrated clear commitment to SGS. The following reward elements were deiberately designed to provide such recognition to non-management employees.

Quality objectives bonus—This cash bonus is paid to individuals or teams for achievement of set quality-related objectives that support the business plan. The set objectives go beyond the normal requirements of the individual's role and are set at the beginning of the financial year. Each manager has a budget from which the quality objectives bonuses are paid.

Gainsharing award—Gainsharing is designed to recognise exceptional contributions or achievements that exceed expectations or goals defined for the individual's job. All non-management employees are eligible for a cash award designed to recognise significant achievements that result in product or system innovation leading to important progress in the completion of a project or particular research. The distinguishing feature of the gainsharing system is that it was designed to recognise contributions that improve directly the operating results of the company. The contribution may be technical, scientific or in research related areas, or an advancement in administrative techniques or procedures that improve efficiency, employee development or lead to cost reduction. The idea must contribute a minimum benefit of $10 000 per annum to SGS in order for the employee to be entitled to the award.

Achievement award—The achievement award is a non-monetary award presented to individuals or teams demonstrating an achievement that meets set criteria. Individual winners receive a prize to the value of $250 and team members $100. Prizes, together with certificates acknowledging the achievement, are made at a special presentation. Managers are supplied with a 'tool kit' of options from which they can select prizes and they are encouraged to consider the likely preferences of employees receiving the award. There are no restrictions on the number of awards that can be presented in any period.

Spot rewards—Spot rewards are spontaneous rewards to the value of $100 provided by managers where they see evidence of behaviour that helps the company to achieve the objectives set in the Towards 2000 program. Spot rewards include items such as a fresh flower arrangement, gourmet hamper, theatre tickets or lunch. The managers are required to document any award given to an employee as a means of reporting and monitoring the reward strategy.

Base pay—The short-term strategy for base pay is to communicate more clearly the criteria for which salary increases are granted and to provide more information in respect to the various classifications within the company. Performance considered to be below satisfactory level is given no increase; performance at satisfactory and above earns increases at the rate of CPI at the time of review. The overall salary structure and performance-based pay is to be reviewed as part of phase two of the reward strategy.

Rewards for managers also received attention at this stage. The following programs were specifically introduced for managers.

Success bonus—This is a bonus is based on actual profit with a threshold set at 95 per cent of budgeted profit and rising for budget and above performance.

Business strategy bonus—The business strategy bonus is set with a threshold of 80 per cent of the target profit together with a minimum of 60 per cent of the business objectives. As with the success bonus, payments increased as profit and business objectives are reached or exceeded.

Excellence in management award—This award is designed to recognise the managers who achieve excellence in all areas of management. A feature of this award is a review process completed by an individual manager's direct reports. The award is given where 100 per cent or greater of the target profit amount is achieved, 95 per cent or better of the objectives in the business plan are met and the manager receives a silver or gold rating in the upward management appraisal process.

Outcomes

The reward and recognition strategy was launched at a national conference in January 1997, followed by training sessions at various levels across the company. The design team members took on the role of implementing and managing the strategy. The team identified three core objectives they hoped the reward and recognition strategy would achieve for the company. Progress against these objectives is described below.

Equity—At SGS the principle of equity is the notion that what employees receive from their employer is equal in value to what they contribute to the company (time, energy, knowledge and skills). Furthermore, what employees receive is equal in value to that received by others doing similar work within the company.

Clarification—Designing and implementing a reward and recognition strategy demanded careful analysis of the objectives to be achieved. It was also necessary to determine what employee behaviours were required to achieve the SGS objectives. This information became the linchpin of the reward and recognition strategy. The business objectives are explained as the strategy is communicated to employees; in rewarding particular behaviours, the company clarifies what it is seeking from its staff. This is particularly important where a company is undergoing a cultural change and staff may be uncertain about what is expected of them. SGS has made significant progress in setting its business goals and objectives, and has expressed them in its statements of vision, mission and core values. The reward and recognition strategy has been one of the most effective ways of gaining support to important elements of SGS' business plan.

Motivation—A key objective was to encourage and inspire people to do their best. Individuals are motivated by different needs at different times. At SGS the reward and recognition strategy allowed for personal needs to be taken into account by incorporating a range of rewards and forms of recognition. In addition, the recognition was given in a timely and expedient way so that employees would understand exactly what behaviour earned the reward.

A preliminary look at the reward and recognition strategy to date reveals the following:

- The ultimate success of the reward and recognition strategy rests with the sector managers responsible for implementing the strategy in their day-to-day decisions. Most have followed the guidelines to provide concise and helpful information to staff for pay decisions, adhered to the grievance procedure in a fair and efficient manner, and implemented the performance appraisal process as planned.
- The HR manager's role is to coach and mentor other managers to ensure that the principles and objectives are followed consistently across the various business units. This requires the HR manager to gain their support and commitment without being seen to undermine any individual sector

manager's decision. It is also essential that the HR manager promotes and monitors the strategy and its impact on the business.

• While a range of human resource issues may be reviewed and modified simultaneously, a successful reward and recognition strategy is highly dependent on a certain level of organisation maturity. Managers need to possess a suitable management style and attitude conducive to SGS' business environment.

Superannuation—A changing landscape

8

Michaela Anderson

Since 1909 the Australian federal government has paid age pensions to eligible persons, meeting its age pension liability from current revenues. In the 1980s increasing consideration began to be given to the effect that Australia's ageing population would have on the government's ability to fund age pensions in the future. This problem is not confined to Australia: Europe, North and South America, Japan, New Zealand and some Asian counties have also been examining the provision of income for an ageing population. Australia is actually in a better position than many countries because of its highly targeted age pension system. The government was also under pressure to increase the level of national savings.

Changes to the funding of retirement began in the industrial relations arena as a result of an agreement between the government and the peak union body, the Australian Council of Trade Unions (ACTU). The parties decided that 3 per cent of wages would be paid into retirement savings funds by employers on behalf of their employees in lieu of a cash-in-hand wages increase. This arrangement was only partly successful and in 1992 the Superannuation Guarantee legislation was passed. It provides for progressive increases over 10 years so that by July 2002 all employees will have an amount

181

equal to 9 per cent of salary being paid into a retirement savings fund which meets the standards set by the government.

This compulsory saving for retirement forms one of the three pillars in the government's retirement income policy. The means-tested age pension remains as a safety net and the third pillar is encouragement of voluntary saving for retirement. Currently about 81 per cent of the workforce have superannuation. There are gaps in the compulsory coverage, particularly with the self-employed.

Central to the federal government's retirement incomes policy is the decision that the contributions made by employers and employees would be paid into privately administered and invested funds rather than into some central government fund. With the system in the hands of the private sector, the need for stricter prudential standards became increasingly apparent, particularly as massive amounts of money—some $304 billion in superannuation and rollover funds in mid-1997—began flowing into funds with the introduction of compulsory retirement savings. Consequently, in 1993 the federal government passed new prudential laws for retirement savings funds.

The chief characteristic of the Australian superannuation system is therefore that, although it is compulsory and heavily regulated and thus very much a government scheme, it facilitates extensive participation by the private sector and the highest degree of competition. It is a private sector competitive scheme operating within a government-mandated and regulated framework.

Today, the employer no longer decides who will get superannuation—it is a matter of law. That law also sets a minimum level of contributions from the employer. The law also restricts the involvement of the employer-sponsor in the management of the company fund.

Taxation

The tax system can be used to influence behaviour, particularly if the government wants to achieve a public policy objective, and it can be used to collect revenue. An examination of the history of taxation of superannuation shows that there is often friction between these two objectives.

The provision of tax concessions for superannuation forms a key part of the government's retirement income policy, particularly for the third pillar of voluntary saving. The objective is to encourage superannuation and thereby limit the demands on the public purse through the social security system. Within this framework it is clear that beyond certain limits, benefits received by individuals would not assist in the achievement of the government policy objective and concessional treatment may cause serious revenue losses. But why provide tax concessions when contributions are compulsory? Tax concessions can be seen as some compensation for the fact that the money is not available until retirement, and as a reward to the present generation for paying taxes to support the present pension payments while also saving enough to free the next generation from paying monstrous taxes for future pensions.

The government can intervene in superannuation at three stages—at the contribution stage, the investment stage and when the benefit is paid. In most countries revenue is collected when benefits are paid. It is simpler and allows for incentives and revenue collection to be introduced most efficiently and more equitably.

All superannuation fund members were once able to receive tax deductions for their superannuation contributions. Deductions were generally available to employers for contributions up to certain limits, and only 5 per cent of a superannuation lump sum payment was included in the recipient's taxable income—the rest was tax free. Pensions and annuities, on the other hand, were fully taxed as income. The tax system favoured lump sums and Australian's obsession with the lump sum was born. This was the golden age for the lucky minority with access to superannuation.

Contribution incentives

After 1975 the incentive diminished for most employee contributions, though, from 1 July 1998, a person will be able to claim a 15 per cent tax rebate for making undeducted contributions of up to $3000 to superannuation.

In relation to employer contributions, deductions were generally available up to certain limits. The effect has been to encourage salaried employees to fund superannuation by way of 'salary sacrifice' arrangements—by having the contributions made from pre-tax salary.

Prior to 20 August 1996 an employer had two options to determine the amount of deduction available for contributions made on behalf of employees. The first option was to use age-based limits. The second option, available where there were ten or more employees, allowed the employer to use the standard contribution method. This method enabled the employer, in some cases, to provide senior employees with contributions substantially greater than the age-based limits and claim a deduction for those contributions. From 20 August 1996 (budget night) the government announced that deductible superannuation contributions that employers make for their employees would be limited to the 'age-based limits'. The age-based limit (or employee's deduction limit) for the 1997–98 year of income is:

Age in years	Deduction limit
Under 35	$10 232
35 to 49	$28 420
50 and over	$70 482

An employer who contributes to an accumulation fund must use the age-based limits. While the amounts are generous, if a young employee (i.e. aged under 35) wants to salary sacrifice, the employer will be able to get a tax deduction up to $10 232, regardless of contributions actually made. This may be a disincentive for the employer to offer salary sacrifice above these age-based limits.

There is slightly more scope in a defined benefit fund for an employer to make a higher contribution for an individual employee, as deductible contributions are allowed based on the sum of the deduction limits of each employee for whom the employer is contributing.

These deduction limits make assumptions about when a person should or could put away large amounts of money for retirement, and some people do make their big money while they are young (e.g. those in some sports). The limits could have an impact on saving activity of individuals, as noted above, and they show the increasing intervention of government. The superannuation guarantee set a minimum contribution level for most of the company's employees, and the 1996 law set the upper limits of superannuation contributions for the company's employees.

Taxing benefits

In the history of super 1983 has to be seen as a mixed year. Under the new rules, lump sum benefits were taxed at the lower of 30 per cent or the recipient's marginal tax rate. So as not to upset anyone, the new rules applied only to that part of the benefit attributable to service after 1 July 1983 and thus was born the great tradition of 'grandfathering', which is another word for complexity.

On a positive note from a public policy perspective, government started to encourage people to keep their superannuation for retirement. An indexed threshold amount was taxed at 15 per cent if taken after age 55 and rollover funds were established to defer tax liability. Also importantly from an individual perspective, the government recognised undeducted member contributions and made them tax free.

Taxing fund income

Prior to 1 July 1988, the income of superannuation funds that satisfied the conditions of the *Income Taxation Assessment Act* was exempt from income tax. Government revenue was only collected when the benefit was paid from the fund—tax was paid by the recipient of the benefit. And that's the way it should still be! But the Treasurer of the day 'brought forward' the collection of revenue, and Income of the fund (deductible contributions, capital gains and investment income) was taxed at the rate of 15 per cent. This was meant to be compensated for by a reduction in tax on the end benefit.

As a result of the 1983 and 1988 changes to the taxation of superannuation, the system is extremely complicated, with a profusion of tax rates applying to the many different components of a benefit. I can find no redeeming public policy reason for the tax having been 'brought forward'—it was a straight out revenue grab. It complicated retirement savings and ultimately allowed that second revenue grab, the surcharge, to be introduced in the name of equity. Experts all agree that taxing at the contribution stage is the wrong way to go for simplicity and equity.

Limiting tax concessions

The reasonable benefits limit (RBL) is the maximum amount of superannuation and similar benefits (e.g. golden handshakes from employers on retirement) that a person is entitled to receive during his or her lifetime on a concessionally taxed basis. From 1965 until 25 May 1988, the Commissioner of Taxation had the statutory responsibility to decide what was 'reasonable'. He issued a plethora of bulletins outlining how he was determining what was reasonable. Broadly, a limit of 7 times final average salary (FAS) applied to lump sums, and a limit of 75 per cent of FAS applied to pensions. This was extremely generous.

Then the government decided to introduce a marginal RBL scale for lump sums and pensions. Members' undeducted contributions were excluded from the RBL. There was more grandfathering. You could see the revenue and equity intention but the whole thing was an administrative nightmare. The legislation didn't see the light if day. Instead in 1990 something very similar, but in my view even harder to explain, was introduced. This limped along until changes in 1994.

The RBL rules we have today are much simpler. The lump sum and pension RBLs are expressed as flat dollar amounts indexed annually to Average Weekly Ordinary Time Earnings. In 1998, the lump sum RBL was $454 718 and the pension RBL $909 435. There are 'transitional rules' to protect past entitlements and the Tax Office keeps a register of benefits received.

Only individual employees can know whether they are going to reach their respective RBL. It will depend on such things as how long they have been saving in the superannuation system, whether they are able to use some of the 'grandfathering' provisions, and how they intend to take the benefit (lump sum or at least half in complying pension).

Taxing contributions (surcharge)

As from 20 August 1996, all employer superannuation contributions (including salary sacrifice contributions) and deductible personal contributions of high income earners are subject to a tax (surcharge) on those contributions up to 15 per cent. For the 1996/97 year of income, the surcharge is phased in over the annual income range of $70 000–$85 000; these amounts are subject to indexation each year. The surcharge affects all types of superannuation plans and golden handshake benefits.

To establish if a person is subject to the surcharge, a person's adjusted taxable income needs to be determined. Adjusted taxable income includes taxable income (as shown on your personal tax return), all employer superannuation contributions, deductible member contributions and certain rolled over amounts (i.e. employer terminated payments).

The $70 000 lower threshold, at which the surcharge applies, includes superannuation contributions. Therefore, where taxable income is $65 000 and employer superannuation contributions are $20 000, the adjusted taxable income is $85 000, which incurs a 15 per cent surcharge on the $20 000 contribution (i.e. $3000).

Should a person in this situation consider repackaging their remuneration? Surcharge may seem a disincentive for salary packaging for superannuation in favour of some other form of packaging, such as fringe benefits. However, there is no guarantee, that the government will not change the definition of adjusted taxable income for surcharge purposes to include fringe benefit items in the future.

Fund design

Changes have also occurred in superannuation fund design—that is, the vehicle in which people save. Fund design is something which the company has traditionally decided.

Funds come in two general designs:

- defined benefit—where the final payment is generally based on a formula involving the member's salary and years of service;
- defined contribution (accumulation)—where the final benefit is the amount contributed by or on behalf of the member plus earnings, less any administration costs.

Some funds were hybrids: often the employer contributions provide a defined benefit and the employee contributions provide an accumulation benefit.

Traditionally, private sector companies and the public sector favoured defined benefits. This has changed over the last decade. The reasons are many but include a more mobile workforce, compulsory superannuation, and regulation which was more difficult to apply to defined benefits. This movement away from defined benefit funds is not confined to Australia.

My own view is that the major cause of change from defined benefit to defined contribution has been changes in work patterns. People no longer stay in a company for a working lifetime and there is a perception that defined benefits suit a pattern of employment that has gone. Of course it is possible to measure an accrued benefit and transfer it to a new fund quite easily, but in Australia we have not got a transfer mentality for defined benefits.

I also believe that high net worth individuals perceive that it is easier to control how much they are saving through superannuation in an accumulation fund, and employers should consider this factor carefully. What is needed is flexibility for contributions, something that is not always found in a defined benefit scheme, but is possible with a bit of creative design.

Diversity of funds

The superannuation industry is now much more diverse than it was ten years ago and the changes are expected to continue as employers and the industry respond to government policy and commercial possibilities and competition.

In general, superannuation funds can be divided into two main types: employer-sponsored and personal superannuation. In the first category are:

- company funds—established by a single employer for its employees;
- public sector funds—established by governments (local, state, federal and public utilities) for public sector employees;
- industry funds—these are multi-employer funds, generally established for a specific industry or range of industries by employer organisations and unions; most industry superannuation funds were established during the last 10 years.

In the second category are:

- retail—offered by a range of financial institutions and sold to anyone eligible to contribute to superannuation, or holding superannuation savings for retirement;
- self-managed funds—funds with fewer than 5 members, officially called 'excluded funds'.

Of course it is never as simple as it seems. Some of these distinctions are getting very blurred. With the implementation of the government's proposal for employees to be given a choice of fund, the industry expects radical change in the composition. One of those predicted changes is the decline in the number of company funds.

For executives, the alternatives to the company fund are usually the retail funds which offer a choice of investment and the self-managed fund.

Do-it-yourself

One of the growth areas in the last 5 years has been the excluded or self-managed funds set up generally by individuals who are self-employed, have a small business or are high net worth individuals. By 1998, there were over 156 600 of them with assets of some $35 billion (11 per cent of the total $304 billion). The attraction is that if you are the trustee of the fund, you can do your own investing. Again it is not as simple as it seems: compliance rules must be followed if you want the tax concessions, administration can be time consuming and advice can be costly. The regulator, the Insurance and Super-annuation Commission, has prepared a guide but a fund would be difficult to set up and maintain without good advice from an independent professional.

There has been a lot of discussion about the use of trusts in relation to these funds. You can't borrow to invest in your superannuation fund. You can, however, set up a unit trust, and use it as a go-between. For example, if you want to invest in a property for $400 000 and only have $200 000 in your self-managed fund, you can set up a unit trust, with the super fund paying for half of the units in the trust. The other $200 000 is borrowed and the unit trust then buys the property.

The investment and tax strategies of self-managed funds vary considerably. Some have quite exotic investments in art, antiques and other collectibles. (The regulator seems to be quite satisfied with this as long as the trustee knows the area thoroughly.) Implementing tax strategies such as managing dividend imputations, or using negative gearing for investments in property, shares or managed funds, require that the executive has full control of the situation.

Choice of fund

The final straw for many employers is that employees can now choose a fund. Control of various areas—who is eligible for superannuation, minimum contribution and vesting levels, and who runs the fund—has gradually been removed from the employer. Until the change announced in the 1997 budget, the choice of what fund would receive employer contributions had remained in the hands of the employer, subject to award obligations for some sections of the workforce. Now the employer must submit five choices to the employee.

The impact on corporate funds will be massive. They will have to compete for members unless the employer uses a 'workplace agreement' to become exempt from the choice rules. The details were not available as of July 1998, causing many companies to ask 'why bother to run our own fund?'. One large employer, the Commonwealth government, has signalled that it intends to move out of the superannuation business and will not offer a 'company fund' to new employees.

Choice of fund will certainly challenge defined benefit funds, even those which provide additional benefits for executives. Some employers believe that medium to large employers should provide one single company fund with a simple benefit design as it can still be a positive influence on employee relations.

Investment options

One of the more interesting pieces of recent research on investment options was conducted by Stephen Jackman and Ben Kerry of William M. Mercer Investment Consulting. They looked at four investment options for two investors—one on average weekly earnings; the other on the top marginal tax rate with an income which would make the surcharge applicable. The investment options were a standard investment account with a bank, superannuation using salary sacrifice and using after-tax contributions, Australian shares and home loan payoff. Each investor was assumed to have $1000 of pre-tax income (indexed from 1977 to allow for increases in salary) to invest at the start of each financial year.

For our purpose of examining whether there has been a change—or a fading—of the effectiveness of saving through superannuation, they looked at the twenty years ending 30 June 1997, reflecting the impact of the tax changes as they occurred, including capital gains tax, dividend imputation and so on. They then assumed that the taxation and superannuation environment as at 30 June 1997 applied for the period 1997 to 2017. This gives us a projection into the future, assuming, of course, that there are no changes to the rules.

For the 20-year period from 1977 to 1997 (the historical comparison), the best investment for both the person on average weekly earnings and the person on top marginal rate was superannuation using a salary sacrifice arrangement (see Table 8.1). This continued to be the case even after taxes were introduced in the 1980s. The next best option was Australian shares. The third best option was superannuation from after-tax contributions, followed by home loan pay-off and finally an investment account with a bank.

Looking into the future, the most interesting part is that superannuation through a salary sacrifice arrangement continues to be the best option, but it is more advantageous for the investor on average weekly earnings. Then the ranking changes. Home loan payoff is ranked second for our investor on top

Table 8.1 Comparison of savings options (ranking 1–5)

	First investor (Average weekly earnings)		Second investor (Top marginal tax rate)	
	Return	**Rank**	**Return**	**Rank**
Historical comparison				
Investment account	$41 000	5	$27 500	5
Home loan	$83 600	4	$58 400	4
Superannuation				
—after-tax contribution	$91 000	3	$62 000	3
Superannuation				
—salary sacrifice	$131 700	1	$131 400	1
Australian shares	$104 900	2	$63 800	2
Comparison based on current taxation and superannuation regime				
Investment account	$43 400	5	$31 500	5
Home loan	$91 500	3	$73 000	2
Superannuation				
—after tax contribution	$81 000	4	$64 500	4
Superannuation				
—salary sacrifice	$104 000	1	$85 600	1
Australian shares	$100 700	2	$70 800	3

marginal rate, followed by Australian shares, superannuation from after tax contributions and an investment account with a bank.

A word of caution about the rankings: the investors' Reasonable Benefit Limit was not considered in this study. For high income earners in particular this could reduce the attractiveness of superannuation. However, exceeding the RBL is not the end of the world. Financial advisers will tell you to view it as a tax planning opportunity.

Spouse comparisons

From 1 July 1997, a person will be able to contribute to a superannuation account opened in the name of their spouse. The person will be able to claim an 18 per cent tax rebate on the first $3000 of these contributions for the spouse, where the spouse earns less than $10 800 per year. The maximum rebate will be $450 and cuts out completely when the spouse's income reaches $13 800. This has been hailed as a move to help women who have time out of the workforce to accumulate superannuation. Although the break in the nexus of paid work and superannuation is welcomed, the change means more for high income groups and it is not the rebate which is the big prize.

There seems to be no limit on the amount that can be contributed to the spouse's account each year, although the rebate is limited. The spouse could therefore accumulate superannuation up to the RBL.

This could be very useful if the working spouse is in danger of hitting his or her RBL. It looks like the advantages of being a traditional 'couple' are improving, as long as you are wealthy. A recent newspaper article demonstrated how a wealthy couple could have almost $2 million in tax-advantaged superannuation. This would be the case if both husband and wife fund up to the pension RBL of $909 435 each.

The spouse contributions are treated as undeducted contributions which means they avoid the 15 per cent fund income tax (only the earnings are taxed) so the full value of the contribution is invested. When the benefit is received, the undeducted contributions are not taxed and the first $90 474 of the benefit is tax free. Undeducted contributions do not count towards a person's RBL.

Anyone can use this strategy by taking the money out of other assets and putting it into the spouse's retirement account, providing the spouse is under 65.

The next step might be to use the tax advantages of income streams in retirement. By buying flexible allocated pensions, a husband and wife could receive a combined tax-free income of around $42 000 (given the 15 per cent rebate allowed on the income). If undeducted contributions are used to purchase the allocated pension, the amount of the tax-free income could be much higher.

Financial advice

Many companies provide information about the superannuation that they provide, most targeted to those close to retirement. If an employer wants to deliver optimum value in remuneration to executives, it will need to provide access to advice rather than information. And this advice needs to be available during the saving phase, not only just prior to retirement. Most of the responsibility for determining retirement saving strategies now rests with the individual and the strategies will be tailored to the individual's circumstances. The options open within superannuation will depend on many factors—what saving the executive already has in the superannuation system, risk tolerance, age, sex, marital status, other investments, planned retirement age, time and inclination run a self-managed fund and so on.

It is important to get the right adviser. A company or an individual seeking to assess the skill and professional standing of the advising company should ask:

- Is the advising company licensed by the Australian Securities Commission?
- What is the adviser's experience in giving advice? Ask for examples.
- Does the adviser charge by fees, commission or both?
- Does the adviser provide written reports?
- What are the educational qualifications?
- Does the adviser have professional indemnity insurance?

Some companies already engage the services of reputable, independent financial planners for their senior staff. Some employers engage planners only when they are about to bundle some senior staff out on early 'retirement'. Some executives will already have sought investment/planning advice independently.

Successive governments have made many changes to superannuation, but it remains a tax efficient and attractive means of saving for retirement, either through employer contributions or a member's own contributions. We should not forget what superannuation provides:

- investment income taxed at 15 per cent (even lower with allowance for imputation credits from Australian company shares); compare this to investments which incur tax at marginal rates;
- from 1 July 1997, a person is able to make contributions for their spouse, and, depending on the spouse's income of the spouse and the amount of the contributions, claim a tax rebate of up to $540 per year, and the spouse has a separate RBL;
- from 1 July 1998, a person is able to claim a tax rebate for making undeducted contributions of up to $3000 to superannuation;
- employers' contributions are tax deductible up to certain limits;
- lump sum benefits paid by superannuation funds are taxed at concessional rates, particularly if over 55 the first $90 474 (1997/98 figure) is tax free;

- most superannuation pensions and annuities purchased receive a 15 per cent tax rebate—about $21 000 per year is tax free.

Conclusion

The role of superannuation in our society has changed from a remuneration mechanism used by companies for selected workers to a central pillar of compulsory saving in the government's retirement income policy. As a consequence, the role of the employer in superannuation has also changed. The employer is no longer in control of fund eligibility, minimum or maximum levels of contributions, or of managing the company superannuation fund. Soon the employee will be able to choose which fund to contribute to.

Superannuation is complex, especially for high net worth individuals, and the rewards for saving in superannuation will vary, as they are linked to individual circumstances including timing, sex, personal relationships and attitude to risk. The employer must ask the executive what role superannuation will play in his or her reward. The best service employers can offer to executives is access to independent financial advice so that they are able to make that very personal decision.

9 Managing diversity

Robin Kramar

The term 'managing diversity' is increasingly being used by Australian managers. Managing diversity is concerned with more than the creation of equal employment opportunity (EEO) outcomes and legal compliance. It is an approach to management explicitly concerned with the integration of people management and business issues, together with the development of a workplace culture that acknowledges the need to manage the similarities and differences between contributors to the organisation. These contributors include not only employees, but also other people who provide labour and ideas such as contractors, consultants, customers and suppliers.

This chapter examines the concept of diversity management and its implications for human resource management practices. The first part identifies the major principles underpinning this approach to management, how it differs from affirmative action and the reasons for the development of this management approach. The second part examines the process of diversity management and the implications for managing a workforce at three levels—strategic, managerial and operational. The strategic level involves a philosophy that acknowledges and values the differences and similarities between people and recognises these differences as critical for organisational success. The managerial level involves the formulation of formal management practices and structures that facilitate the expression of this philosophy. The third level is concerned with the implementation of these practices and therefore is concerned with the ability of individuals to manage and work with diverse contributors. One of the issues that needs to be examined during the implementation stage is the barriers which could be encountered.

The nature of diversity management

Diversity management is a process of management, particularly human resource management, underpinned by a set of values that recognise differences between people as a strength for management. The concept of diversity management incorporates four notions, set out below.

- *Managing the differences and similarities between individuals.* Managing diversity involves managing similarities and differences at the same time. This process of managing can be examined from the subjective or objective point of view. Subjectively, diversity refers to a sense of 'otherness' based on those human qualities that differ from our own. Objectively, it refers to the vast array of personal and cultural differences that constitute the human race. The management of these differences involves managing relationships between individuals with different personal and cultural characteristics, and the associated tensions that often exist.
- *Specification of the dimensions of diversity.* These dimensions can be considered in terms of two categories known as the primary (or observable) and the secondary (underlying or non-observable) dimensions of diversity. The primary dimension includes such immutable characteristics as gender, age, race, physical abilities/qualities, race and sexual orientation. The secondary dimension includes characteristics that can be changed, such as educational background, marital and parental status, geographic location, income, religious beliefs, work, functional background, organisational tenure, personality characteristics and military experience. These dimensions shape individuals' perceptions of their environment and their method and style of communication (Loden & Rosener 1991, p. 21; Jackson, May & Whitney, 1995). A program designed to manage diversity therefore requires identification of the specific dimensions being addressed in the program. For instance, a diversity management program could identify parental status and an older workforce as dimensions being specifically targeted by the program.
- *Management of a collective, all-inclusive mixture of differences and similarities along a particular dimension* (Thomas 1995, p. 246). For instance, the management of the dimension of parental status is not just dealing with the management of those employees with pre-school age children, school and university age children or aged parents, but it is also dealing with a collective mixture of employees with these responsibilities as well as those employees without these responsibilities. This process involves acknowledging that employees

without dependent children could resent the provision of employment conditions, such as leave without pay, special family leave or child care facilities for those employees with dependants.

- *A process of managing 'inclusion', rather than a process of assimilating different groups to a dominant organisational culture.* This process requires mechanisms that allow the effective involvement of all organisational members in the process of diversity management and the development of a new workplace culture. Such an approach also requires acknowledgment of the need to define what 'differences' will not be valuable for the organisation. One way this can be done is to use the mission and the corporate values as the basis of decisions.

Diversity is not neutral. It requires an acknowledgment that differences between employees exist in the workplace, and these differences must be managed. 'Without an environment that works well for all employees, diversity works against you, simply because you do not have an enabling environment' (Thomas 1991, p. 49).

Different from affirmative action and equal employment opportunity

Although diversity management is often explained as the next generation of affirmative action (Kramar 1996), it is more appropriately considered as an approach to management. The conceptualisation of diversity management in terms of affirmative action and EEO outcomes orients the framing of issues to aspects of legal compliance and the development of policies that remove discrimination against specified groups. In Australia, groups identified by federal and/or state legislation are defined in terms of personal characteristics such as gender, race, physical ability, ethnic heritage and family responsibilities. Discrimination and affirmative action legislation require the removal of policies and the prevention of behaviour that hinder individuals with particular personal characteristics having fair and equitable access to employment opportunities and the rewards associated with this employment.

The requirements of the federal *Affirmative Action (Equal Employment Opportunity for Women) Act 1986* (the Act), emphasises legal compliance and the submission of annual reports to the Affirmative Action Agency (the Agency). The scope of the Act is narrow because it only requires employers with 100 or more employees to remove direct and indirect discrimination from their employment policies and practices. The coverage of the Act is restricted to one target group only (women), and to one type of stakeholder (managerial and non-managerial employees). Although it requires some participation of employees, particularly women and their representative trade unions, this participation is limited to a process of consultation about the development of an affirmative action program.

The administrative requirements of the Act encourage the integration of human resource issues with business issues. The new reporting form distributed by the Agency is designed to assist employers to comply with the Act and to provide a strategic planning model that links affirmative action to organisational goals and objectives. Although the form explicitly links affirmative action programs to business goals, the link reflects a cascading down of policy. The link is framed in terms of the policies designed to promote affirmative action contributing to the achievement of established business goals, rather than issues associated with equality and equity influencing the business goals of the organisation.

The Commonwealth government's Industry Task Force on Leadership and Management Skills reported on its examination of the process of managing for diversity. The Task Force report, known as the Karpin Report (1995), made recommendations for action in six areas associated with diversity. These were:

1 women in senior and executive management;
2 women on boards of publicly listed companies;
3 women and management education;
4 women and small business;
5 the management of cultural diversity;
6 indigenous people's labour market participation and business activity.

Burton (1995, p. 67) demonstrates that a managing for diversity approach is consistent with the Karpin Report's recommendations for effective management in a future competive environment. For instance, managers need to move from a short-term tactical focus to a longer-term strategic focus and they need to shift from valuing homogeneity to acknowledging diversity as a source of difference. Training materials have been developed to encourage the development of skills and values consistent with a managing for diversity approach among Australian managers (Edith Cowan University 1996).

Aspects of the diverse nature of the workforce are already recognised through leave for childcare responsibilities (e.g. maternity, paternity and adoption leave, taking sick leave to care for ill dependants and management development programs specifically designed for women). In addition, some organisations, such as the Australian Public Service, recognise the need of some groups to take religious holidays that differ from those of Christian members of the community. However, these policies do not represent a diversity management approach. These policies provide for equal treatment in terms of making concessions so that employees with certain personal or domestic arrangements can assimilate into the prevailing employment patterns. The quest for EEO has been sought through 'laws and practices that demand similar treatment' (Chen 1992, p. 32). These policies do not start from a focus on organisational success or from a recognition that there is a need to acknowledge that organisational success can be achieved through utilising different employment patterns and practices for different groups.

This point is illustrated very clearly by Krautil who makes reference to wild animals in the zoo. She says:

Imagine your organisation is a giraffe house. Equal opportunity has been very effective widening the door of the giraffe house to let the elephant in, but home won't be best for the elephant unless a number of major modifications are made to the inside of the house. Without these changes the house will remain designed for giraffes and the elephant will not 'feel at home'. (Krautil 1995, p. 22)

Reasons for the development of the concept of diversity management

The need for a diversity management approach is argued for in terms of four issues. These are framed in terms of a 'business case' associated with competing effectively in the labour market, as a source of competitive advantage, as a means of effectively adapting to change and also on ideological grounds.

The arguments in terms of the 'business case' focus on the changes expected in the composition of the workforce. A popular reason given for the implementation of diversity management in western industrial countries is the expected changes in the demographics of the population and the workforce (Loden & Rosener 1991; Thomas 1991; Loden & Loeser 1991). Projections of the changes in the population and the workforce indicate women, older workers and workers from a wider variety of ethnic and cultural groups will constitute a larger proportion of the workforce and a larger source of new labour. In Australia, it is predicted male and female workers in the 45–54 year age group will increase their representation in the workforce during the period to 2005 by 33 per cent and 51 per cent respectively. During the same period, representation of workers in the 55 to 64 years age group will increase from 7.6 per cent to 9.1 per cent (Patrickson 1994).

These changes are similar to those predicted in other western industrialised countries. For instance, in the United States it is predicted that over the next 20 years Hispanics, blacks and Asians will account for about 87 per cent of the growth of the workforce and women will represent almost half of the workforce (Loden and Rosener 1991, p. 7). Similarly, the percentage of the workforce aged over 65 years will increase from the current 12 per cent up to approximately 22 per cent in 2030 (American Association of Retired Persons 1995, p. 3).

It is argued these changes will increase competition among employers for skilled labour and consequently have implications for the way employees will be managed (Thomas 1991; Rodgers 1993, p. 26). It will become important that employers be seen as employers of preferred choice. One way of becoming such an employer will be by providing employment conditions that are attractive to prospective employees and by developing and marketing jobs in such a way that they deal with the concerns of these people.

A second reason for a diversity management approach is a recognition that as markets become increasingly international, and as the demography of the population changes, so will the demographic characteristics of customers. It is argued customer service and products can be more effectively provided if an organisation's workforce mirrors its customers (Loden & Rosener 1991). For instance, in areas with high representations of migrant groups, organisations providing customer services such as real estate agents and bank branches will staff their agencies/branches with employees drawn from these migrant groups—or at least with an understanding of their language and culture.

A third reason often used for a managing diversity approach is that it facilitates organisational and cultural change. The continuing major changes in world economies and markets require organisations to be adaptable and flexible in the way they operate. Adaptability can be achieved in a number of ways, including ensuring a heterogeneous group of individuals is involved in making business and human resource management decisions. This will limit the influence of groupthink and cloning.

A team of people from a variety of backgrounds is more able to contribute to an organisation's competitive advantage by improving marketing, through enhanced creativity and innovation and improved problem solving (Cox & Blake 1991). If predictions are correct that the percentage of the population, and therefore potential customers aged 65 years and over, will increase from the current 12 per cent to 20 per cent in 2026 (ABS 1991), the importance of including older workers as members of these teams is apparent. Older workers also have corporate memory, wisdom and a longer time perspective which could contribute to organisational effectiveness.

A fourth reason for the development of a managing diversity approach is one which reflects an ideology around the contribution of individuals. This is consistent with the human resource management direction based on the notion of matching the needs of the individual to those of the organisation, and integrating human resource decisions with business decisions (Storey 1992). Proponents of this approach place emphasis on maximising the potential of individuals as gifted and creative, an emphasis which is consistent with managing diversity. Such an approach to employee management requires determination and evaluation of commonly held stereotypes about these groups and it challenges the view that individuals outside the dominant culture are deficient.

The Karpin Report acknowledged the value of a less homogeneous managerial workforce as a means of dealing with an increasingly competitive environment. The report predicted that by the year 2010 senior managers would have more diverse personal characteristics than they do in the 1990s. Furthermore, in 2010 senior managers would come from a wider range of ethnicities and citizenships compared to the senior manager in the 1990s who is typically male and Anglo-Celtic with Australian citizenship. It was also predicted that these senior managers of the future would be required to work in 'nondiscriminatory environments', will require skills to manage customers from diverse cultural backgrounds, and have greater cross-cultural awareness (Industry Task Force on Leadership and Management Skills 1995, p. 136).

Management of diversity

As mentioned previously, the management of diversity operates at three levels: the strategic level recognises diversity as critical for organisational success; the managerial level is associated with the formulation of management practices and structures that facilitate the effective operation of diversity; the operational level in which the practices are implemented in the workplace. The building of a culture that supports diversity requires that the following issues be addressed at each level.

Strategic

The key aspects of this level involve issues such as specifying and building the desired organisational culture, improving management systems, developing leaders for the future and developing business strategy with awareness of the nature of the population and workforce changes. This section briefly examines the processes associated with managing these desired outcomes in relation to older workers.

The building of a culture concerned explicitly with managing older workers as contributors to the organisation requires understanding three dimensions of culture: the nature of the existing culture, the dimensions of the desired culture and the way in which the roots of the existing culture hinder the development of the desired culture. The dimensions of the existing culture can be established through a cultural audit. Thomas (1991) suggests this audit can be done by either an outside consultant—who can bring a degree of objectivity—or, in circumstances when trust is high within the organisation, by organisational members, with the assistance of an outside consultant. This process can involve in-depth interviews, written surveys, reviews of relevant organisational documents (such as reports, manuals, memoranda), focus groups and direct observation of organisational members' behaviour. The data collected are then used as the basis for drawing inferences about the attitudes of organisational members toward the issue of diversity.

Among the steps associated with building a culture that values diversity are: first, organisational values must be clarified so they reflect respect of the needs of individuals; and second, the need for mutual adaptation by individuals and the organisation and involvement of all contributors in decision-making. These values could then shape policies about management development and organisational structure. When the organisation is considered as a community of contributor relationships (Saul 1996), it is formally acknowledged that individuals can contribute to organisational performance and success through a variety of relationships that differ in terms of their intended purpose and expected duration. Contributions can be made as part of the strategic or flexible workforce, as customers or as contractors. Saul (1996, p. 19–36) argues that different management styles and expectations are required for different contributors, and that there will be movement between the relationships associated with different types of contributions. For instance, older workers could choose to move from full-time employment to the role of consultant:

by doing so, they still provide expert advice and knowledge of the practices within the organisation to existing members, and at the same time, better meet their own needs.

The next component of the cultural audit involves assessing formal procedures such as human resource policies. This assessment provides the means to examine the extent to which the organisation's policies actually support or hinder the desired culture, particularly a culture that values diversity. For instance, policies about hours of work should be based on satisfying the needs of the business, as well as the individual. This can be achieved in a variety of ways and may involve job sharing, telecommuting or contracting the work out. It could also involve scheduling meetings at times which do not conflict with responsibilities outside the workplace. In the case of older workers, it could suit them to work fewer hours so they are able to develop interests that they can pursue during retirement.

Esso has explicitly linked diversity management to its business through its mission statement and three of its six core values. The mission is to be Australia's most successsful petroleum exploration and production company. Two core values, *teamwork* and *concern for the individual*, and the critical success factor for achieving the third core value of *achieving business excellence* (maximising the productivity of our people), provide the means of linking diversity management and strategic management.

Esso conducted a culture audit to provide the company with an assessment of employee perceptions of the extent to which members of Esso behaved in terms of the six core values, and the effectiveness of its formal and informal people management processses. The culture audit surveyed 27 per cent of the Esso workforce and provided data for the development of priority areas for action at the managerial level (Krautil 1995, p. 24–25).

Managerial

Once the review of human resource policies has been undertaken it is necessary to formulate policies to provide for—and support—diversity management. These policies include procedures and criteria for such things as employment structures and working hours, recruitment and selection, career paths, promotion, performance management systems (particularly performance indicators), training and development, mentoring, communication and difference management, the nature of competencies (wisdom, continuity, sense of history), reward systems, succession planning, and support services such as elder care for family members and employee assistance programs.

This stage involves integrating these policies to support the philosophy promoted by diversity management. This can be done in a variety of ways. For example, Honeywell uses a management practices index to correlate management styles and perceptions on bias. Four main areas are used to delineate management style: *building rapport, supporting development, acknowledging value* and *recognising individuality*. These dimensions are included in selection, appraisal and pay settings, and employees are assessed and rewarded partly in terms of these dimensions.

At Digital the aim is to make the principle of managing diversity an integrated part of management practice. It is part of management duties and is built into the manager's career structure. Digital's performance appraisal and reward systems take account of how managers meet affirmative action and EEO goals (Hall 1996, p. 15). Similar arrangements exist in Westpac where managers need to meet EEO targets as well as their traditional quarterly financial targets (Gillespie 1995).

At Esso, the data from the cultural audit provided information for the review of human resource policies. It demonstrated that many policies including in areas such as recruitment, training, working conditions, compensation, hiring, benefits, termination and transfers and promotion needed to be reviewed. The first step taken was to assist supervisors to create a supportive environment and to clarify those behaviours considered unacceptable. In addition, a workshop for supervisors was developed to enable them to understand their managerial style and to develop a style consistent with supporting diversity. Themes of valuing and managing difference were also integrated into training courses that deal with people issues or management. Furthermore, with the assistance of employee relations staff, individual departments developed diversity initiatives consistent with their respective business priorities (Krautil 1995, pp. 26–7).

Operational

Managers and supervisors are critical change agents in the process of building a culture that values diversity on a number of dimensions, including age. They also play a central role as educators and trainers. Managers and supervisors must implement the policies designed to create an effective diverse workforce, if there is to be any chance of creating a culture in which every employee has the opportunity to do his/her best work. It is therefore critical that individuals who understand the nature of diversity are selected for these positions and that their supportive behaviour is recognised in performance indicators and organisational reward structures.

Responses to diversity

The response of managers and employees to diversity can take a number of forms. Thomas (1995, pp. 249–52) identifies these in eight response options appropriate in different circumstances. Only one of these responses—*foster adaption*—unequivocally endorses diversity. However, Thomas claims each response could be appropriate in certain circumstances. For instance, in situations where older and younger workers differ substantially about how work should be done, the response of segregation could be the most appropriate.

The eight responses identified by Thomas are exclusion, denial, suppression, segregation, assimilation, toleration, building relationships and fostering mutual adaption. He defines these responses in the following way:

- *exclusion*—this involves keeping members of diverse groups out or expelling diverse groups once they have been included (e.g. selection criteria that identify candidates with high potential for success can also limit the amount of diversity in an organisation).
- *denial*—individuals may ignore diversity dimensions as a means of denying the differences between individuals. Thomas (1995, p. 249) expresses this as 'They look at a green jelly bean and see only a jelly bean. Examples include managerial aspirations to be colour-blind, gender-blind, or school-blind'.
- *suppression*—individuals are encouraged to suppress their differences. For example, individuals with unique social views may be encouraged not to express their philosophies for the sake of maintaining good team spirit or minimising conflict.
- *segregation*—this refers to clustering members of particular groups in certain occupations or departments.
- *assimilation*—attempts to transform members of a diverse group into clones of the dominant group are examples of assimilation. Many elements of affirmative action programs promote assimilation. Similarly, when an organisation makes an acquisition, differences between the acquired and the parent organisations are sought to be minimised by making members of the acquired organisation like the members of the parent organisation.
- *toleration*—in this situation different groups acknowledge the right for other groups to exist, but they take steps to minimise the interaction between the groups.
- *building relationships*—this approach assumes that building a good relationship will overcome differences. Although this approach has the potential to foster acceptance and understanding of differences, often it is used to minimise differences.
- *fostering mutual adaption*—this involves all parties accepting and understanding differences and diversity, recognising that such an approach will probably require changes in the culture and systems of the organisation.

Communication of the policies, support systems

Successful programs have been found to communicate the importance of the diversity philosophy in a variety of ways. These include personal intervention by top management, targeting recruitment of non-managers, internal advocacy groups, emphasising EEO statistics and profiles, providing for managing diversity training networks and support groups, and providing specific strategies that explicitly seek to manage work and personal needs such as family needs (Galagan 1993).

Barriers to managing diversity

Barriers to managing diversity can arise from a number of areas. These include inexperience with the process, the nature of communication and decision-making in organisations, misdiagnosis of management issues and attitudes—including thinking of diversity in terms of identity group representation (Thomas & Ely 1996, p. 80). These barriers need to be addressed to effectively implement policies designed to promote diversity,.

Diversity, with regard to such issues as age, lifestyle preference and priorities with respect to families, has always existed in organisations; however individuals often suppress it to conform to an accepted employee stereotype. Because it was always suppressed, organisations are having trouble dealing with diversity around race and gender issues (Solomon 1991, p. 91), and in future, they will also have difficulties managing issues around age.

The nature of organisational decision-making and management selection acts to prevent the entry of managers with diverse personal characteristics. Managers prefer working with individuals similar to themselves because of ease of communication and sense of comfort (Kanter 1977). This dynamic has been labelled *homosocial reproduction* and could prevent the selection and promotion of older workers.

Galagan (1993) lists six barriers that further inhibit effective management of diversity: *prejudice* (equating difference with deficiency), *poor career planning*, a lonely, hostile or unsupportive *environment* for non-traditional managers; lack of *organisational know-how* by non-traditional managers, people more *comfortable* with their own kind, and difficulties in *balancing* family and career. She also identifies a tendency for managers to reach conclusions without understanding the problems. A pertinent example is the view that high female staff turnover is related to family commitments. In fact she found only 7 per cent of female managers leave for family reasons, while 73 per cent leave because they see limited opportunities for women in companies.

In addition to the problems of misdiagnosis there are major attitudinal barriers to effective management of diversity. These include a denial of the issues, a lack of awareness, restrictions on bad news further up the organisation, a lack of trust in how others will react to diversity issues; a need to be in control of all of one's job; compulsion to fix them not us; issues outside own reality; and past actions to address diversity which were well intended but failed to develop an individual for a job, and/or others were not well developed with them.

Thomas (1991) claims resistance can emanate from a variety of factors associated with perceptions and attitudes in the workplace, and from a lack of strong leadership and direction. He identifies factors such as insufficient motivation resulting from perceptions that diversity management is a legal, moral or social responsibility, rather than as a business issue; from a commitment to assimilation; insufficient understanding of organisational culture; the presence of attitudes such as racism and sexism; a detrimental view of affirmative action and a belief that efforts to introduce diversity are an attempt to introduce affirmative action; lack of a strategic direction; a desire to avoid risk; insufficient leadership; lack of power to succeed; inadequate change management skills; too many other activities and the way work is done.

Problems can often arise when diversity management programs do not acknowledge the 'other' (e.g. white, young male). For diversity management to be effective all groups in the workplace need to perceive that employment policies operate to satisfy their needs as well as those of individuals with different personal characteristics. Therefore a diversity program specifically addressing the needs of older workers—by introducing special pre-retirement planning and paid leave for medical attention—should also explain how existing policies—such as funding of management education programs and fitness centres—address the needs of many young males. All groups benefit and can be seen to benefit as much from diversity programs as do older members of the organisation, women and ethnic and Aboriginal groups. Policies designed to enable different groups to work effectively need to be developed and communicated as ways of achieving organisational objectives for this to happen.

Conclusion

Diversity management will provide an opportunity to manage a *heterogeneous* workforce which will probably include a higher proportion of older workers, and at the same time increase organisational performance. This approach to management requires building a culture that supports diversity among organisational contributors through strategic processes such as a cultural audit. It also involves the development of human resource policies that attempt to deal explicitly with stereotypes of older workers and the employment conditions required to enhance their performance. Finally, to be effective, the reaction of other contributors to the presence of older workers and other barriers needs to be identified and addressed. Unlike affirmative action programs, the stimulus for diversity management will primarily be the continuing search for organisational effectiveness.

References

American Association of Retired Persons (AARP) 1995, *The Aging Workforce: Managing an Aging Workforce*, AARP, Washington.

Australian Bureau of Statistics 1991, *Projections of the populations of Australia, States and Territories*, Series D projections (Catalogue no. 3220).

Burton, C. 1995, 'Managing for diversity: Report to Karpin', in Davis, E.M. and Harris, C. (eds), *Making the Link*, no. 6, Affirmative Action Agency and the Labour Management Studies Foundation, Sydney; pp. 66–71.

Chen, C. 1992, 'The diversity paradox', *Personnel Journal*, January, pp. 32–5.

Cox, T.H. & Blake, S. 1991, 'Managing cultural diversity: Implications for organisational competitiveness', *Academy of Management Executive*, vol. 5, no. 3, pp. 45–56.

Edith Cowan University 1996, 'Gender issues in management', Curriculum material produced for the Industry Task Force on Leadership and Management Skills, *Enterprising Nation*, AGPS, Canberra.

Galagan, P. 1991, 'Tapping the power of a diverse workforce', *Training and Development Journal*, March, pp. 38–44.

—— 1993, 'Leading diversity', *Training and Development Journal*, April.

Gillespie, J. 1995, 'How to be heard by business—A customer centred and cost benefit approach to diversity policies', Recruiting, Developing and Retaining the Corporate Woman, IBC Conference, 30 and 31 October.

Hall, P. 1996, *Affirmative Action and Managing Diversity*, Monograph no. 5, Australian Government Publishing Service, Canberra.

Jackson, S.E., May, K.E. & Whitney, K. 1995, 'Understanding the dynamics of diversity in decision making teams', in Guzzo, R.A. and Salas, E. (eds), *Team Effectiveness and Decision Making in Organisations*, Jossey-Bass, San Francisco, CA; pp. 204–61.

Kanter, R.M. 1977, *Men and Women of the Corporation*, Basic Books, New York.

Kramar, R. 1996, 'Equal employment opportunities', in Warner, M. et al. (eds), *International Encyclopaedia of Business and Management*, Routledge, London.

Krautil, F. 1995, 'Managing diversity in Esso Australia', in Davis, E.M. and Harris, C. (eds), *Making the Link*, no. 6, Affirmative Action Agency and the Labour Management Studies Foundation, Sydney; pp. 22–8.

Loden, M. & Loeser, R.H. 1991, 'Working diversity: Managing the difference', *The Bureaucrat*, Spring, pp. 21–5.

Loden, M. & Rosener, J.B. 1991 *Workforce America! Managing Employee Diversity as a Vital Resource*, Business One Irwin, Homewood, Illinois.

Patrickson, M. 1994, 'Workplace management strategies for a millenium', *International Journal of Career Management*, vol. 6, no. 2, pp. 25–32.

Rodgers, J.O. 1993, 'Implementing a diversity strategy', *Limra's Market Facts*, May/June.

Saul, P. 1996,'Managing the organization as a community of contributors', *Asia-Pacific Journal of Human Resources*, vol. 34, no. 3, pp. 19–36.

Shea, G. 1991, *Managing Older Employees*, Jossey-Bass, San Francisco, CA.

Solomon, C.M. 1991, 'Are white males being left out?', *Personnel Journal*, November, pp. 88–94.

Stone, D. L. & Collela, A. 1996, 'A model of factors affecting the treatment of disabled individuals in organizations', *Academy Management Review*, vol. 21, no. 2, pp. 352–401.

Storey, J. 1992, *Developments in the Management of Human Resources*, Blackwell, Oxford.

Thomas, R.R. Jr. 1991, *Beyond Race and gender: Unleashing the power of your total workforce*, Amacon, New York.

—— 1995, 'A Diversity Framework', in Chemers, M.M., Oskamp, S. & Costanzo, M.A. (eds), *Diversity in Organizations: New Perspectives for a Changing Workforce*, Sage Publications, New York.

Thomas, D.A. & Ely, R.J. 1996, 'Making difference matter: A new paradigm for managing diversity', *Harvard Business Review*, September–October, pp. 79–90.

Industry Task Force on Leadership and Management Skills 1995, *Enterprising Nation* (Karpin Report), AGPS, Canberra.

Profiting from diversity: The Westpac experience

Jacqueline Gillespie

Westpac was founded in 1817 and is proud to be Australia's first bank. The company currently employs some 32 000 people in Australia and overseas. It is represented through approximately 1300 branches, agencies and service centres worldwide, including 1100 in Australia.

Until the early 1990s, banking was a stable, protected industry. Westpac, as with other Australian banks, experienced increased competition and a fast pace of change following deregulation of the industry in the mid-1980s. Some of the key changes affecting Westpac's operating environment are shown in Table G1.

The late 1980s and early 1990s was a difficult period for Westpac, and Australian banks generally. Westpac's performance culminated in a loss of $1.2 billion in 1992, a result that few financial institutions in the world have recovered from. The arrival of Bob Joss as managing director in 1993, together with subsequent changes in senior management, signalled significant change; and the profit of $1.1 billion in 1996 confirmed Westpac's economic turnaround.

Westpac's vision is to 'deliver better solutions to customers'. It does this increasingly through a range of delivery channels and services. The branch network remains an important point of entry for customers; however, technology-based services such as

Table G1 Impact of deregulation on Westpac's operating environment

Before deregulation	After deregulation
rationing credit	selling credit
bank on every corner	multiple channel delivery
limited technology	extensive technology
appointments only	house calls
restrained image advertising	aggressive product promotion
withdraw cash for groceries	withdraw groceries to access cash
media apathy	media focus
employment for life	employability

ATMs, telephone, kiosk and Internet banking now provide customers with many choices on how to satisfy their banking needs.

The human resource strategy of the bank is deliberately designed to support the overall vision of the bank, and to assist Westpac's transformation following its economic turnaround. The strategy is to deliver better solutions to customers by gaining a performance edge through people. This link between the business objectives and human resource management is built around four themes:

- developing a culture that directly supports the achievement of delivering better solutions to customers;
- improving the management capability of the organisation;
- continuously improving the overall portfolio of talent; and
- building a relationship with employees that releases discretionary effort.

Profiting from diversity

The links between solutions for customers and performance through people have been an important platform for the development of a diversity strategy within the bank. In the late 1980s, the focus for diversity was based on compliance. Since then, the focus has changed to emphasise how managing diversity can positively impact on customers, performance and the overall success of the business. All the key drivers for introducing a managed approach to workforce diversity in Westpac were business issues focusing on customers, employees, culture, control, community and cost.

Customers—understanding customers better, Westpac needs to have a workforce that reflects the diversity of its customer base. Diversity in the workforce helps Westpac serve the customer more effectively as well as develop products and new services that meet their needs.

Employees—workforce diversity helps Westpac position itself as an employer of choice, attracting the best people in the marketplace. It also ensures that employees perceive it as a good place to work. In these respects, it aims to have employees feel they are valued as employees and have equal access to employment opportunities.

Culture—workforce diversity helps transform Westpac's culture to one that deliberately values skills and performance. This provides a significant basis from which the company can harness the commitment and energy of all employees.

Control—managing workforce diversity ensures that the company complies with its legislative requirements and that all managers and employees are aware of their responsibilities.

Community—a genuine and systematic approach to workforce diversity enhances Westpac's image and reputation in the community as a good corporate citizen. It also demonstrates that the company acts with honesty and integrity as an employer.

Cost—the management of an effective diversity program assists in reducing turnover, providing for improved morale and better productivity. These all result in significant employee effectiveness and cost savings to the company.

Introducing managed workforce diversity

Westpac had always complied with affirmative action legislation; however, it was not until the early 1990s that diversity was seen as a significant factor influencing business performance. With Joss' arrival and his observation of the lack of women in Westpac's senior levels, and in Australian business generally, this awareness was followed by action. Joss made his views public, both internally and externally. He recruited Anne Sherry, a high profile woman from the federal government's Office of the Status of Women, to assist Westpac improve its record in this area. In 1994, Joss and his senior team set a series of goals for the organisation; there were three primary areas of focus with regard to workforce diversity:

- increase the percentage of women in management;
- increase the number of women in non-traditional female areas;
- increase the employment of people with disabilities.

Joss also introduced a measurement process for each business unit. Together with the usual financial and business measures, a quarterly *Women in Management* report was used to track statistical progress within each business unit. Over time, statistics have also been introduced to map employment of males and females, people from non-English speaking backgrounds, people with disabilities and women returning from maternity leave. These are included in the board report and also given to the executive team. Individual business units are provided with quarterly statistics and they can now request more targeted information statistics to enable them to analyse their affirmative action progress against individual business unit goals. These reports highlight key issues and trends for women and other groups within the workplace. For example, the annual *Workforce Indicators Report* to executive management highlights trends in many of the statistics by gender.

Outcomes

Since December 1993, Westpac has made significant progress toward the achievement of the three workforce diversity goals set by the senior management group. Table G2 shows the percentage increase in women occupying management positions from December 1993 through to December 1996. Overall, there has been a 13 per cent increase in female managers across the four levels of management.

The company focused on increasing female representation in traditional male dominated functions, particularly sales and credit. This included such roles as personal banking manager, regional customer service manager and business banking manager. The results over the three-year period are shown in Table G3. Westpac introduced a specific project aimed at increasing employment opportunities for people with disabilities. Fifty people have been employed in various jobs under this project as at July 1997.

Table G2 Percentage increase of women in management

| | Number of women as % of management | | | | | |
	Dec. 1993	Dec. 1994	Dec. 1995	Dec. 1996	July 1997	% Increase
Junior management	13.8	18.5	24.4	27.3	29	15.2
Middle management	5.4	8.4	11.7	14.3	15.2	9.8
Senior management	7.4	11.9	11.2	12.4	11.4	4
Specialist management	14.7	16.6	18	23.5	23	8.4
All	11.5	15.5	20.3	23.3	24.5	13

Table G3 Percentage increase of women in traditional male management roles

| | % of women in non-traditional roles | | |
	December 1993	June 1996	% increase
Personal banking manager	11	28	17
Regional customer service manager	18	28	10
Business banking manager	1	11	10

How were the outcomes achieved?

These outcomes were achieved through two main channels. First, the principles of equal employment opportunity (EEO) were integrated into existing human resource management processes and systems. Second, specific initiatives were implemented to address areas of identified employee and business need.

Human resource management procesess and systems

Policy—Human resource policies and practices are continually reviewed to respond to the dynamic changes within the workforce. Westpac's policies are updated and communicated in the employee guidelines on a quarterly basis to ensure they accurately reflect 'the way we do things around here'. The objective is to communicate the company's commitment to a workplace based on merit and ensure staff understand the variety of policies and programs available to them. Diversity policies include EEO/workforce diversity, discrimination, harassment, home-based work, job share, parental leave (including paid maternity and adoption leave), family leave, family care, career management and hours of work.

Selection—Westpac is committed to merit-based selection processes. The following selection policies and practices have been introduced to ensure equal employment opportunity within the company:

- all vacant positions (including executive levels) are advertised internally, prior to advertising externally to allow all staff to have access to opportunities for promotion;
- at least one suitably qualified woman must be included on the shortlist for all management positions;
- objective, behavioural-based techniques, including targeted selection interviewing, role plays, assessment centres, aptitude testing and work samples have been implemented as a process for selection; and,
- preferred external recruitment consultants, demonstrating commitment to EEO, have been selected and briefed on these policies.

This approach to selection, particularly the use of assessment centres, has been a critical factor in increasing the number of women in management roles.

Training and development—A range of training and development programs have been implemented to raise awareness, educate and ensure managers understand the legislative framework. The training and development opportunities include such programs and workshops as:

- *Springboard Program*, aimed at assisting women prepare for management and supervisory positions by empowering them to take active control of their lives and career objectives;

211

- *Moving into Management* is designed for high potential women in junior to middle management positions and aims to assist participants identify their strengths and development needs;
- *Managing Flexibly* and *Managing Diversity* workshops assist managers realise the potential of a diverse workforce and how to manage it more effectively; and
- *Harassment Prevention* briefings cover the bank's diversity policies and the resolution process.

The Managing Diversity and Managing Flexibly workshops have briefed over 7000 executives, managers, supervisors and employees to date. The participants are then responsible for educating their teams on EEO and diversity issues.

Succession planning—Westpac has a formal succession planning process that involves the managing director and group executive spending a day offsite each quarter reviewing the top 200 high potential executives in the bank. The executive resource review ranks people's performance against core competencies and identifies potential successors for critical positions. Included in this process is a specific focus on the identification of high potential women.

Performance management—The integrity of the performance management system is integral to ensuring that all staff are appraised fairly and equitably. The appraisal system is based on achievement of defined objectives and competencies identified as critical for the role. Employees are appraised on their performance annually and their remuneration is based on the resulting performance rating.

Diversity initiatives

A range of specific initiatives have been introduced to ensure Westpac provides support to business and employee needs in relation to diversity.

Consultation—Consultative processes aim to identify employee needs and business unit requirements. Recent projects have included the 1995 Part-time Employment Survey, Leonie Still's 1996 report on Women in Finance, the 1995/97 Enterprise Development Agreement, 1996 review of the Employee Assistance Program (ACCESS), a 1995 Language and Qualifications Survey, annual Executive Opinion Survey and the introduction of exit interviews.

Family care initiatives—Work and family initiatives have been implemented to assist employees juggle competing demands. This is an area where the company wanted to demonstrate its commitment to integrating work and family needs into the business. Initiatives include the following:
- Introduction of Family CareLink, an independent information and resource service designed to assist staff make dependent care arrangements for their children, elderly relatives and dependants with disabilities. This

service is provided free to employees and includes: information on availability of childcare (including vacation, family day and long day care and
before/after school care); advice on residential and home service for the
elderly and dependants with disabilities; information on relevant government assistance; and guidance on how to access and assess the quality of
service.

- A work-based childcare initiative resulting in an on-site, employer-
sponsored childcare centre for employees in Adelaide's mortgage processing centre. The centre supports the strategy of recruiting employees
wanting flexible working hours. A second on-site centre is due to open in
Jaunary 1998 in suburban Sydney to service the needs of over 800
operations centre staff.

- As a result of research undertaken in 1996, Challenge Bank (Westpac's
regional bank in Western Australia) sponsored a pilot of 10 childcare places
in the employer-sponsored family day care program. Family day care
provides licensed childcare in a home environment for up to four children.
The WA pilot will continue for 12 months with a view to extending this
type of childcare further in Westpac.

- All Westpac business units are encouraged to consider the benefits of
flexible work initiatives such as job sharing and home-based work. A job-
share register has been developed to assist staff identify prospective job
sharers with compatible competencies and skills. The ultimate goal is for
job sharing to become an option that individuals can confidently pursue
within their own business units. Similarly, following the successful pilot of
home-based work by the Westpac information technology business unit,
further career opportunities for employees are arising within this unit.
Approximately 100 employees in the bank now formally work from home
in a full- or part-time capacity.

- A project to improve the conditions of work, and career and training
opportunities for part-time workers was established as part of the 1995
enterprise development agreement. Westpac introduced a minimum 64
hours of work per four-week cycle for all new part-time employees in
exchange for an increase in the part-time work ceiling, with part-time
employees receiving pro-rata full-time employment benefits. These moves
were in response to Westpac's research showing that higher attrition
rates—and therefore higher costs—were directly related to the lower
number of hours worked. The notion of 'mutality' required mutual agreement between the employee and the business for hours of work to change:
this gives part-time employees more control over their rostered work
hours and helps them balance work and family commitments. The project
is now focused on enhancing the skills and quality of the part-time
workforce and providing part-time jobs at more senior levels of the
organisation. Currently there are 69 part-time management positions in
the bank.

- Westpac introduced paid maternity leave in July 1995, the first privately owned bank to do so. This benefit applies to full- and part-time employees with a minimum 12 months continuous service and was introduced to increase the numbers of women returning from maternity leave. For the 12-month period from July 1995 to June 1996, retention rates for women eligible for paid maternity leave were 12.2 per cent higher than for women who were not eligible. Further strategies to retain women include publication of Westpac's *Great Expectations* booklet to provide practical advice and information on strategies to assist in life and work changes; and distribution of employment-related and general organisation information through the mail for duration of the leave. From March 1997, employees (full- and part-time with a minimum 12 months continuous service) who are 'primary carers' are entitled to six weeks paid adoption leave if they are adopting a child. The benefit of paid paternity leave is currently under review.
- The Disability Project commenced in 1995 to improve product and service delivery to people with a disability, and to increase employment opportunities for people with a disability. Westpac employs 50 people across the bank in a variety of roles through the Disability Project and incorporated many of the requirements of the *Disability Discrimination Act* and Australian Standards *AS 1428.1* into all new centralised banking sites. This includes the mortgage centre, the customer service centre and telephone banking. The company is also developing an action plan around product and service delivery to be lodged in the Human Rights Commission

Challenges

Westpac has made significant progress in the area of workforce diversity. The company has received public acknowledgment for its achievements: Westpac was the Silver Award winner in the 1997 Corporate Work and Family Awards and received a Women's Network of Australia Advancement Award.

While there has been significant progress in managing diversity, there have been challenges to the implementation of its program. These include:

- new acquisitions and regionalisation have increased the complexity of policy development and strategy execution;
- the number of diversity initiatives sometimes provide competing priorities for business units and limit their capacity to focus on immediately relevant issues;
- the need for greater management accountability in managing and communicating workforce diversity policies and programs in their areas;
- the barriers for women moving into non-traditional areas of the bank need to be more fully understood;

- culture change is slow, especially perceptions of diversity difference between men and women in the organisation.

Critical success factors and lessons

The future of Westpac's diversity program is clearly constructed. The work to date has enabled an increase in the numbers of women in management and non-traditional roles, as well as increasing employment opportunities for people with a disability. The level of awareness about the issues for managers and employees is high.

The public and clear commitment and support given by Managing Director Bob Joss has been critical to the diversity program. This has been reinforced by the business units' quarterly reporting on women in management and the regular discussions and updates at board, group executive and management council level. The 1994 appointment of Ann Sherry also ensured these issues had a high profile within the organisation and externally. Westpac's commitment to supporting a workforce diversity unit, linked closely to the HR policy unit, ensured the integration of EEO into policies and the resources to pursue focused EEO initiatives. All of these and related initiatives have had a strong business focus and business case.

Predictably, business units progressed at different rates in the acceptance and implementation of the policies and programs. The next phase is to pursue the development of further links between the business, the customer and the workplace. The changing dynamic of the Westpac customer base is proving to be a stronger impact than ever before on the need to have a workplace that more clearly reflects the company's general customer base. In particular, the increasing number of women who are small business owners, the large number of Asian businesses, as well as lobby groups representing people with a disability, means that our workplace must respond. Customers are demanding that their needs be understood and are willing to use the media to demonstrate when this has not happened.

The shift in direction is that business managers increasingly want to drive the agenda from a business need. The workforce diversity unit is moving toward a partnership approach with Westpac's regional banks to develop strategies to meet the needs of the customers. For example, Queensland regional bank has developed a strategy for increasing its market share of the women in business segment: to support this business direction, it has implemented a 12-month action plan to ensure the workplace reflects the needs of this market and can deliver against those needs. Similarly, NSW regional bank is now targeting the recruitment of people with specific skills who can meet the needs of this market, whether it is in languages spoken or understanding the cultural expectations of business. Financial markets in the institutional and international banking group found that women generally do not study disciplines such as finance, mathematics, commerce and economics. A number of initiatives are being adopted to address this: 'Uni Link' awards prizes to women studying these courses; courses in securities and other specialist subjects are being introduced; senior managers are involved in career information sessions at universities and other venues; newspaper advertising is targeting careers in financial markets; and graduates from disciplines other than those which are financial market orientated are being assessed.

If Westpac is to continue attracting and retaining customers—as well as the best employees—the challenge is now to tackle some of the broader cultural issues within the organisation. This will include a business by business focus on barriers to workforce diversity, and acceptance of the challenge provided by issues that employees, customers and community groups raise with Westpac. These range from concerns for integrating work and life, lifestyle and sexual preference, and employment opportunities for Aboriginals and Torres Strait islanders.

10 Managing an international workforce

Alan Fish

Recent developments in economic, political and trade relationships have heightened the need to manage people across international boundaries. With the emergence of APEC and NAFTA, the re-focusing of traditional trade relationships, such as ASEAN and the European Community, the emergence of China and the re-emergence of Eastern Bloc countries, having human resource management that supports effective international business operations has become vitally important.

The management of staff across international boundaries requires an understanding of how management practice supports business strategy. International human resource management (IHRM) practices should be designed to ensure that: organisational learning results from international appointments; business strategies are supported; staff are appropriately prepared for and aware of their overseas business responsibilities; and organisations identify people for international appointments from appropriate sources (Fish 1995).

These outcomes can be facilitated by managing four issues. First, staff needs, competencies and family requirements need to be identified. Specifically, it is necessary to identify an individual's cross-cultural management competencies and the extent to which these will enable effective performance in foreign locations. Second, it is important to identify what motivates staff to accept an overseas move. Third, the needs of the family, particularly those of the spouse/partner and children must be addressed. Finally, an individual's ability to adjust to the overseas business and cultural environment needs to be assessed because this ability is critical for the development of effective business relationships.

Effective management of an international workforce also requires an understanding of overseas industry practices, economic factors, political concerns, foreign business practices and laws, and the cultural values and mores. This chapter examines issues associated with managing an international workforce and addresses the need to manage individual, organisational and broader national issues.

Individual considerations

Four issues are critical for the management of individuals on international assignments; these are:

- effective preparation for the assignment;
- transfer between assignments;
- adjustment to the overseas assignment;
- eventual movement to newer and improved employment experiences as a consequence of the overseas experience.

The management of these four issues can be understood in terms of the processes involved in the individual's experience. These processes have been outlined in Nicholson's (1987) role transition model shown in Figure 10.1. Individuals need to *prepare* for the new job and social requirements by developing realistic expectations, as well as by being aware of their possible motives and feelings. The next stage in the career transition cycle involves the way individuals *encounter* the overseas assignment. This experience is influenced by personal capabilities such as their self-confidence in coping in new environments. The third stage, *adjustment*, concerns the extent to which the individual is able to undertake role innovation, manage relationships and undertake personal development. The final stage of the transition process is *stabilisation*, characterised by sustained trust, commitment and effectiveness with tasks and people. Movement through these stages can be fostered through induction and support programs.

Career transitions are often not effectively managed. Individuals often experience poor adjustment to new roles, cultures and jobs and this results in poor performance. It is therefore critical to provide precise attention to and understand these issues (Black, Gregersen & Mendenhall 1992; Fish & Wood 1993, 1994; Fish 1995).

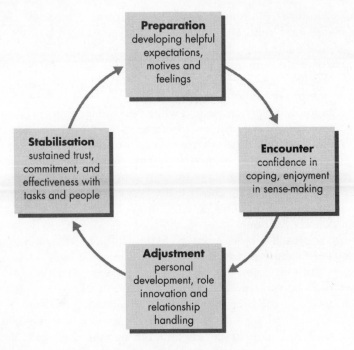

Figure 10.1   Career transition cycle

Organisational considerations

It is important to acknowledge differences in industry, economic, financial, and HRM practices if organisations are to adjust effectively to a new environment. In addition, an appreciation of differences in general political and business practices, including local laws and regulations and the cultural values that underpin business and social behaviour patterns in foreign locations are important for ultimate success in foreign business dealings. Another matter to consider when managing people on international assignments is the approach which has been adopted to managing international assignments.

Cross-cultural business and HRM practices

An understanding of the different approaches to managing people on international assignment has been provided by Heenan and Perlmutter (1979). They developed a classification continuum of IHRM, based on the extent of the influence of the home culture dominance. This classification system focuses on issues such as where decisions are made and which individuals get the job. Different issues need to be managed with each approach.

The classification continuum commences with an *ethnocentric* approach where home country culture dominates. This is represented by little understanding of—or willingness to learn—new business and cultural practices. Business practices are centralised and key decisions made at the parent company. The subsidiary has little if any autonomy and key positions are held by parent company personnel.

The next approach is *polycentric*, and while the parent company culture still dominates, some minor adjustments to business and HRM practices occur. High quality host country nationals begin to appear in the business, for example, though key positions are retained by parent company personnel, and host country staff rarely gain promotion to head office. This restriction creates potential problems in retaining good quality host country nationals, establishing a strong presence in the host country and as a consequence maintaining sound host country relations.

The third approach is *regiocentric* which aims to blend the parent company's interests with those of its subsidiaries on a regional basis. Hence, little change from the polycentric approach is seen, except that host and third country nationals become more visible.

The *geocentric* approach represents a fully integrated, global/transnational approach. Decision-making is decentralised to the subsidiary or regional management, and a broad range of staff are found throughout the career structure of the business. Management staff are likely to be selected, prepared and managed with sophisticated inter-cultural business ability and awareness as the driving force. Managers gain experience and exposure to the firm as a whole in developing their international business expertise, and are drawn from a variety of organisational and cultural backgrounds. Business firms using this approach usually operate under a globally integrated business strategy, with key personnel moved strategically to gain the appropriate experience for appointment to more senior corporate management positions. The career moves of Australian Jack Nassar, a senior executive with Ford International, for example, follow this pattern.

This classification has been further developed by subsuming regiocentric as a subset of polycentric and creating a category termed *contingency*. Contingency practices pursue an eclectic approach, with decisions regarding which of the previous strategies to pursue reserved until such time as foreign business and cultural environments have been assessed.

Adler and Ghadar (1990) propose that different ways of managing an international workforce are developed according to the firm's international business activity. Table 10.1 shows the way international business activity and human resource practices can be integrated. However, their model is limited in a number of respects. It does not fully specify individual and business cultural adjustment issues; nor does it fully acknowledge the transitional, discontinuous, recursionary and different approaches of IHRM activity.

The model does suggest how organisations might move from one international growth phase to another, and how appropriate HRM activity can complement such movement. For example, firms in phase I (domestic) might wish

Table 10.1 International business activity and human resource management

	Phase I Domestic	Phase II International	Phase III Multinational	Phase IV Global
Primary orientation	Product/service	Market	Price	Strategy
Strategy	Domestic	Multidomestic	Multinational	Global
Worldwide strategy	Allow foreign clients to buy product/service	Increase market internationally; transfer technology abroad	Source produce and market internationally	Gain global strategic competitive advantage
Staffing				
Expatriates	None, few	Many	Some	Many
Why sent	Junket	To sell, control or transfer technology	Control	Co-ordination & integration
Who sent	–	OK performers; sales people	Very good performers	High potential managers & top executives
Purpose	Reward	Project—to get job done	Project & career development	Career & organisational development
Career impact	Negative	Bad for domestic career	Important for global career	Essential for executive suite
Professional re-entry	Somewhat difficult	Extremely difficult	Less difficult	Professionally easy
Training & development	None	Limited	Longer	Continuous throughout career
Language & cross-cultural management				
For whom	No one	Expatriates	Expatriates	Managers
Performance	Corporate	Subsidiary	Corporate	Global
Appraisal	Bottom line	Bottom line	Bottom line	Strategic positioning
Motivation Assumption	Money	Money & adventure	Challenge & opportunity	Challenge, opportunity, advancement
Rewarding	Extra money to compensate for foreign hardships	Extra money to compensate for foreign hardships	Less generous global package	Less generous global package
Career	Domestic	Domestic	Token international	Global
Executive passport	Home country	Home country	Home country, token foreigners	Multinational
Necessary skills	Technical & managerial	Plus cultural adaptation	Plus recognising cultural differences	Plus cross-cultural interaction, influence & synergy

Source: From Adler & Ghadar 1990

to expand overseas. When moving into phase II (multidomestic), organisations establish an overseas presence and extend their HRM practices by appointing parent company national (PCNs) to their overseas operations. The exchange is usually one-way—head office staff are sent overseas but integration of host country nationals (HCNs) is minimal. The management philosophy is largely ethnocentric in nature, with HCNs in junior supervisory roles being directed by parent company management personnel and practices. Phase II firms rarely send the most capable managers overseas, and unfortunately have traditionally placed little value on the experiences and skills gained (Adler & Ghadar 1990). Herein lies the problem of an inability to acknowledge the need for changes to management practices and philosophies when moving into a different stage of business operation.

When moving into phase III (multinational), firms have developed beyond a mere overseas operation. They are more sophisticated, operating in diverse areas and in some instances producing diverse products. These types of firms endeavour to centralise and stabilise operations and tend to pursue a mixture of polycentric and regiocentric management practices. Human resource management practices, while culturally sympathetic, still allow PCNs to dominate. In other words, some concessions are made to host country cultures but a full commitment to change has not been made, even though international experience is normally well regarded in these firms. Business practices are not fully adapted to the different cultural requirements, and continue to be based on parent company rituals which can lead to adjustment problems for the business and its managers in non-familiar territory.

Movement into phase IV (global) witnesses a maturing of the business enterprise. It is involved in competition which is diversified on product, price, market and business strategies, reflecting adaptation to broad global considerations as well as adjustment to specific needs in particular areas. Human resource management strategies here demand international exposure with highly sophisticated international management development practices including: being multilingual, cultural sensitivity, and the skill to identify the specific needs of environments, and an ability to respond quickly to those needs.

These four phases provide a useful means of identifying the links between business activity and HRM practices. However, four other matters need to be addressed to better understand the process of managing an international workforce. These are the international business growth stages; international key players; dual issues in cross-cultural adjustment and dual responsibility for international HRM practices.

International business growth stages

The idea developed by Adler and Ghadar that firms grow through various stages of international business, and each stage requires different types of HRM interaction, is intuitively appealing. However, not all firms operating internationally 1) desire to grow through such stages, 2) need to grow through them, or 3) should necessarily be capable of growing through them. It should be acknowledged that firms can remain at a given stage of international business activity and develop within that stage. For example, the formation of joint ventures, consortiums, the development of multinational enterprises, or simply going it alone, will each see the need for different HRM practices. However, all need cross-cultural HRM awareness if they are to respond effectively to the needs of their particular relationship in specific foreign business locations and with particular international institutions.

On this basis, IHRM practice is not something that arrives when a firm becomes a multinational, as implied by some writers (e.g. Dowling, Schuler & Welch 1994). Rather, it is a process that all firms, irrespective of their level of international operation, need to address if they are to be successful at their chosen level of international business activity.

Key international players

The growth and development of firms internationally is achieved in part by the involvement of key international players. At early stages of international business growth and development, the *itinerant traveller* is usually involved, someone sent out from the parent company with something akin to missionary zeal. As firms move into different stages of international involvement, different types of people become important. Such people include *expatriates* or parent company nationals, *inpatriates* consisting of host country nationals, *repatriates* or parent company nationals, and *transpatriates*, people whose involvement has taken them through a variety of international business experiences. Ultimately, there are *transnationals*, people who have recognised the critical importance of adjusting behaviour to suit various stages of international business. Underpinning such key players are the executives who determine and design international strategies and supporting HRM practices (Fish, 1995).

The decision about who is the most appropriate person for a foreign appointment needs careful consideration. According to Fish (1995), the choice among a PCN, a HCN or a third country national (TCN), as well as the development of the transnational management mindset, should be driven by four factors:

1 stage and type of international business development;
2 general sophistication of a firm's management practices and the need to internationalise their HRM practices;
3 cultural distance of the offshore business location;
4 intended international growth of the firm.

In addition, the decision also needs to take into account the parent company's business strategies. Companies may be involved in a joint venture, a consortium arrangement, a multinational operation or simply be exporting. The overseas experience should not be linked to a single purpose, nor should an expatriate be necessarily seen as the best person for an overseas role. The effective employment of HCNs and TCNs and their development in assisting cultural diversity and understanding should be recognised as a legitimate strategy to assist international business growth.

Involvement of non-parent company nationals will then assist with business acceptance and also assist the organisation adjust to overseas needs. Equally, it will help with individual adjustment problems by having someone in an important overseas role who is familiar with the respective culture.

Two levels in cross-cultural adjustment

Separate issues associated with individual and organisational levels of adjustment are often forgotten when organisations venture off-shore. Not recognising the need to adjust to changed circumstances can and does contribute to substantial failures, for both business and individuals alike.

The process of adjustment to a culture is paramount for individuals both prior to and on arrival in their new enviroment. With some understanding of what to expect on arrival, *anticipatory* adjustment can be made, but *in-country* adjustment is always demanded—and demanding.

Anticipatory adjustment includes understanding factors such as how previous overseas experiences might assist in developing new cognitive maps when going somewhere new, and how awareness of a new environment—in terms of lifestyle changes and the characteristics of the new business environment—will assist with initiatives to cope with stress. The process of anticipatory adjustment is important, especially in circumstances when staff have not been overseas prior to the appointment. False or misleading information contributes to failure for both the staff member and an accompanying spouse/partner. The selection of a PNC, a HCN or a TCN as the most appropriate appointee will influence what preparation is required prior to departure.

In-country adjustment requires dealing with considerations such as relationship and perception skills, and job, business and environmental induction. The issues to be considered include the extent of change required as a consequence of cultural differences and novelty, and the needs of an accompanying spouse/partner in coming to terms with a new environment and circumstances. This adjustment essentially involves four stages with the potential for problems at each stage. Black et al. (1992) characterise these stages as:

1 *honeymoon* generally lasts for up to two months and is represented by a fascination of the new culture and what it has to offer; something new is invariably welcomed and the fascination with it can be intoxicating;

2 *culture shock*, the next stage, lasts up to 12 months and is represented by periods of disillusionment and frustration because the job, its setting and the overall experience has not lived up to expectations; the reality of cultural distance can be quite demoralising;

3 *adjustment* is the next stage and can take two to three years to pass through; it is represented by adaptation and acceptance of and by the new culture;

4   *mastery* can take up to five years and is represented by an ability to function not only in a given culture but across a variety of cultures.

The other aspect of adjustment involves organisational practices. Ethno-centric attitudes to business operations should not be carried internationally. It is easy to assume that successful domestic practices will be appropriate in an overseas business, but this might not be the case. The impacts of economic, legal, government, and general business practices of the host countries need to be dealt with in order to be accepted by foreign business and cultural communities (Fish & Wood, 1997c).

Responsibility for IHRM practice

The movement of staff between countries requires individuals and organisa-tions to acknowledge that they share responsibility for effective transition. Organisations can facilitate an individual's experience of the stages of prepara-tion, encounter, adjustment and stabilisation through human resource poli-cies and practices such as selection, training, induction, appraisal and career advancement. Individuals also bear responsibility for movement through these stages by honestly assessing their competencies, motivation and experience for the overseas posting; they also need to address family and personal issues. These responsibilities occur at each stage of Nicholson's role transition cycle shown in Figure 10.1. Table 10.2 outlines some of the areas of organisational and individual responsibility which can facilitate movement through the role transition cycle.

Organisational context responsibility

Clearly, human resource policies and practices such as selection, training and development, job design, career development, performance appraisal and compensation need to be consistent, reinforce each other as well as the business objectives, and take account of individual career needs. In the

Table 10.2   Responsibilities of organisations and individuals

Step in cycle	Organisational context responsibility	Individual development responsibility
Preparation	selection, training, job design	cross-cultural competencies, motivation, family/partner situation
Encounter	induction, socialiation	induction
Adjustment	appraisal, compensation, training	personal and professional development
Stabilisation	career advancement	preparation for next move, commitment to stay

international context a number of practices can be adopted to improve the effectiveness of these policies and practices.

International staff selection

As firms have recognised the need to respond to local and international business requirements, they also need to acknowledge that they cannot continue to rely on their traditional domestic sources of staff, particularly management staff. While awareness is increasing of the factors that contribute to the effective selection of international managers, the predictors of success in the position are less clear. In this respect, Zeira and Banai (1984) argue that 'selection of international executives should be broadened to include an analysis of the expectations of the host environment in addition to those of the parent company'.

Traditional international selection practices have relied heavily on technical skills and domestic business success coupled with length of service. However, this focus limits the poll of potential international manager. As Mendenhall and Oddou (1988, p. 82) state, 'technical competence has nothing to do with one's ability to adapt to a new environment, deal effectively with foreign co-workers, or perceive and if necessary imitate the foreign behavioural norms'.

More appropriate selection criteria for international staff would include a person's ability to adapt to a foreign setting, concern for their impact on others, understanding of the behavioural patterns of host country nationals, and understanding of the differences between the home and the host cultures. Gordon and Teagarden (1992) add personal motivation, cross-cultural relations skills and family awareness. Effective selection can be promoted by using multiple selection methods, ensuring individuals have role clarity at the time of selection and are aware of the skills necessary to operate in the overseas environment (Fish & Wood 1996). The selection process for domestic staff may not always be the most appropriate strategy as HCNs and TCNs may be more effective choices.

Training and development

The importance of effective training and development is emphasised by Temporal and Burnett (1990, pp. 62–3): 'As sensitivity to local conditions is required for management success, the development of managers in MNEs is less likely to be successful in terms of their foreign-based performance if it is restricted to the organisation's home country and culture.'

Although initiatives are increasing, there is still no extensive Australian evidence of a shift in international management development activity (Karpin Report 1995). Training should be directed at activities that allow international managers—or those earmarked for such involvement—to identify the attitudes and behaviours required in various cross-cultural circumstances. Such training could involve technical knowledge, socio-cultural differences between the home and host culture, foreign business practices and the processes associated with establishing foreign business and community relations (Fish & Wood 1996).

Job design

Poor job design can lead to poor cross-cultural business relationships which, in turn, may result in an inability to establish the firm in the international marketplace. This can lead to: loss of market share, less than satisfactory profits and an inability on the part of the international manager to understand the role in a culturally distant land. Poor job design also means that inappropriate messages, regarding consideration given to overseas assignments, are sent to staff, making it difficult in the future to attract quality internal applicants for important overseas business positions (Fish & Wood 1996). It is important to recognise the strategic purpose of an off-shore role, and to ensure an appropriate mix between what is expected of the role incumbent and how the person goes about the job.

Fish (1995) identifies five issues critical for appopriate job design in the international context:

1 understanding the rationale and strategic purpose of a particular job;
2 ensuring the job incumbent is clear about what is expected in the job;
3 ensuring the job incumbent has appropriate job discretion;
4 minimising the potential for any role conflict;
5 providing for organisational learning to occur as a consequence of job performance.

Unless these issues are addressed when determining the overseas role, the person in the position may experience difficulty fitting into the new environment, leading to setbacks in gaining acceptance in the host business community.

Career development

The impact of an overseas posting on an individual's career needs to be understood. Overseas studies by Feldman and Tompson (1993), Feldman and Thomas (1992), Adler and Ghadar (1990), and Fish (1995) in an Australian study, have all shown there is a distinct lack of attention to this issue. Fish (1995) identified a number of problems that could arise due to failure to address the career implications of an overseas move. These included lack of job opportunities following an overseas assignment, loss of professional status, loss of career and promotional opportunities, and professional jealousy by those who have not had overseas opportunities.

In a European study, Forster (1992, p. 612) points to similar findings and argues that, 'One of the principal problems reported was finding a suitable promoted post for the expatriate in the home operation.' Clearly, as involvement in international business is becoming increasingly important, it becomes imperative that one is successful at it. It is likely that in the future managers will need overseas experience to ensure their own career success (Fish & Wood 1996). On this basis Fish (1995) identifies a range of practices designed to increase the effectiveness of the posting. These include:

- an informed rationale for overseas appointments,
- using the experience as a development activity, rather than as an ad-hoc reaction to short-term problems, and
- identifying the overseas appointment as a legitimate part of an organisation's formal career structure.

Integrating career management with an organisation's selection and training processes in these ways helps establish an effective international focus. Such attention provides for more informed development opportunities, leading ultimately to the development of a transnational mindset as staff gain experience and know-how in and across a variety of business and cultural settings.

Performance appraisal

Butler, Ferris and Napier (1991) suggest the need for accurate international performance appraisal because the process communicates expectations to the international manager, facilitates global strategy and has the potential to identify areas for strategy development. However, using the traditional domestic process in an international environment is fraught with danger: 'A firm's standard domestic appraisal cannot generally measure expatriate performance in overseas assignments effectively and accurately ... . Therefore, firms should examine expatriate performance within the context of the overseas assignment' (Gregersen, Hite & Black 1996, p. 713).

International enterprises need to address and emphasise a variety of potentially competing interests in the appraisal approach. In this respect, there is a need to establish medium to longer term appraisal periods, and to acknowledge: i) the legitimate input of host country national managers, ii) the impact of different legal, economic, technical and cultural demands on performance in foreign locations and iii) the effects of issues such as the use of domestic appraisal forms, who the raters are and their actual knowledge of and relationship with the expatriate's circumstances (Gregersen, Hite & Black 1996). Such a focus will assist in a more informed appreciation of the international manager's effectiveness by tuning appraisal practices to the peculiar demands of specific overseas settings and matching this with the international business strategies of the firm.

Compensation

International compensation practices have long been a cause of concern and conflict: 'If there is one area of multinational personnel policy that can be designated the most complex, it has to be the area of compensation. The problems to date defy a simple solution and cause much intra-organisational resentment' (Phatak 1989, pp. 130–1).

Issues of motivation, market competitiveness and equity have traditionally been the guiding principles in designing reward systems, the aim being to attract and retain the best people for the business. Internationally, the aim should not simply be for some perceived notion of extra income (Fish & Wood 1997a); rather the arrangement is to 'compensate' the individual in monetary and non-monetary terms for any actual or perceived losses resulting from an overseas assignment. Essentially, international reward systems have been designed to achieve outcomes (Fish 1995) such as

- facilitating movement to foreign locations;
- attending to any disruption in the family lifestyle;
- providing incentives to undertake an assignment to a particularly difficult location and
- assisting with specific situations in the foreign location such as expensive housing costs, cost of living adjustments, children's education, entertainment requirements, balancing salary with local requirements and resolving tax equalisation issues.

Non-monetary issues such as career advancement, professional development and reducing the impact on the family also need careful consideration. If these issues are not resolved, inequities may occur between the international manager and those at home as well as between the international manager and local staff in foreign locations.

Individual development responsibility

Individual development responsibility is associated with ensuring that candidates for overseas appointments have the appropriate background, competencies and motivation to undertake the new role. Overseas appointments require people who are committed to an ongoing career with the organisation and have addressed personal and family issues associated with the move (Fish 1995).

International management competencies

Understanding cross-cultural management competencies is important for three reasons: i) for managers to appreciate that particular competencies—beyond ethnocentric conceptualisations of the management role—are required when operating within and across cultural business environments; ii) to provide a management development framework to assist identification, preparation, management and repatriation of staff; and iii) to provide a framework through which organisations can learn and develop as a consequence of their international business operations and the experiences of its international manager (Fish 1995).

Traditional studies have pointed to specific, measurable personality traits. Tucker (1978) for example in an American study identified skills associated with open-mindedness, respect for others beliefs, trust in people, tolerance, personal control, flexibility, patience, social adaptability, initiative and risk taking. A British study undertaken by Barham and Wills (1992) categorised international management skills into three groups: 1) 'doing competencies', such as the ability to champion international strategy, operate as a cross-border coach, and act as an inter-cultural mediator and change agent; 2) 'being competencies', associated with recognising the cognitive complexity and emotional energy needed when operating overseas; and 3) 'psychological maturity', associated with a need to develop and re-orient oneself to differences in morality and orientation to time, and to possess a curiosity to learn.

These are each important; however, there is nothing uniquely international in them—one would reasonably expect to find them in a competent domestic manager. Adler and Bartholomew (1992) identified the characteristics distinguishing the traditional international manager from the emerging transnational manager. The new transnational manager has a global perspective and awareness of cross-cultural interaction, has had various types and levels of foreign experience, and has an ability to adapt to and respond to local needs, and specific business and cultural needs.

A study of Australian organisations (Fish & Wood 1997b) identified four cross-cultural management competencies:

1 transformational management skills associated with changing management mindsets from domestic to international considerations;
2 interactional management skills associated with understanding human resource management, leadership and motivational practices across international settings;
3 transactional management communication skills associated with representing and selling the business presence overseas; and
4 foreign language competence.

Foreign language competence

Mead (1990, p. 213) argues that: 'the manager who has fluent control over the other culture's language has direct access to members of that culture.' Foreign language competence is likely to contribute significantly to acceptance of an individual in a new cultural setting and have positive spin-offs for the organisation at the same time. Furthermore, as language usage is contextually bound, culture, class, gender and age all influence usage. People with only rudimentary knowledge of a foreign language may communicate poorly and use inappropriate terminology. Their basic command of the language may in turn lead to poor business and individual relationships (Fish & Wood 1997b).

International career motivation

While ensuring that appropriate compensation is in place as argued earlier, it is also imperative that intrinsic issues of international career motivation beyond pure extrinsic matters are considered: 'A good reward system must contain both monetary and non-monetary rewards ... and reward systems need to be considered in the light of the strategic roles these employees can play in the global competitiveness of their firms' (Black et al. 1992, p. 214) It is thus important that both the organisation and the candidates understand why an overseas appointment might be accepted. Fish and Wood (1993, 1994, 1997a) argue that the idea of an overseas appointment has a great deal of romantic appeal and people may be attracted for no reason other than the 'status' associated with being 'our man in Hong Kong'. The appeal may be countered by the prospect of a harsh location, the costs associated with changes to lifestyle, family disruption, what refusal might mean to an ongoing career, lack of attention to the skills likely to be derived as a result of the appointment and the possibility that the appointment will not contribute to career development and progression within the organisation (Fish & Wood 1997a).

Fish and Wood (1997a) found that international career advancement and professional development were key intrinsic motivators; monetary satisfaction and international career support were important extrinsic motivators for Australian managers in accepting an overseas posting. The intrinsic motivators though, played a more dominant role in the process.

Hence, an awareness of the factors that motivate managers to accept an off-shore move are likely to assist managers in coming to terms with the move and its ongoing career implications and assist organisations in identifying and selecting the most appropriate person.

Commitment—A factor which could cause an interest in an overseas posting is an individual's commitment to the organisation and its goals. In a study of Australian expatriates, Fish (1995) identified two forms of commitment that influenced an organisation's ability to retain managers. These were commitment to the parent company and commitment to the foreign affiliate. Attitudes associated with perceptions of enhanced career mobility, both domestically and internationally, and potential problems associated with balancing dual allegiances and attraction to the host country were identified as important issues to be dealt with following an international assignment. That is, unless organisations manage careers effectively, managers may seek greener pastures once they have returned home. Alternatively, international managers become so attached to the overseas lifestyle that, rather than return home, they opt for longer appointments or seek opportunities with other firms to remain off-shore.

Spouse/partner situation—An issue of particular significance is the need to cater for the adjustment needs of an accompanying spouse/partner. Concerns associated with disruption to the family and a spouse/partner's career, as well as to children's education, need to be addressed early. In addition, special attention needs to be directed to lifestyle adjustment and how the spouse/partner will come to terms with new living standards and different customs and roles (Tung 1982).

The spouse/partner is separated from friends and family more than is the expatriate international manager. The manager has the safety net of the business community and is partly sheltered from the day-to-day personal rigours of adjusting to the requirements of living in a new cultural environment. It therefore makes a great deal of sense to include spouse/partner preparation and adjustment in the IHRM agenda of business enterprises. Fish and Wood (1997d) confirm the need for improved attention to spouse/partner preparation and adjustment, and point to issues associated with both anticipatory adjustment (preparation) and in-country adjustment (see Table 10.3).

Table 10.3 Spouse/partner preparation and adjustment factors

Anticipatory adjustment	In-country adjustment
Quality of life adjustment	Lifestyle induction
Effective host country social behaviour	Inter-cultural communication networks
Business awareness	Business environment empathy
Personal/family impact	

Source: Fish 1995

Adler (1991) also argues for more informed attention and suggests that a spouse/partner being generally 'comfortable' with his/her immediate surroundings is of itself insufficient. Adjustment issues that go beyond a basic understanding of the new cultural setting need to be attended to. Adler (1991) describes this as the development of 'a meaningful portable life'. Given that the spouse/partner has, in most situations, left something quite significant in the form of a life-long career or social relationships, or both, behind, involvement in the overseas environment beyond mere shopping and restaurant excursions would seem critical to effective adjustment and ultimate success for the overseas assignment (Fish & Wood 1997d). A further Australian study (De Cieri, Dowling & Taylor 1991) suggested the introduction of company programs to provide spouse assistance and social support, address culture shock, recognise problems with perceived cultural distance, attend to the development of self-esteem, deal with life-satisfaction issues and finally to address family relationship satisfaction.

Overall, there is strong support for Australian organisations to invest more time and resources in the development of a more meaningful life for an accompanying spouse/partner in the foreign business environment. The medium to long-term benefits are improved retention rates on foreign assignments, less stress on the spouse and the expatriate, improved business image and presence, and significant potentional cost-savings from reducing the likelihood of a failed assignment.

Conclusion

The increasing move toward global businesses will require a more internationally focused HRM activity. For this to happen, work role transitions required in a variety of cross-cultural business settings need to be examined. Organisations need to ensure that appropriate IHRM practices are consistent with the organisation's business strategy. In addition, attention needs to be given to individual and family cross-cultural adjustment needs.

Organisational benefits resulting from an integrated perspective to IHRM include increased organisational learning, increased market exposure, retention and commitment of key staff, increased effectiveness and productivity, organisational growth and survival and improved international public relations. Individual benefits to be derived include increased job satisfaction, career advancement, successful repatriation and personal growth.

References

Adler, N.J. 1991, *International Dimensions of Organisational Behaviour*, Boston, PWS-Kent.

Adler, N.J. & Bartholomew, S. 1992, 'Managing globally competent people', *Academy of Management Executive*, vol. 6, no. 2, pp. 52–65.

Adler, N.J. & Ghadar, F. 1990, 'Strategic human resource management: A global perspective', in R. Peiperl (ed.), *Human Resource Management: An International Perspective*, de Gruyter, New York, pp. 235–60.

Barham, K. & Wills, S. 1992, 'International Management Competencies', in P.S. Kirkbride, K. Rowlands & B. Shaw (eds), *Proceedings of the Third Conference on International Personnel and Human Resource Management*, Ashridge Management College, England, vol. 1, section 2.

Black, J.S., Gregersen, H. & Mendenhall, M. 1992, *Global Assignments: Successfully Expatriating and Repatriating International Managers*, Jossey-Bass, San Francisco, CA.

Butler, J.E., Ferris, G.R. & Napier, N.K. 1991 *Strategy and Human Resource Management*, South-Western, Cincinnati, Ohio.

De Cieri, H., Dowling, P. & Taylor, K. 1991, 'The psychological impact of expatriate relocation on partners', *International Journal of Human Resource Management*, vol. 2, no. 3, pp. 377–414.

Dowling, P., Schuler, R.S. & Welch, D. 1994, *International Dimensions of Human Resource Management*, Belmont, Cal.: Wadsworth.

Feldman, D.C. & Thomas, D.C. 1992, 'Career Management Issues Facing Expatriates', *Journal of International Business Studies*, vol. 23, no. 2, pp. 271–94.

Feldman, D.C. & Tompson, H.B. 1993, 'Expatriation, repatriation and domestic geographical relocation: An empirical investigation of adjustment to new job assignments', *Journal of International Business Studies*, vol. 24, no. 3, pp. 507–29.

Fish, A.J. 1995, 'Expatriate career practices in Australian business enterprises: An East-Asian focus', PhD thesis, Graduate School of Business, University of Sydney.

Fish, A.J. & Wood, J. 1993, 'A challenge to career management practice', *International Journal of Career Management*, vol. 5, no. 2, pp. 3–10.

——1994, 'HRM and international expatriate management: A strategic link for Australian Business', *International Journal of Career Management*, vol. 5, no. 4, pp. 25–36.

——1996, 'A review of expatriate staffing practices in Australian business enterprises', *International Journal of Human Resource Management*, vol. 7, no. 4, pp. 846–65.

——1997a, 'An evaluation of factors motivating Australian business managers to undertake expatriate assignments to the East-Asian business region', *Career Development International*, vol. 2, no. 1, pp. 36–45.

—— 1997b, 'A review of cross-cultural management competencies in Australian business enterprises', *The Asia-Pacific Journal of Human Resources*, vol. 35, no. 1, pp. 37–52.

——1997c, 'Realigning international careers—a more strategic focus', *Career Development International*, vol. 2, no. 2, pp. 99–110.

——1997d, 'Managing spouse/partner preparation and adjustment—Developing a meaningful portable life', *Personnel Review*, vol. 26, no. 6, pp. 445–66.

Forster, N. 1992, 'International managers and mobile families: The professional and personal dynamics of transnational career pathing and job mobility in the 1990s', *International Journal of Human Resource Management*, vol. 3, no. 3, pp. 606–23.

Gordon, G.D. & Teagarden, M.B. 1992, 'Corporate selection strategies and international manager success', *Proceedings of The First International Conference on Expatriate Management*, Hong Kong Baptist College.

Gregersen, H., Hite, K. & Black, J.S. 1996, 'Expatriate performance appraisal in US multinational firms', *Journal of International Business Studies*, vol. 27, no. 4, pp. 711–38.

Heenan, D.A. & Perlmutter, H.V. 1979, *Multinational Organisational Development*, Reading, Mass.: Addison-Wesley.

Karpin, D. 1995, *Enterprising Nation: Renewing Australia's Managers to Meet the Challenges of the Asia-Pacific Century*, Report of the Industry Task Force on Leadership and Management Skills, AGPS, Canberra.

Mead, M. 1990, *Cross-Cultural Management Communication*, Chichester, Wiley.

Mendenhall, M. & Oddou, G. 1988, 'The overseas assignment: A practical look', *Business Horizons*, September–October, pp. 78–84.

Nicholson, N. 1987, 'The transition cycle: A conceptual framework for the analysis of change and human resource management', *Research in Human Resource Management*, vol. 5, pp. 167–222.

Phatak, A.V. 1989, *International Dimensions of Management*, 2nd edn, Boston, Mass.: PWS-Kent.

Temporal, P. & Burnett, K. 1990, 'Strategic corporate assignments and international management development', *Journal of Management Development*, vol. 9, no. 5, pp. 58–64.

Tucker, M. 1978, *The Measurement and Prediction of Overseas Work Assignments in the Navy*, US Navy Contract Number N00600-73-D-0780, Centre for Research and Education, Denver, CO.

Tung, R. 1982, 'Selection and training of personnel for overseas assignments', *Columbia Journal of World Business*, vol. 16, no. 1, pp. 68–78.

Zeira, I. & Banai, M. 1984 'Present and desired methods of selecting expatriate managers for international assignments', *Personnel Review*, vol. 13, no. 3, pp. 29–35.

Case Study H

Human resource issues involved in establishing a joint venture in Indonesia

Jasmine Sliger

Indonesia is undergoing rapid growth in the financial services industry. This case study examines the efforts undertaken to manage human resource issues associated with establishing a joint venture in the financial services industry by an Australian organisation. It focuses on the selection process, the identification of training needs, managing family/partner issues, cultural adjustment processes and induction. Although the case indicates effective ways to manage people during the establishment of a joint venture, it demonstrates these practices are not sufficient for the successful continuation of the business.

Background

Martin Leehman had been at Harmers, a leader in the financial services industry since 1970. During his time with the company, he led Harmers to become a powerful force in the marketplace. Due to its sound leadership, high technical expertise and its stability as an Australian company the turnover rate was minimal—people simply did not leave this conservative company. It prided itself on its intellectual property and sound business ethics.

By the early 1990s, its expertise was highly regarded throughout Australia. It was clear that at some point it would begin to saturate the market. Harmers had been successful in other joint ventures, and it was time to go off-shore to Asia. Could their valuable expertise be used in an Asian country? Could they penetrate one of the most difficult markets in the world?

Politically the time was ripe, every sentence out of Prime Minister Keating's mouth had Asia in it. All professional business organisations were conducting workshops on 'How to do business in Asia'. International human resource committees began to crop up within these organisations offering valuable culture-specific workshops on Korea, Japan, Indonesia, Malaysia and China. There was a strong push by the government along with strong incentives for Australian companies. It was Paul Keating's firm intention that Australia become a major player in the Asia-Pacific region.

As with many joint ventures, it started with a connection within the organisation. One of Harmers' middle managers, Patricia Chang, had strong personal connections in Indonesia. Connections, although useful, do not necessarily a joint venture make! Once Patricia Chang's connection was verified, Martin Leehman, members of the senior management team and R&D began to do their homework on the viability of establishing a joint venture with an appropriate company in Indonesia.

Such a joint venture would require government sanction. Obtaining the necessary approval was a very time-consuming and costly process requiring many visits to Indonesia. It involved meetings with several ministers both in Indonesia and here in Australia. Feasibility studies were undertaken, in part to determine how the technical skills could be translated into the Indonesian culture. The timing was right as Indonesia was undergoing rapid technical growth in the financial services industry and could look to Australia for world-class expertise. Through much relationship building, many meetings, and R&D studies, it was determined that extending the business was a realistic opportunity and that there could be good returns in it for Harmers. Fifteen months later, the joint-venture company was established.

The selection process

On one of the visits of ministers from Indonesia, an official asked whether Harmers would be ready to send a team over within six weeks once the 'green light' was given. Mary Wilson, the human resources manager, knew of the groundwork being done by Leehman and his team. She was aware of the human resources implications of such a development.

Wilson wanted to scour the 1000 Harmer employees to find the best of its talent in deciding who should go to Indonesia. Technical expertise and intellectual property would be Harmers' greatest asset. However, the specialised nature of the project—and the fact that it was their first joint venture in Asia—meant that a team with outstanding people skills was required. To identify those who had these skills, plus a positive attitude towards relocating off-shore, the best selection scenario would have been to call for self-nominations. But it was crucial to the company that its competitors and the press not get wind of what was going on.

Instead, a working party was formed, consisting of Mary Wilson and other divisional managers. Branch managers were asked to submit names of people they considered suitable, based on criteria set by the working party. A consultative approach was then used between the working party and the managers. Due to the technical expertise required, the entire team was to be selected from within the company.

Because of the distance, degree of cultural difference, number of people involved and the cost of relocating Australians to Indonesia, it was expected that the careful selection and preparation of these employees and their families would be critical to the success of the venture from day one. Accordingly, specialist assistance was sought in the form of a cross-cultural psychologist, a specialist in communications and cross-cultural team-building, and a management consultant with cross-cultural training experience, particularly in pre-departure training. This specialist advice proved invaluable in streamlining the selection process and identifying key issues for Wilson and her colleagues to address immediately.

The greatest challenge was getting senior management to agree to spend the money on these activities, as the final go-ahead had not yet been received. Wilson's argument was that the ministers had said once the 'green light' had been given, there would be only six weeks before the team left for Indonesia. This was insufficient time for the team members to come to terms with all of the joint-venture issues and to participate in cross-cultural training. Six weeks would give them only enough time to move house.

Mary Wilson's influence and commitment to the process gave sufficient leverage for her to persuade management to give their support to the program. Even if this venture did not proceed, it would be an investment towards similar opportunities in the future.

Harmers had used specialist remuneration consultants to prepare job descriptions and advise on appropriate remuneration structures. The job descriptions for the overseas postings were begun but could not be completed as, with the contract still not approved, the roles had not been clarified.

The approach

Among the tools and techniques used to prepare the relocatees was an Australian version of the Overseas Assignment Inventory (OAI). The OAI is an international tool, consisting of a self-response questionnaire completed by the employee candidate and partner/spouse. It is a standardised instrument that describes 14 attitudes and attributes necessary for successful personal adjustment to a different culture as well as yielding valuable information for discussing motivations and expectations prior to the assignment.

Additionally, it provides an objective and consistent means of assessing an individual's ability to adjust to a different cultural environment. Responses were subsequently verified in a private interview with each couple by both consultants. On the basis of the findings, the consultants assigned risk ratings to each couple ranging from 'low to moderate' to 'very high'. These findings were then reported back to Mary and the working party for further discussion and final decision.

The OAI and the in-depth interviews provided a good basis for selecting candidates for the project. The OAI also identified many training and development issues. First and foremost were issues of living in another country. As in Maslow's hierarchy of needs, you can't think about self-esteem if you don't have a roof over your head! Family issues such as accommodation, medical facilities for children, support for pre- and post-natal mothers, business entertainment requirements, children's education and welfare, and opportunity for university level study were of chief concern to candidates.

Many training needs were immediately identified. These included knowledge of cultural differences in management. For example, how do those I will be dealing with operate? How are they motivated? What are some of the culturally appropriate ways of showing emotion and trust? Other issues included cross-cultural problem solving and acquiring the necessary people management skills. Dealing with personal difficulties such as isolation for partners and managing stress within the relocated family were also identified.

From the interviews, it was evident that some couples would need further pre-departure counselling in certain areas such as partner communications, stress management in overseas assignments, cross-cultural dynamics of male–female relationships and cross-cultural adjustment issues (e.g. ethnocentricity and general lifestyle adjustment).

The first thing to be addressed was the family concerns with accommodation. The company agreed for Wilson to go to Indonesia to review housing, schooling and medical facilities. Through the connections established in Indonesia, Mary was taken to various areas for staff housing. Issues that were critical were the standard of hygiene of the facilities, travelling time for employees and the consequent level of isolation for the accompanying partner. Mary videoed all the facilities so the families could get an idea of what it was going to be like to live in Indonesia. Having been there herself, she was more aware of the range of family issues. During face-to-face meetings, she used the videos as a mechanism for providing specific information, along with her first-hand observations.

Meanwhile in Indonesia, there had been some political developments. Some factions were concerned that due to the superiority of the Australian technical expertise, Indonesia, through its partner in the venture, might lose face in the eyes of its citizens and neighbours in the region. This anxiety led to another round of meetings and although the ministers at the highest level wanted things to go ahead, other political factions continued to offer resistance.

In subtle ways Harmers was not receiving the necessary co-operation. There began to be doubts over the usefulness of Patricia Chang's connections.

Some cultural adjustment was necessary in doing business with the Indonesians. Much time is spent in building relationships and getting to know each other. In direct business contexts, time is seen as limitless and flexible, the concept often being referred to as 'rubber time'. Other issues such as dealing with favours, gift giving, dealing with bribes and the nature of business meetings, were discussed at length at senior team meetings. During one visit, the overseas entourage expected that Harmers people would be assigned to their party 24 hours a day over a weekend; duties included driving visitors around on personal shopping sprees. At every stage, Martin Leehman gave full support to his team even though some members questioned the way business was done.

The training program

Companies involved in joint ventures often send only a few people overseas at a time, to work with the host country nationals.

Ultimately, a dozen employees and their families were accepted for the joint-venture project. The training program ran for seven days; during the first few days for the employees, the areas of team building, communication skills and project management were covered. Mary Wilson and some senior managers made an appearance and participated in some of the activities. It was important that the company show strong support for the employees and their families. At the end of this phase, the team had bonded strongly and there appeared to be a lot of enthusiasm for the overseas project.

The last three days were dedicated to international issues and partners were invited to attend. Culture-specific and general issues were worked through and areas of cross-cultural communication and business ethics were part of the program. Later, there was a one-day follow-up for the team-members, specialising in cross-cultural team-building, change strategies and stress management.

At the end of the program, two candidates were deselected because of their attitude towards working in a different culture and some concerns regarding tolerance. As their technical expertise was crucial to the team, the positions needed to be filled urgently. It was decided to appoint people from outside the organisation.

The training program was conducted on the understanding that there would be further training in Indonesia. The process utilised the latest in management development tools, including the team management index (TMI) and several project management simulations. TMI looks at how people like to work together. Work preferences are measured and the TMI profile provides feedback on how each person relates to others, how they gain and give information, how they make decisions and how they organise themselves and others. Its use in team development has been well tested and found to be very effective.

The waiting game

Preparatory work continued despite the fact that approval had still not been given. Management introduced projects and research to prepare the ground-work for departure and relocation. The team leader and Patricia Chang, together with their respective partners, had already moved to Indonesia. There was a lot of work to be done, starting with a major presentation to the ministry. Some members of the team from Australia prepared for the presen-tation and were flown to Indonesia to assist the two already there. By appear-ing on Indonesian TV, Patricia Chang managed to give Harmers high exposure. This made the politically resistant factions quite nervous but clearly raised Harmers' profile.

Time passed, and it appeared that nothing was happening. This discour-aged Martin Leehman, who had backed the project and Mary Wilson from the beginning. Martin was also being pressured by the board. A series of meetings was scheduled but subsequently cancelled by the ministry following an incident in the news where Indonesia was mentioned unfavourably by an Australian official. In the Asian international press, issues that may seem inconsequential to Australians in Australia take on a deeper significance for Australian companies working in Asia.

Several weeks later, an official letter came stating that the government was not going to approve the joint-venture project The team was devastated. As it turned out Patricia Chang's connections were not as valuable as they had first appeared. It looked as if Chang was not now able to deliver, and this per-ception began to divide the team. The team leader, however, had become acquainted with another powerful leader in the ministry. Eventually, this person proved to be a valuable link for the company.

Martin Leehman retired and was replaced by Michael Hoffman. Although Hoffman was familiar with the project and the surrounding issues—and sup-portive of the joint venture—decisions had to be made regarding the cost involved and the timeframe for decisions. The team leader's new contact was flown to Sydney for discussions with company representatives. The under-standing was that the plug would be pulled if sufficient return was not seen for the investment within a specified period. If there was no progress, the office would be closed down and the relationship managed from Australia.

There were many attempts to prevent closure of the Indonesian office, but after three and a half years, and with no sign of a break-through, the decision to close was made and the two employees were called back to Australia. As a sign of recognition for the continuing commitment of the two families already in Indonesia, Wilson flew across to break the news personally. Although it was hard to hear, they appreciated the personal communication from Mary Wilson. It was also critical that they work together to plan their transition back to Australia. She reassured both employees that positions would be available to them upon their return to Australia.

The learning experience

There are many lessons to be learned from this attempt at setting up a joint venture. First, as is often the case, this joint venture started because an employee had certain contacts. However, the relationship with the joint-venture partner should not have proceeded without much closer involvement and supervision by the managing director or a senior manager.

Second, personal contacts can bring both rewards and problems. Harmers' employee in the venture proved to be a double-edged sword: although her personal investment in the project and her contact offered opportunities to the company, the closeness of the connection could also have clouded objectivity. Too much information and therefore power lay in the hands of one employee.

On the positive side, it is important to note that this episode did not affect the loyalty or commitment of the team members. All are still with Harmers except for Patricia Chang, who chose to leave. Management has no regrets over the investment in processes leading up to selection, preparation and training of its employees in this specialised area of business. All the employees have taken on new and challenging work within the company. The investment on their training and development allowed them to be open to new possibilities.

Off-shore expansion offers major opportunities for growth and those companies which have done their homework, even had their fingers slightly burned, are best placed to take advantage of the opportunities.

Today Harmers continues to have good relations with Indonesia, with the links maintained from Australia. The connection that the team leader had fostered is now stronger than ever. Several trips are made annually to Indonesia. This particular joint venture is closer to eventuating than ever in the past, and the company has built powerful international strategic alliances in the region. It has since also established a few successful joint ventures but not in the Asian region—yet.

11 Developing an ethical culture

Ron Miller

Organisations in fields as diverse as business, government, education, health and not-for-profit are increasingly involved in transitions that are taking place faster and faster. These transitions are being managed with re-engineering, cultural change, reorganisation, acquisition, divestiture, alliances, technology shifts—and occasionally, bankruptcy Extra effort is required from the workforce as organisations make these transitions; and employees with little experience in handling change are faced with new demands, new methods and new relationships. In many cases, they are asked to proceed on trust. At the same time, major transitions have the potential to reduce employee trust when it is most needed. Employee trust is not commanded: it is won and maintained on the basis of decision by decision and action by action. In the context of rapid change, trust previously taken for granted needs to be re-established.

Organisations with an ethical culture—reinforced by actual behaviour and performance—generate a higher level of trust. This is a key reason why many enterprises are directing effort into defining their ethics and communicating the outcomes to employees to educate and assist them to understand the importance of ethical behaviour. This is reinforced by the increasing community awareness and expectations, government regulations—including penalties—and global business standards.

Positioning ethics

The term *ethics* comes from the Greek *ethos* meaning custom, usage or character. Ethics has been a topic of debate and discussion for centuries, focusing on issues such as morality, integrity, honesty, truth and virtue. Studies have identified forms of ethics in most cultures. One common value is the relationship of an individual to others, referred to as the 'Golden Rule' in Christian societies. Almost all organisational codes of conduct have a strong element of the notion of 'do unto others as you would that they do unto you', where 'others' includes an ever-growing list of stakeholders from employees, to customers, shareholders, the community, the environment and government.

Ethics in a commercial and business sense is generally promulgated as a code of conduct. That code is usually derived from the organisation's values, vision and mission. The values and vision are developed from the culture of the organisation. Culture can be defined as a body of beliefs, traditions and guides for behaviour shared among members of a society or group. The organisational culture expresses shared assumptions, values and beliefs and is the social glue which binds the organisational fabric together. At a time when private and public sector organisations are finding their actions coming under more and more scrutiny (and accountability) from their employees, the media and the community in general, the issue of corporate ethics is becoming an increasingly important aspect of the public face of the organisation.

Many organisations have found that ethics is good business. Trusting employees—and behaving ethically towards them—flows into the marketplace, creating a competitive advantage. Successful organisations recognise that their employees are basically honest and want to do the right thing. They then educate and train them about ethical behaviour and provide support as needed in ethical dilemmas. In effect, they are providing their employees with the necessary support to say 'We are too good to have to cheat to get the business.'

The higher level of interest in ethics has been driven by various events. In the United States, federal government legislation has caused organisations to review their behaviour, often formalising a position of ethics officer, to take account of their codes of conduct and the responsibility for compliance with federal laws. Other drivers have been significant fines levied on corporations and jailing of corporate officers.

In the development and implementation of ethics, there appears to be a strong division between compliance and ethics. Compliance is identified as meeting the laws, regulations and standards as defined or identified by law and legal requirements, that is adhering to legislation and the general requirements for doing business. Compliance is reinforced in the USA by sentencing guidelines. Corporations that have been fined for improper actions can have their fines reduced based on what previous actions they have taken to support ethical behaviour. The steps can include an ethics department, code of conduct, training, implementation programs and other industry-specific actions.

There is a growing recognition that corporations are exposed to charges of unethical behaviour when corporate performance standards are set at such a level that actions of dubious ethics provide the only means of meeting corporate objectives. It must be made clear that people are not to use their position to gain monetary rewards or influence external situations by actions such as bribery, and that they need to avoid situations that involve conflicting interests. In this respect, the Northrop Grumman Corporation is often cited as a leader in the field of corporate ethics. They espouse the value 'We're not really in the business of teaching people to be ethical. We're teaching ethical people how to make tough decisions'.

Treviño and Nelson (1995) summarise what CEOs and ethics officers agree to be important about ethics:

> They believe that ethics is essential to business—that good business is built on honest relationships and on a reputation for integrity and trust. They assume that most people are basically good and they prefer to work for an ethical organisation. They also believe that these same people welcome guidance and the organisation's development and communication of a strong set of values. And they believe that people want to see good conduct rewarded and misconduct punished. Finally, they have found that moral leadership and open communications are essential building blocks of an ethical organisation. (p. 306)

This statement is consistent with the stance taken by Phil Condit, president and CEO of the Boeing Company, who said at a 1996 Ethics Officers Association Conference in Seattle:

> Ethics cannot be a stand-alone program. It has to be integral to and embedded into the operation of the company. Unless senior management is deeply involved and committed, the challenge is impossible. People will look at the day-to-day actions and see if they add up. It cannot break down anywhere along the way. Ethics is part of every second of the day.

By way of illustration, he outlined Boeing's Four Principles:

1 *Integrity*—Do what you say you are going to do.
2 *Customer satisfaction*—Without satisfied customers, none of this matters.
3 *Shareholder value*—A good return to investors encourages them to invest in the company.
4 *People working together*—The Mission statement for working on the 777 aircraft was 'Working together to develop a preferred aircraft'.

Condit concluded with the comment: 'There is no priority in these four principles. All must be done all the time. The customer judges if the job is well done.'

The Ethics Resource Center conducted a survey of US employees on the effects of ethics programs in American business (Ethics Resource Center 1994). The report concluded that

> Corporate ethics programs appear to have distinctly positive impact on employee behaviour and their opinions about the ethics of fellow employees, management, their companies and even themselves. The most positive effects were reported in companies which had all three program components—codes of conduct, ethics training and ethics officers.

Vision, mission, core values

Ethics practice originates with an organisation's vision, mission and core values. These give focus, direction and composition to the expression of the required behavioural standards. The emphasis is on the long-term interests of the organisation, together with its relationship to all relevant stakeholders over this period. Most mission, vision and values statements identify how the enterprise will serve its stakeholders and maintain long-term profit through fair and honest actions with all of its constituencies. Core values typically refer to obligations to shareholders, employees and customers, usually expressed in terms of delivering value, excellence, innovation, commitments and integrity.

Integrity is a vital element in ethics: it is often recognised as a most valuable corporate asset, maintained by the organisation keeping its word and performing according to commitments. There are three key foundations for an organisation's commitment to integrity to be seen as credible: first, adoption of the principles of honesty, fairness and respect for individual and community freedoms; second, employees are not placed in situations that lead to a conflict between their personal values and interests and those of the organisation; and finally, the corporate pursuit of sales and profits is undertaken within the expressed ethical framework.

Figure 11.1   Northern Telecom's core values

---

1 We create superior value for our customers.
2 We work to provide shareholder value.
3 Our people are our strength.
4 We share one vision. We are one team.
5 We have only one standard—excellence.
6 We embrace change and reward innovation.
7 We fulfil our commitments and act with integrity.

Developing an ethical culture

Organisations embarking on an ethics program start at different stages of development. Some may commence by exploring how to go about introducing a program; others may review and improve an ongoing activity or revitalise a neglected process. In each case, the usual requirements for a change or transition need to be in place: these include senior management's active commitment and support; an internal 'champion' to provide leadership and energy to new initiatives; appropriate funding to ensure activities can be completed; and communication to all affected stakeholders of the enterprise.

The development and implementation of an ethics culture will typically consist of three phases:

- Phase 1—analysis and evaluation to determine plan and direction
- Phase 2—develop content and implementation of plan
- Phase 3—review progress and make corrections.

Phase I—analysis and evaluation to determine plan and direction

Establishing a plan and strategy with as much organisational input and commitment as possible—particularly from the most senior levels—is a necessary prerequisite. This early development of a sense of ownership facilitates later implementation. It may be necessary to commence with an external agency undertaking an initial review and evaluation. This provides an objective and unbiased perspective that builds credibility for developing the overall plan and direction.

The review and evaluation of the analysis is best done by building representation from all areas (functions and business units) and levels (board, executive, management and employees) within the organisation. Determining the current ethics performance and identifying historical experience assist in establishing a base from which to build. They also provide an understanding of the constituents' real and perceived view of the organisation's ethics and its past performance. This process, and the outcomes, help to identify the behaviours that will be required for the future. A typical outcome of this preliminary stage is a statement of policy and direction that draws directly from the organisational vision, mission and core values.

There are three keys to this stage of the process. First, ethics is a matter of observed behaviour. Most behaviour is habit based; looking behind observed behaviours provides a basis for understanding the causes of individual and collective actions. The objective is to instil a sense of ethical behaviour that becomes the 'corporate glue' binding the organisation together with its own unique identity. In this respect, it underpins and affects all operational activity. In the human resource area, activities include performance planning and appraisal, salary administration, equal employment opportunity, industrial relations and occupational health and safety.

Second, progressive organisations manage and give leadership to all stakeholder relationships. These include relationships between the organisation and employees, shareholders, suppliers, contractors, customers, governments and community groups. These relationships all need to be based on a consistent, identifiable and corporate-wide ethical approach.

Third, a more detailed plan can be generated once an understanding of the current situation is established and compared with the proposed ethics strategy. Successful ethics plans include important stakeholder considerations with an emphasis on ease of implementation. Implementation considerations need to recognise that ethical behaviour is not practised throughout the organisation until all employees understand and appreciate the behaviour required of them individually and collectively.

The common elements of effective ethics programs include issues such as:

- standards and procedures;
- individual responsibilities;
- ethical considerations in assigning authority;
- methods for feedback and resolution of ethical issues;
- discipline, corrective and preventative actions required.

The plan that emerges from this first phase should consider issues such as: a code of conduct outlining what is expected of all employees in their behaviour on behalf of the organisation; the administrative system that will reinforce these expectations, including any processes for employee assistance to report or resolve ethical issues, and for internal arbitration and appeal; implementation and maintenance actions such as the introduction of an ethics officer, employee education and communication; and how the enterprise plans to evaluate its commitment to ethics.

Phase 2—develop content and implementation of plan

The content for organisational ethics is generally defined in policy statements and promulgated through a formal statement of the code of business conduct. The code of conduct becomes a vital link between the organisational leadership and employees. Anecdotal evidence suggests that the better the code, the better the performance. The following issues are typical of the content headings included in a formal code of business conduct publication.

- Responsibility to Ourselves and Our Environment
- Protecting Shareholder Value
- Competing with Integrity
- Interacting with Government
- Conducting International Business
- Putting the Code to Work
- Questions and Answers

Figure 11.2 displays the code of conduct developed by Australia's Western Mining Corporation (see Francis 1997, p. 151). Of particular interest is the importance of the code of conduct to Western Mining Corporation employees as stated in the preamble to the code.

Many organisations have found that the introduction of an ethics office provides an important ingredient for the overall success of the program. Figure 11.3 illustrates how US-based electronics firm Texas Instruments defines the role of its ethics office.

Figure 11.2   Western Mining Corporation's code of conduct

The reputation and integrity of WMC will only be maintained if every one of us acts, and is seen to act, in a way that is exemplary of the high standards of business we set for ourselves. Accordingly, **the Code of Conduct is the most important document issued by WMC to its employees.** Every one of us must understand and comply with our Code.

Our Code of Conduct applies to directors and all employees of WMC.

Our Code of Conduct is not just a document. It is our corporate creed.

You can apply the Code of Conduct in any particular situation by asking yourself *'What is the **right** thing to do?'*

The Code of Conduct consists of five 'minimum standards':

1 We respect the law and act accordingly.
2 We conduct ourselves with integrity, are fair and honest in our dealings and treat others with dignity.
3 We do not place ourselves in situations which result in divided loyalties.
4 We use WMC's assets (including funds, equipment and information) responsibly and in the best interests of WMC.
5 We are responsible for our actions and accountable for their consequences.

Figure 11.3   Role of Texas Instruments' ethics office

The Texas Instruments Ethics Office is a resource that exists to:
1 Define and communicate TI's ethical and legal expectation.
2 Provide guidance in resolving issues, interpreting policies/practices/laws and making appropriate changes in policies and practices.
3 Provide a safe place where TIers, customers and suppliers can seek information and raise issues.
4 Provide leadership and facilitate value-based decision making that enables trusting relationships.
5 Enhance TI's reputation, internally and externally, through outreach efforts.

The transition to an ethically based culture requires significant empowerment of individual employees. Behaviour in organisations where the existing culture is focused on control is usually characterised by compliance (Walton 1985); a significant investment in training and education is then required to enable people to make decisions and take initiatives without reference to a higher authority. The transition is likely to be easier in an enterprise whose culture encourages and reinforces employee empowerment. In this case, the move to introduce a culture of ethics is likely to proceed similarly to other change processes where the introduction stresses awareness and provides communication processes that enhance learning and provide support.

Phase 3—review progress and make corrections

As with any transition, the best progress comes from programs that communicate policies, procedures and responsibilities clearly and frequently to all employees. Targeted communications must meet the needs of a variety of audiences and their particular learning styles. Although the message that each employee is responsible for ethical behaviour is consistent throughout the organisation, its presentation needs to be different for executives and managers compared with clerical and administrative staff or factory-floor employees.

Establishing standards and evaluating performance is part of the job of management at all levels. Some organisations use annual compliance reports as a means of safeguarding (and emphasising) the external implications of unethical behaviour. Western Mining Corporation has a code of conduct advisory committee, chaired by an executive director. Part of the committee's role is to annually select a cross-section of senior officers to report to the managing director confirming that they have individually endeavoured to comply with the code, promoted it within their areas of responsibility, have no matters covered by the code outstanding in their areas, and have included proposals to maintain awareness and need for compliance in the business plan for the coming year. A similar procedure is used by Caterpillar Tractor Company (see Figure 11.4).

Figure 11.4 Illustrative compliance reporting procedure

Reporting Code Compliance—Caterpillar Tractor Co.

Before the close of each year, the company's General Counsel will prepare an appropriate listing of senior company managers who are to be asked to report on compliance. Those on the list will be required to complete a memorandum, by year-end: (1) affirming knowledge and understanding of the Code; and (2) reporting events or activities which might cause an impartial observer to conclude that the Code hasn't been followed. These reports should be sent directly to the General Counsel. Reports will be treated in confidence.

Employees may also be encouraged to do a quick ethics test when confronted with situations that provide them with doubt or concern:

- Is the action legal?
- Does it comply with our values?
- If you do it, will you feel bad?
- How will it look in the newspaper?
- If you know it's wrong, don't do it!
- If you're not sure, ask!
- Keep asking until you get an answer!

The role and contribution of HRM

Human resource managers have a responsibility to help prepare the organisation and its employees to perform in an ethical way. All successful performance is based on defined expectations to be performed by qualified and skilled people who are appropriately trained and rewarded. The same is true of ethics. What constitutes ethical behaviour must be defined and communicated to employees: this commences at recruitment and continues through all aspects of training in the standards and expected ethical behaviour on a regular basis. Employee performance must be measured against the code of conduct and given appropriate forms of recognition. Ethics is a discipline, having standards of performance and one which can be taught with behaviour observed and corrected or rewarded as needed. Figure 11.5 (p. 254) illustrates the expectations required of Caterpillar Tractor Company.

Other aspects of the human resource contribution can be much more operational. Actions can include the establishment of an ethics advice call line. An essential element of this service is that callers have the right to remain anonymous, although they are encouraged to identify themselves. Employees need to have the confidence that their questions are taken seriously and, if reporting a concern, that they will be protected from any retaliation.

Code of conduct

A code of conduct is the document that gives clear direction for individual behaviour. For many organisations, it is the main reference for defining expected performance. A code of conduct can include as many or as few sections as required by the culture and organisation style. The code structure will usually include beliefs, guidelines, rules, definitions, rationales; these are often accompanied by illustrations and questions and answers. Figure 11.6 (p. 255) shows the American federal government's code that specifies 14 principles of ethical conduct for its employees.

Typically, the code of conduct is introduced by a general statement of company philosophy and commitment to ethical standards. Emphasis is placed on the observance of laws and regulations and can include specific examples. The code of conduct content adopted by the Australian Institute of Company Directors is an appropriate example (see Francis 1997, ch. 6). The preamble states:

> The Institute of Company Directors' Code of Conduct is intended to provide guidance to directors and to assist them in carrying out their duties and responsibilities effectively and in accordance with the best professional standards. It sets out the standard of conduct which the Institute expects from its members.
>
> The principles in the Code are relevant to directors of all companies, as well as to directors of government business enterprises and not-for-profit organisations. They apply to both executive and non-executive members.
>
> Fellows and members of the Australian Institute of Company Directors have agreed to be bound by the Principles in this Code.

Figure 11.5   Caterpillar Tractor's expectations of employee behaviour

Human Relationships as Defined by Caterpillar Tractor

1 We aspire to a high standard of excellence in human relationships. Specifically, we intend:

2 To select and place employees on the basis of qualifications for the work to be performed—without discrimination in terms of race, religion, national origin, color, sex, age or physical or mental disability.

3 To place people on jobs which are truly productive and necessary for achievement of approved objectives.

4 To show each employee the purposes of his or her job and work unit and require that work be done well.

5 To ask that people give their best efforts, including their ideas and suggestions for innovation and continuous improvement.

6 To maintain uniform, high standards of work and offer people opportunities to make the best use of their abilities.

7 To encourage self-development and assist employees in mastering their current jobs and improving their job skills.

8 To protect people's health and lives. This includes maintaining a clean work environment as free as practicable from health and safety hazards.

9 To provide employees with timely information concerning company mission, vision, operations and results, as well as other work-related matters in which they logically have an interest.

10 To compensate people fairly, according to their contributions to the company, within the framework of national and local practices.

11 To develop human relationships that inspire respect for, and confidence and trust in the company.

12 To operate the business in such a way that employees don't feel a need for representation by unions or other third parties.

13 Where employees have elected in favour of—or are required by law to have some form of—union representation, Caterpillar will endeavour to build a sound company-union relationship.

14 To seek to provide stable, secure employment consistent with the long-term success of Caterpillar.

15 To refrain from hiring persons closely related to members of the board of directors and administrative officers. When other employees' relatives are hired, this must be solely the result of their qualifications for jobs to be filled. Nepotism—or the appearance of nepotism—is neither fair to employees, nor in the long-term interests of the business.

16 To make decisions at the lowest level in the organisation at which they can be competently resolved.

17 To develop a climate that encourages good people to want to work for, and build careers with, Caterpillar.

18 To give special effort to work directly with each other in a helpful, friendly way, avoiding bureaucracy and other hazards common to large organisations.

The Institute expects that Members and Fellows will seek to uphold and promote the values of: Honesty; Integrity; Enterprise; Excellence; Accountability; Justice; Independence; Equality of Shareholder Opportunity.

Figure 11.6 US government code of ethical conduct

Fourteen Principles of Ethical Conduct for Employees of US Government

1 Public service is a public trust, requiring employees to place loyalty to the Constitution, the laws and ethical principles above private gain.
2 Employees shall not hold financial interests that conflict with the conscientious performance of duty.
3 Employees shall not engage in financial transactions using non-public Government information or allow the improper use of such information for private interest.
4 An employee shall not, except as permitted by the Standards of Ethical Conduct, solicit or accept any gift or other item of monetary value from any person or entity seeking official action from, doing business with, or conducting activities regulated by the employee's agency, or whose interests may be substantially affected by the performance or nonperformance of the employee's duties.
5 Employees shall put forth honest effort in the performance of their duties.
6 Employees shall not knowingly make unauthorized commitments or promises of any kind purporting to bind the Government.
7 Employees shall not use public office for private gain.
8 Employees shall act impartially and not give preferential treatment to any private organization or individual.
9 Employees shall protect and conserve Federal property and shall not use it for other than authorized activities.
10 Employees shall not engage in outside employment or activities, including seeking or negotiating for employment, that conflict with Government duties and responsibilities.
11 Employees shall disclose waste, fraud, abuse and corruption to appropriate authorities.
12 Employees shall satisfy in good faith their obligations as citizens, including all financial obligations, especially those—such as Federal, State or local taxes—that are imposed by law.
13 Employees shall adhere to all laws and regulations that provide equal opportunity for all Americans regardless of race, color, religion, sex, national origin, age or handicap.
14 Employees shall endeavour to avoid any actions creating the appearance that they are violating the law or the ethical standards set forth in the Standards of Ethical Conduct. Whether particular circumstances create an appearance that the law or these standards have been violated shall be determined from the perspective of a reasonable person with knowledge of the relevant facts.

The code of conduct should also address external relationships with key stakeholders such as customers and suppliers. Sections related to customers tend to emphasise issues concerning customer trust, representation and confidentiality. Some large organisations go so far as to define the limits of acceptable customer gifts and entertainment. With regard to suppliers, the code of conduct will stress the need for employees to be impartial and objective in their dealings, and not to accept or solicit any personal benefit that might compromise normal commercial relationships. Again, issues of confidentiality are also usually included.

All large corporations recognise the importance of educating their employees on the requirements for doing business in a global marketplace. Emphasis is put on a world composed of differing races, religions, cultures, customs, political philosophies, languages, economic resources and geography. Success in the international arena requires that these differences be respected and that recognition of human pluralism be viewed as a corporate strength, where no organisation (or nation) has a monopoly on wisdom. Employees are thus encouraged to learn and benefit from human diversity in their commercial dealings. These issues are clearly illustrated in the guiding principles of Japan's internationally focused Toyota Motor Company as shown in Figure 11.7.

Figure 11.7   Toyota Motor Corporation's guiding principles

Guiding Principles of Toyota Motor Company
1 Be a company of the world.
2 Serve the greater good of people everywhere by devoting careful attention to safety and the environment.
3 Assert leadership in technology and customer satisfaction.
4 Become a contributing member of the community in every nation.
5 Foster a corporate culture that honours individuality while promoting teamwork.
6 Pursue continuing growth through efficient, global management.
7 Build lasting relationships with business partners around the world.

The ethics officer

The role of the ethics officer is evolving, and requires significant independence, influence and credibility to be effective. The officer generally establishes partnerships with legal and human resource departments and has ready access to the chief executive officer and other senior executives and managers. In many organisations this can be achieved by requiring a formal half-yearly or annual report to the board or its audit committee. Ideally, employees should see the ethics officer as the 'conscience' of the organisation.

Members of the Ethics Officers Association feel very strongly that their office should be kept separate from management operations to retain and protect the integrity and impartiality of the position. Such separation is also consistent with the view that ethics officers do not have the responsibility or accountability to make judgements or decisions on what does or does not constitute ethical behaviour; their role is to be a resource to employees and provide advice as required. Nevertheless, the position has the potential for defined performance measurement. This can range from the position having a direct contribution to such issues as litigation and media reports, through to assessing employee attitudes and reactions to issues of ethical behaviour.

The ethics officer's role commences with setting up effective processes for communicating and reinforcing the corporate values. Visible leadership is required from the top, with the ethics officer ensuring the transmission and support for these messages. Such leadership positions the company's reputation as an asset alongside other corporate assets.

Competitive business pressures are likely to lead to issues, questions and concerns for a range of employees, and they will not always be certain of the appropriate course of action. The ethics officer can provide a structured, proactive method or process to support employees when demands appear to conflict. In effect, the role provides a resource that employees can use to understand the organisation's ethical expectations when they are in doubt. At the same time, ethical behaviour cannot be seen as solely the responsibility of the ethics officer. He or she is there as a resource to guide people to make decisions and behave in a way consistent with the corporation's values and interests.

Ultimately, people are proud to work for—and identify with—an organisation that takes a strong stand for integrity. Employees need to know that they should be sensitive to a range of commercial and social relationships and what their obligations are. Simply staying out of jail is not sufficient!

Conclusion

The past few years have seen almost weekly coverage of prominent organisations and their leaders being exposed to significant ethical issues. Politicians, government agencies, public servants, CEOs and major corporations have all had to account for—and in many cases, pay significant penalties for—incorrect or questionable behaviours. The community is increasingly critical of such behaviour, and has called for more rigorous social accountability. The reputation and standing of any organisation can be put at risk, and dissipated, by a single careless act.

While many boards, chief executives and managers will claim to be conducting their business in line with appropriate behavioural standards, ethical performance currently lags in three major areas; there is:

1 a lack of identification and definition of what constitutes ethical behaviour;
2 a subsequent lack of training and commitment from employees; and
3 an absence of recognition and reinforcement for ethical conduct within organisations.

Successful ethical organisations have developed a code of conduct jointly with their employees, giving a sense of ownership. These are sufficiently pre-scriptive to identify expected behaviour. Employees are trained in the expected behaviour with an emphasis on the positive benefits; nevertheless, penalties are defined. Training is regular and audits are conducted as required. Training is also provided for methods and techniques in making ethical decisions; what is acceptable, appropriate and ethical to one person may not be so for another in the same organisation. The aim is for consistency and adherence to agreed values, principles and guidelines to minimise the risk of conflicting priorities and potential exposure.

Figure 11.8   Northern Telecom's guideline questions for ethical analysis and decision-making

1   What is my character? Is maintaining my ethical integrity important to me?
2   What is the ethical problem? What are the morally significant facts?
3   What are my values? Do they conflict?
4   What are my duties? Do they conflict? Do they conflict with my values?
5   Have I looked at the problem from the perspective of all the affected parties?
6   What is the ethical culture of my firm? What support structures do I have?
7   What ethical principles or factors apply in this situation? Whom might my decision injure?
8   What is the ideal outcome? Can it be achieved?
9   What alternative courses of action do I have?
10   What is the most likely outcome for each alternative course of action?
11   Have I considered the long-term effects of each outcome?
12   What is the symbolic significance of the alternative courses of action?
13   Which outcomes are consistent with my values and duties? Are any of them in conflict with the ethical culture of my firm? Do any of them violate ethical principles?
14   Is this a situation where an exception should be made to my values, duties and/or ethical principles? What factors might warrant such an exception?
15   What should be my decision?

How do we know the right principles? It might be said that a sense of right and wrong is part of our basic makeup. We inherently know what is the proper thing to do from what is the wrong way to act. Why then does unethical behaviour take place? In corporate life ethical behaviour can often be put aside as an expedient to achieve a short-term goal. Maybe ethical prin-ciples lie dormant in our thinking and need to be aroused and brought to the forefront of our thought, to guide the correct behaviour.

The practice of progressive management and leadership starts from the premise that people inherently have the capability to perform well. They need only an explanation of the results of their task, the required education, resources, guidance, and finally evaluation with recognition. Following this concept through in an ethical context leads to the conclusion that employees need to know what behaviour is expected, to have the necessary education on how to behave—together with appropriate coaching—and then receive feedback on the results of the effort.

The challenge of remaining in effective contact with the workforce becomes greater as organisations progress through outsourcing, identifying and managing intellectual capital, and moving to being 'virtual'. Employees who have less direct contact with their supervisors and managers will require more and clearer articulation of standards of ethical performance, especially as external influences increasingly affect organisational performance. Successful organisations will recognise this need and devote time and energy to improving the education and support for their employees. The issue is not *if* our ethical posture should be improved, but *how soon* and *how well* can the results demanded by employees and external stakeholders can be achieved.

The various perceptions of the organisation by its constituents and stakeholders are critical. In many circumstances, how the firm is viewed may be more important than what it does. Good reputations take time to build and consolidate; all of this hard work can be damaged or lost overnight.

References

Ethics Resource Center 1994, *Ethics in American Business: Policies, Programs and Perceptions*, Ethics Resource Center, Washington, DC.

Francis, I. 1997, *Future Direction: The Power of the Competitive Board*, Pitman Melbourne.

Treviño, L.K. & Nelson K.A. 1995, *Managing Business Ethics: Straight Talk About How To Do It Right*, John Wiley & Sons, New York.

Walton, R. 1985, 'From control to commitment in the workplace', *Harvard Business Review*, March–April, pp. 77–84.

12 Sources of information

Margaret Patrickson

The original version of this chapter appeared in volume 1 of this book published in 1995 and began with an overview of the major reference books to be found on library shelves and likely to be consulted by the typical human resource practitioner. Since that time, however, there has been a revolution in how all information, including human resource management information, is created, stored, and accessed. Purchasing one's own collection of reference books, or travelling frequently to the library, may no longer be the preferred or even the most cost-effective choice for those seeking to acquire up-to-date reference material.

The personal computer has taken over as an efficient place to begin seeking HR information and useful reference material can often be obtained rapidly without having to leave one's office. Today's HR manger typically has easy access to a computer networked to the world which can be used to research just about anything that has been published. At the minimum, careful use of the internet before venturing forth can significantly reduce the time spent searching for information.

Effective utilisation of this network requires familiarity with electronic data sources, compiling information on available library catalogues and borrowing policies, investing in access to appropriate CD Rom software, subscribing to regularly updated electronic database systems, and adopting a strategic approach to information search. Material can be downloaded from the internet on most topics by payment of a small fee charged to a credit card.

Internet access can be augmented with helpful new publications, as, despite this change, it is unlikely that ownership of books will be totally jettisoned. There will always be a need for significant and reliable reference works and these will continue to be well thumbed inclusions on the bookshelf. Most practitioners will reallocate information support dollars to electronically delivered material as long as it is readily accessible and available when needed, and to establishing borrowing arrangements with nearby libraries when needing data on specific topics.

Joining a library to supplement a personal book collection is an inexpensive method of maintaining and expanding knowledge on specific areas with limited usability before becoming dated. It helps if the library catalogue can be accessed through remote means. Universities collections provide the greatest selection of information on human resource management matters and most will permit their graduates to become registered borrowers for a small fee. Become a registered borrower and obtain the software to install the catalogue.

Successful library users have generally invested time to learn how to use the catalogue. Most catalogues are arranged by both author, topic (or keywords), or journal title. Next clarify the parameters of your search. Is your needed information restricted to Australian sources? English language? Do you need the information within a specified time frame? How much information do you need? If you are not seeking to access the work of a particular author, then begin by selecting the key words which describe the information being sought.

Once you have clarified your limits you can begin in earnest. Most Australian libraries use the Dewey classification system. Books on human resource management can normally be found in the mid-600s, usually around 658.2 or 658.3. Libraries generally divide their collections into reference material, which can only be accessed within the library, and the general collection, which can be borrowed by registered users. As its name suggests, the reference collection consists of major reference guides which are not available for removal from the library, though they can be copied. Here you will find the major definitive overviews and glossaries. Frequently, they carry the words encyclopedia, handbook, standard, guide or similar, in their title and generally they cover a broad field. Many of these contain information which is universal in application though some may be restricted to their country of publication. If you are seeking for specific information you may need to consult all English-language publications which includes British and North American handbooks in addition to those originating in Australia.

The general collection in most libraries contains books and published reports available for loan. A comprehensive comment on such a broad and extensive range of publication material is impossible and the following comments refer only in general terms to the material available. Non-reference texts have usually been written to address particular topic areas and are designed to provide a summary of the topic, its component parts, and its historical development. Edited books form part of such collections, bringing together contributions from a number of authors on a similar area and are useful if you want to compare ideas from different perspectives.

As well as lists of titles, most electronic catalogues will also supply details of availability. For example, is the book on the shelves and available for borrowing or it is on loan to another customer? Almost all libraries will allow you to reserve a book for borrowing once returned by others and advise you when it is available for collection.

Periodicals still form the best source for up-to-date information on a specific topic. They range from scholarly publications featuring research evidence and theoretical debate, such as the *Asia Pacific Journal of Human Resources*, through to more professionally focused journals, such as *HR Monthly*. During the last few years, production of journals has increasingly been supplemented by additional information delivered electronically on CD Rom. A number of these databases are relevant to human resource management.

Overviews of journal publications in management can be obtained through ANBAR Management Intelligence, ABI/Inform, the Business Periodicals Index (BPI), and the Business Periodicals Ondisc (BPO). ANBAR contains citations and abstracts from over 400 international journals in all areas of management but its strength is in HRM. It is probably the best source for British publications; coverage began in 1989. ABI/Inform abstracts over 1000 international journals in all areas of business, with strengths in general management issues and United States sources; it begins in 1987. The Business Periodicals Index has a strong overlap with ABI/Inform, citing around 350 international newspapers and journals in all areas of business. The author has found the best source to be the BPO since it provides full text of some 500 journals indexed on ABI/Inform. The full text of articles, including graphics, can be printed on a laser printer but printing costs are high.

Other useful CD Roms include ABIX which sources Australian newspapers and journals; its prime focus is financial issues. DATADISC contains reviews of all companies listed on the Australian Stock Exchange and is sourced from annual reports and company annoucements. In a similar vein is The Annual Report File, produced by the Australian Graduate School of Management at the University of South Wales which contains annual reports of some 500 Australian companies. AUSTROM contains 13 different Australian data bases from AFPD (the Australian Federal Police Digest) to APAIS (Australian Public Affairs Information Service) to FAMILY (Australian Family and Society Abstracts) most going back to the mid–1980s.

Specific Australian business discs are also emerging. The Australian Institute of Management has developed AIMMAT which contains citations and abstracts on management and training since 1991. Both IREL and WORKLIT contain citations and abstracts of issues in industrial relations. Occupational health and safety is covered by both OSHROM, which contains four international databases in the area of occupational health and safety, and WORKSAFE which features Australian information. Worksafe also hosts a website at http:/www/allette.com.au/ ~wsa1 which provides full texts of standards and guidelines for applying health and safety regulations.

Some HR managers may also find useful bases from other disciplines. PSYCLIT sources psychological journals since 1971 and SOCIOFILE sources sociological data which can be useful in providing information concerning societal trends here and abroad. Demographic and population data are also available on CLIB91: Matrices and CLIB91: Profiles.

Much material similar or identical to that on CD Rom can also be accessed by computer if Netscape software is installed. ANBAR intelligence delivers biweekly updates of newly published abstracts on management and full transcripts can be ordered if the abstract sounds promising. MCB press provides online information of over 100 articles published through their various journals. Alternatively, you can obtain a plethora of information through the netsearch facility. Simply click on the infoseek icon, type in the key words to search the internet and then click on seek. Worldwide information sources can be perused on everything connected to your topic. In addition, the majority of publishing houses now operate websites. To find out the latest news on releases, call up the home page for the publisher and request information on new publications. In human resource management, for example, this could include information on new books out, details of local, international and overseas conferences, compensation glossaries—in fact whatever may be relevant to the specific topic being investigated. You can spend many hours surfing the net, and you can order newly published books directly through local and overseas publishers.

The computer has revolutionised our information-seeking behaviour and is likely to continue to do so. How easy it now is to find out what we need to know and to learn to use the facility. E-mail, with its capacity for attaching documents, can extend the internet process by using electronic transmission to share standard documents and files with domestic and international colleagues. Data prepared by one organisation can be made available to others quickly and without difficulty if such distribution is authorised.

Committed computer enthusiasts maintain that the need for books lies in the past and will soon pass into history. However, this author believes there will always be a need for one's own copy on the shelf. Most of us are so attached to the idea of having a book as the major reference source that it is difficult to conceive of us being willing to retreat from retaining some reliance on the printed page.

Nonetheless, given the escalating cost of new books it is likely that many will prefer to rely either on our professional journals or the internet for keeping up to date on new research findings, and rely on books for guidance with respect to new HR practices or for expanding our knowledge of particular topic areas. Attending seminars and conferences can help supplement journal findings as often the seminar provides the opportunity to tap into emerging ideas which have yet to be published as well as the added benefit of meeting other practitioners and sharing their experiences.

In the following section, and with these considerations in mind, the author has compiled a list of recent publications likely to be of interest to HR practitioners. They are arranged into sections covering both general and various specific components of human resource practice.

Reference texts

'Reference texts', as the name suggests, represent the source guide of general reference material on human resource management and are often the starting point when seeking information on either general or specialised issues in the HR field.

One of the major useful references in human resource management includes *The Handbook of Human Resource Management* edited by Ferris, Rosen and Barnum and published by Blackwell in the UK. This book contains over 30 chapters, each written by different authors, which together cover the major components of the field of HRM. Blackwell also produces an *Encyclopedic Dictionary of Human Resource Management* edited by Peters, Greer and Youngblood in the United States. In Australia CCH produces a two-volume reference guide as well as other regularly updated guides to what's happening in HR at the local level which are described in more detail in the final part of this section. Other useful references include *The Human Resource Glossary* by William Tracey which provides a list of definitions of all key terms in the HR field and the WG and L book of *Human Resources Forms* edited by Asquith and Marx and published by Warren Gorham and Lamont in 1990. A similar Australian-based handbook of *Employment Contracts and Personnel Forms* was developed by the Centre for Professional Development in 1996.

Specialised handbooks are also available. Some of the best known include *The Gower Handbook of Training and Development* edited by John Prior, with the second edition published in 1994; *The Compensation Handbook* by Rock and Berger and published by McGraw-Hill, now in its third edition; *The Encyclopedia of Team Development Activities* edited by Pfeiffer and Nolde and published by Pfeiffer and Co. in the USA; the *Handbook of Training Strategy* by Sloman and published by Gower in 1994; and more recently *Designing and Implementing Successful Diversity Programs* by Lawrence Baytos, published by Prentice-Hall. Prentice-Hall also produces a yearbook, with the latest edition— 1997/1998—edited by Mary Cook containing 16 chapters; McGraw Hill's *Personnel Policy Handbook* by William Hubbartt is a useful guide for developing HR manuals. Recent useful reference books in the United States which aim to address typical HR dilemmas include *The Human Resource Problem Solver's Handbook* by Joseph Levesque, published by McGraw-Hill, and *The Staffing Problem Solver* by Mark Dorio, published by Wiley.

Loose leaf reference services provide an alternative to books as they allow subscribers to keep an updated reference collection and reduce the need to personally visit the libarary. CCH is the largest Australian supplier of this service with publications offered in equal opportunity law and practice, equal opportunity cases, a business advisory guide, cases in Australian company law, corporate news, corporate and securities legislation, the corporate practice manual, the employment law guide, the enterprising bargaining manual, the Australian law reporter, the guidebook to workers' compensation, occupational health and safety law, hazard alert, and general management, in addition to their well-known series in human resource management.

Australian general texts

Though the number of general HR texts written overseas continues to expand, there have been few new original Australian texts produced in the last five years. Most new overseas publications take a strategic perspective and confirm the earlier emergent trend towards a more strategic focus for human resource management. By the mid-1990s this strategic orientation, whereby activities undertaken by human resource managers are required to reinforce and support broader organisational strategy, has become accepted as the preferred framework in which to position human resource management texts both in Australia and overseas.

International developments have encouraged Australian HRM practices to follow developments in the rest of the world, while our economic and legal environments have stimulated some differentiation of our activities. The 1990s have seen a steady growth in HR books from Britain, the United States, Canada, New Zealand and Australia, targetting students and practitioners. Such a broad field cannot be comprehensively covered in this short chapter, and so a brief overview of those HR texts which are set within our own business environment is presented.

The majority of locally produced HR texts are now in new editions. Stone's third edition of *Human Resource Management* was published by Wiley in 1998. Like previous editions the approach is pragmatic, with chapters dealing with strategic human resource management, managing change and workplace relations, HRM and the law, incentive compensation, job analysis, job design and quality of working life. Its practical focus makes it a popular text with part-time students who are already experienced members of the workforce and who therefore find it easier to identify with the author's assumption that readers understand typical working environments.

McGraw-Hill published Clark's second edition of *Australian Human Resources Management* in 1992 and Nelson published the second edition of *Strategic Human Resource Management* by Nankervis, Compton and McCarthy in 1996. Each contains new chapters which reflect the increasing importance of the strategic approach to managing people and broaden the geographical setting in an effort to compare Australian practice with our neighbours in the Asian Pacific basin.

Stone has compiled a new edition of his collection of readings, and Nankervis and Compton also published a book of readings in 1994; each of these provides an excellent supplement to the text it is designed to accompany. Both books of readings contain chapters by leading academics and practitioners from both Australia and overseas, and some chapters reproduced from leading HR journals.

The third edition of *Human Resource Management in Australia* by Kramar, McGraw and Schuler was published by West Publishing and Addison Wesley Longman in 1997. The book aims to fulfil a number of needs by integrating a practical perspective with a strong background in theory and research. It is a useful source for more recent research, and will assist you to critically evaluate current human practice within your own organisation.

Specific topics

Employment relations

As the 1990s has unfolded, employment relations, which seeks to bring together the previous divergent approaches of industrial relations and human resource management, has blossomed as an expanding field in its own right rather than remaining a component of the more traditional human resource management. This development is illustrated by the emergence of a number of new texts specifically aimed at this area. Best known and specifically developed for the Australian context is *Employment Relations* by Margaret Gardner and Gill Palmer, published by Macmillan in 1992; a second edition released in 1997 updates the earlier material and adds two new chapters on company policies regarding performance and pay, and occupational health and safety.

Tom Keeney and Di Kelly have written an alternative published by Harcourt Brace in 1996 which contains a number of useful explanatory tables and contains an excellent section on the regulatory structure of work organisation. Another useful contribution in this area, which is especially helpful in its coverage of the employment implications of many new production systems such as cellular manufacturing, is John Mathews' book *Catching the Wave* published in 1994 by Allen and Unwin.

International human resource management

During the 1990s international HRM has emerged as a field in its own right, reflecting the growth of Australia's international trade and an expanding interest in international HR practices, in order both to compare practices here and abroad and to manage people across national boundaries. Little information had been collated to assist students in this area prior to the 1980s and international practices were rarely accorded a book focused solely on this activity. However, specialised new texts devoted to this field have been issued in the 1990s. The second edition of Dowling, Schuler and Welsh *International Dimensions of Human Resource Management*, released by Wadsworth in 1994, aims to assist students to develop a more systematic approach to practice, with an appendix urging more research in this area. Another publication was introduced by de Gruyter in 1995 specifically for the Asian-Pacific market:

Human Resource Management on the Pacific Rim edited by Moore and Devereaux Jennings. Either or both of these would provide helpful coverage of many of the problems and issues facing practitioners in this field.

Specialised areas

Each specialised area—traditionally encompassing recruitment and selection, health and safety, diversity management, training and development, performance appraisal together with remuneration and benefits planning and administration—has developed its own literature base through publication of specialised books and journals. This chapter cannot hope to cover such a broad range but recommends that all practitioners continually update material to ensure that practices are in line with changing legislation and developments in performance management and reward administration.

Government has emerged as a key player in the provision of guidelines for appropriate HR practices. Both federal and state departments concerned with occupational health and safety, and the administration of claims for injury and rehabilitation through Workcover, are excellent sources of literature to assist with setting up and maintaining an up-to-date and effective occupational health service. Similarly, given that most states now have legislation widening the grounds of illegal discrimination, appropriate information can generally be obtained from the relevant state or federal department. However, the government has been less active in supplying literature to assist with issues of work organisation and in providing guidelines which would help companies achieve a more strategic approach to matters of people management and development. Much of the current emphasis on empowerment and organisational restructuring and flattening has led to an increasingly professional approach to performance management in Australia but assistance with implementing these new developments is largely through professional journals rather than government.

Perhaps the fastest growing area in terms of specifically targeted publications is that of total quality management (TQM), but organisations differ in whether TQM is located within the sphere of HRM or under the umbrella of another function—such as engineering, or production. If you are interested in this field, you may need to peruse a broad literature base and not restrict your search to HRM. Space limitations preclude any detailed coverage of this field but Longman's 1995 publication by Gilmour and Hunt contains a useful bibiography which may offer a good place to begin.

Information on specific HR topics can also be obtained through other media, such as films and video, and feedback from organisations suggests that video presentations rather than print can be especially helpful in introducing new ideas to a wide audience. Seven Dimensions offers a number of training videos positioned in the Australian context which you might find useful in following up ideas within your own company.

Periodicals and journals

Subscribing to periodicals can be such an expensive activity that most individuals choose to restrict their subscriptions to those which offer immediate utility and access the remainder through either library membership or by downloading items of interest from the internet. More and more journals offer online access in addition to printed copy, but for many individuals overseas journals may not be the most cost-effective source given that only a proportion of the content would have direct relevance. The main benefit of online access is that you can acquire only the article(s) that is of immediate concern. With these comments in mind, the following remarks refer largely to locally produced journals. Overseas periodicals such as *Personnel Review*, *Human Resources Management*, and the *International Journal of Human Resource Management* provide a wealth of information on recent developments in HRM both nationally and internationally, but locally produced journals have the local reader in mind and often address international issues from a local perspective.

HRM periodicals tend to fall into two types—those predominantly dedicated to publishing research information or promoting scholarly debate and those directed predominantly at practitioners which generally contain shorter articles and focus on the application of new developments with human resource practice in organisations. Members of the Australian Human Resources Institute receive both types included in their annual subscription. The *Asia Pacific Journal of Human Resources* aims to fulfil scholarly requirements, with all articles published in its main section undergoing blind peer review. It is widely read both here and overseas and contains many useful contributions which address emerging issues of international focus. In addition to the regular articles, there is always a briefer section devoted to issues of HR practice, plus a section on book reviews. It comes out three times a year whereas *HR Monthly*, as its name indicates, is issued on a monthly basis. This magazine-style publication aims to keep practitioners up to date on changing HR practices, details of forthcoming events, distinguished visitors, and points of concern in HRM.

Journals are also produced by other professional organisations in the HR field. The *International Employment Relations Review* contains articles of interest to those working in employment relations. The *Journal of Industrial Relations* is available to its members local and overseas members and *Training and Development in Australia* is provided to members of the Institute of Training and Development. Interesting articles can also be found in journals which address issues of more general management, such as the *Australian Manager* or the *Journal of the Australian New Zealand Academy of Management*. *Business Review Weekly* often contains useful case studies for debate and analysis.

Videos

Given the potential of videos to illustrate behaviours through demonstration, they are emerging as a major force in workplace-related training. Seven Dimensions in Melbourne is the dominant Australian supplier, with a number of short videos produced in Australia and employing local actors. Most are aimed at developing interpersonal skills such as being assertive, establishing customer value, dealing with conflict, empowerment, team-building and interviewing, and their average length is between 10 and 25 minutes. They provide an extremely helpful visual illustration of desired behaviours which can be adapted as models.

Though not locally produced, the BBC videos are equally effective and many include a touch of humour to make their point. A significant advantage is their use of well-known names such as Michael Porter and Ricardo Semler. Examples include the *Borderless World, The Competitive Edge, The Maverick Solution,* and *A Prophet Unheard*, and most run for about 30 minutes.

Compared with written material, videos are generally expensive to rent or purchase so they tend to be mainly used for training large numbers of people in repeated small-group learning situations.

Conclusion

Overall, there have been significant shifts in data sources available to HR managers. One major shift has been towards greater reliance on electronic access to information, and thus a reduction in the proportion of material delivered through the print medium. The other major direction change has been towards a greater emphasis on strategic fit of HR activity to ensure that HR practices are aligned with the overall strategic thrust of the firm in which they are pursued.

Few new general HRM texts for the Australian market have been produced; rather those previously in existence have been updated with new material and new editions. It is doubtful that the local market can sustain higher numbers of general reference works. Given the increasing utilisation of the internet, video and interactive learning through the electronic classroom, this author believes the future trend will be in generating publications which address specific areas of new knowledge and practice, such as performance management, and salary packaging. Production of material may also increase on strategic HR issues associated with developing management areas.

Journals should continue to be the preferred source of research and debate and it is recommended that all readers ensure they maintain their knowledge base through joining and maintaining their membership of the relevant professional body.

References

Asquith, N. & Marx, G. 1990, *W,G and L Human Resources Forms,* Warren, Gorham and Lamont, Boston, MA.

Baytos, L. 1995, *Designing and Implementing Successful Diversity Programs*, Prentice-Hall, Englewood Cliffs, NJ.

CCH Editors *Human Resource* Update, CCH, Melbourne.

CCH Editors 1993, *Human Resources Management*, CCH, Melbourne.

CDP Editors 1996, *The Handbook of Employment Contracts and Personnel Forms*, CDP, Melbourne.

Clark, R. 1992, *Human Resources Management*, 2nd edn, McGraw-Hill, Roseville, NSW.

Cook, M.F. 1997, *The Human Resources Yearbook*, Prentice-Hall, Englewood Cliffs, NJ.

Dorio, M. 1994, *Staffing Problem Solver, For Human Resource Professionals and Managers*, John Wiley & Sons, New York, USA.

Dowling, P., Schuler, R. & Welch, D.E. 1994, *International Dimensions of Human Resource Management*, Wadsworth, Belmont, CA.

Ferris, G.R., Rosen, S.D. & Barnum, D.T. 1995, *Handbook of Human Resource Management*, Blackwell, Cambridge, MA.

Gardner, M. & Palmer, G. 1997, *Employment Relations,* 2nd edn, Macmillan, Melbourne.

Gilmour, P. & Hunt, R.A. 1995, *Total Quality Management*, Longman, Melbourne.

Hubbartt, W.S. 1993, *Personnel Policy Handbook*, McGraw-Hill, New York.

Keenoy, T. & Kelly, D. 1996, *The Employment Relationship in Australia*, Harcourt Brace and Company, Sydney.

Mathews, J. 1994, *Catching the Wave*, Allen & Unwin, Sydney.

Moore, L.F. & Devereaux Jennings, P. 1995, *Human Resource Management on the Pacific Rim*, de Gruyter, Berlin and New York.

Kramar, R., McGraw, P. & Schuler, R. 1997, *Human Resource Management in Australia*, Addison Wesley Longman, Melbourne.

Levesque, J.D. 1992, *The Human Resource Problem Solver's Handbook*, McGraw-Hill, New York.

Nankervis, A.R., Compton, R.L. & McCarthy, T.E. 1996, *Strategic Human Resource Management*, 2nd edn, Nelson, Melbourne.

Nankervis, A.R. & Compton, R.L. 1994, *Readings in Strategic Human Resource Management*, Nelson, Melbourne.

Peters, L.H., Greer, C.R. & Youngblood, S.A. 1997, *The Blackwell Encyclopedic Dictionary of Human Resource Management*, Blackwell, Cambridge, MA.

Pfeiffer, J.W. & Nolde, C. 1991, *The Encyclopedia of Team Development Activities*, Pfeiffer and Co., San Diego, CA.

Prior, J. 1994, *Gower Handbook of Training and Development*, 2nd edn, Gower, Aldershot, UK.

Rock, M.L. & Berger, L.A. 1991, *The Compensation Handbook*, 3rd edn, McGraw-Hill, New York.

Sloman, M. 1994, *A Handbook for Training Strategy*, Gower, Aldershot, UK.

Stone, R. 1994, *Readings in Human Resource Management*, vol. II, Jacaranda Wiley, Milton, Qld.

—— 1995, *Human Resource Management*, 2nd edn, Jacaranda Wiley, Milton, Qld.

Tracey, W.R. 1991, *The Human Resources Glossary*, AMACOM, USA.